GLOBAL BIOETHICS

D1615296

WITHDRAWN

The panorama of bioethical problems is different today. Patients travel to Thailand for fast surgery; commercial surrogate mothers in India deliver babies to parents in rich countries; organs, body parts and tissues are trafficked from East to Western Europe; physicians and nurses are migrating from Africa to the US; thousands of children or patients with malaria, tuberculosis and AIDS are dying each day because they cannot afford effective drugs that are too expensive.

Mainstream bioethics as it has developed during the last 50 years in Western countries is evolving into a broader approach that is relevant for people across the world and is focused on new global problems. This book provides an introduction to the new field of global bioethics. Addressing these problems requires a broader vision of bioethics that not only goes beyond the current emphasis on individual autonomy, but that criticizes the social, economic and political context that is producing the problems at global level.

This book argues that global bioethics is a necessity because the social, economic and environmental effects of globalization require critical responses. Global bioethics is not a finished product that can simply be applied to solve global problems, but it is the ongoing result of interaction and exchange between local practices and global discourse. It combines recognition of differences and respect for cultural diversity with convergence towards common perspectives and shared values. The book examines the nature of global problems as well as the type of responses that are needed, in order to exemplify the substance of global bioethics. It discusses the ethical frameworks that are available for global discourse and shows how these are transformed into global governance mechanisms and practices.

Henk ten Have is Director of the Center for Healthcare Ethics at Duquesne University, Pittsburgh, US.

'*Global bioethics* is eloquent in its critique of the moral myopia of mainstream bioethics and is a must for any reader seriously concerned with the role bioethics should play in the face of globalization.'

Jan Helge Solbakk, University of Oslo, Norway

'Unlike other authors of the Northern hemisphere, the meaning of bioethics for Henk ten Have goes beyond the biomedical field. The inclusion in the framework proposed by the author of topics related to health care, social inclusion and preservation of the environment provides a new historical mark that puts this book in the pleasant academic surprises of this early twenty-first century.'

Volnei Garrafa, University of Brasília, Brazil

'A comprehensive and penetrating account of how Bioethics could be extended to become Global Bioethics through an ambitious and visionary ethical and multi-disciplinary discourse. Addressing biological, social, political and ecological determinants of health from bio-centric and eco-centric perspectives is offered as a new bridge towards sustainable improvement in the health of people and our planet.'

Solomon Benatar, University of Cape Town, South Africa;
University of Toronto, Canada

GLOBAL BIOETHICS

An introduction

WITHDRAWN

Henk ten Have

Routledge
Taylor & Francis Group

LONDON AND NEW YORK

First published 2016
by Routledge
2 Park Square, Milton Park, Abingdon, Oxon OX14 4RN

and by Routledge
711 Third Avenue, New York, NY 10017

Routledge is an imprint of the Taylor & Francis Group, an informa business

British Library Cataloguing-in-Publication Data
A catalogue record for this book is available from the British Library

Library of Congress Cataloging-in-Publication Data
Names: ten Have, H., author.
Title: Global bioethics : an introduction / Henk ten Have.
Description: Milton Park, Abingdon, Oxon ; New York, NY : Routledge, 2016. | Includes bibliographical references and index.
Identifiers: LCCN 2015031281 | ISBN 9781138124097 (hbk) | ISBN 9781138124103 (pbk) | ISBN 9781315648378 (ebook)
Subjects: LCSH: Bioethics.
Classification: LCC QH332 .H38 2016 | DDC 174.2--dc23
LC record available at http://lccn.loc.gov/2015031281

ISBN: 978-1-138-12409-7 (hbk)
ISBN: 978-1-138-12410-3 (pbk)
ISBN: 978-1-315-64837-8 (ebk)

Typeset in Bembo
by Saxon Graphics Ltd, Derby

For Nancy and Carien

CONTENTS

ACKNOWLEDGMENTS

Working in bioethics means collaborating with students to discuss and clarify ethical issues. It is engaging in research, participating in committees and contributing to public debate. Increasingly, it involves travelling. This is not just a response to an invitation to make a presentation but more often an occasion to explore what kind of bioethical issues are significant in other parts of the world, and how these issues are perceived, interpreted and addressed. What I have learned about global bioethics is first of all the result from meetings, exchanges and discussions with colleagues and friends from all over the world. In the 1990s, working at the Radboud University Nijmegen in the Netherlands, many international activities could be initiated such as the Bioethics Summer School and the European Master in Bioethics with colleagues in Belgium, Spain, Switzerland and Italy. In 2003, I was fortunate enough to be appointed as Director of the Division of Ethics of Science and Technology at UNESCO. This not only turned my life around (though Paris is not the worst place to live) but it shocked and transformed my conception of bioethics. In hundreds of missions from Abidjan to Stellenbosch, from Jakarta to Jeddah, from Winnipeg to Panama and Buenos Aires, and many places in-between, I faced the reality of moral queries, the struggles of physicians and patients, the dilemmas of policy-makers, and the power as well as fragility of bioethics. It was the time to draft the Universal Declaration on Bioethics and Human Rights. Here I learned that global bioethics is not simply an academic enterprise (although being an expert in bioethics is certainly helpful). It implies political skills, diplomatic manoeuvring, lobbying, advocacy and activism. My colleagues in UNESCO contributed to broaden my thinking, experiences and skills. They also taught me the reality and urgency of global bioethics. Thanks go especially to Pierre Sané, Georges Kutukdjian, Dafna Feinholz, Jan Helge Solbakk, Susana Vidal and Christophe Dikenou. The opportunity to elaborate on the concept of global bioethics through teaching and research was offered by Duquesne

University. I would like to thank the President of Duquesne University, Charles Dougherty, himself a bioethicist, for his continuous support. Thanks also to James Swindal, dean of the McAnulty College and Graduate School of Liberal Arts for creating the conditions to write this book. Special thanks go to my colleagues in the Center for Healthcare Ethics; Gerald Magill, Peter Osuji, Joris Gielen, and Glory Smith. The research for this book was tremendously facilitated by the help of research assistants. Graduate students Michael Afolabi, Gary Edwards, Jennifer Lamson, Amanda Mattone, Barbara Postol, Carrie Stott, Rabee Toumi, Jillian Walsh and Aimee Zellers all contributed over the years, and enthusiastically supported the development of global bioethics. Thanks to Thomas Gerkin for making the Index. Gumberg Library at Duquesne with its enormous collection of materials and resources should be thanked (especially Ted Bergfelt). I would like to thank three persons in particular. Gary Edwards and Rabee Toumi meticulously read most of the manuscript, provided criticisms and comments. Michèle Stanton-Jean did the same from her experiences in health policy; without her as IBC chair during the negotiations in UNESCO, the Declaration would probably never have been adopted. I am grateful to them for their useful feedback.

Chapter 3 draws upon previously published work: Henk ten Have (2012) Potter's notion of bioethics. *Kennedy Institute of Ethics Journal* 22(1): 59–82. Chapters 4 and 7 elaborate on ideas from my first publications on global bioethics: Henk ten Have (2011) Global bioethics and communitarianism. *Theoretical Medicine and Bioethics* 32: 315–326; Henk ten Have and Bert Gordijn (eds) (2013) *Handbook of Global Bioethics*. Springer Publishers, Dordrecht. Thanks to Bert Gordijn for the many occasions provided to discuss global bioethics, and for his encouragement to write this monograph.

Henk ten Have
Summer 2015
Pittsburgh/Amsterdam

ACRONYMS

ADHD	Attention Deficit Hyperactivity Disorder
AMA	American Medical Association
ASBH	American Society for Bioethics and Humanities
CAB	Committee on Animal Biotechnology
CBD	Convention on Biological Diversity
CIOMS	Council for International Organizations of Medical Sciences
CITI	Collaborative Institutional Training Initiative
EGE	European Group on Ethics in Science and New Technologies
EU	European Union
FAO	Food and Agriculture Organization
FGM	Female genital mutilation
GDP	Gross Domestic Product
GM	Genetically Modified
HCEC	Health Care Ethics Consultation
HIV/AIDS	Human Immunodeficiency Virus Infection/Acquired Immune Deficiency Syndrome
HUGO	Human Genome Organization
IBC	International Bioethics Committee
ICESCR	International Covenant on Economic, Social and Cultural Rights
IMF	International Monetary Fund
IPR	Intellectual Property Rights
IVF	In Vitro Fertilization
MDGs	Millennium Development Goals
MSF	Médicines sans Frontières – Doctors without Borders
NGO	Non-governmental organization
NIH	National Institutes of Health
PEPFAR	President's Emergency Plan for AIDS Relief

SARS	Severe Acute Respiratory Syndrome
SCI	Science Citation Index
TAC	Treatment Action Campaign
TRIPS	Trade-Related Intellectual Property Rights
UAEM	Universities Allied for Essential Medicines
UDBHR	Universal Declaration on Bioethics and Human Rights
UDHGHR	Universal Declaration on the Human Genome and Human Rights
UDHR	Universal Declaration of Human Rights
UN	United Nations
UNAIDS	Joint United Nations Programme on HIV/AIDS
UNDP	United Nations Development Programme
UNESCO	United Nations Educational, Scientific and Cultural Organization
UNICEF	United Nations Children's Fund
UNITAID	International Drug Purchasing Facility for HIV/AIDS, tuberculosis and malaria, established by countries such as Brazil, Chile, France, Norway and the United Kingdom
US	United States
WEMOS	a non-profit foundation in the Netherlands, advocating the right to health globally
WHA	World Health Assembly
WHO	World Health Organization
WMA	World Medical Association
WTO	World Trade Organization

BOXES

FIGURES

1

BIOETHICS REALITY CHECK

The customs officer is carefully studying the passport:

> 'Why are you visiting Israel?'
> 'I've been invited for a bioethics conference in Zefat.'
> 'A bio ... what?'

Bioethics may be an unusual term but it is not difficult to explain its meaning. One can easily mention some of the issues that are widely discussed and make headlines in the newspapers and social media: cloning, organ transplantation, genetic testing, mercy killing or the right to refuse treatment. The officer looks at me now. She understands what I am talking about. She starts telling me that her father, who is rather old, is in intensive care in the major hospital in town. The family does not know exactly what is going on with him. They are suspicious because the doctors don't provide much information. Her two brothers insist that everything will be done to keep the father alive, but she and her sister wonder whether he himself really wants to be in this situation. She is puzzled about what would be best for her father. At that moment she stamps the passport and wishes me a good conference. I have no time to tell her that bioethics nowadays is addressing many new topics. The conference is actually about the ethics of disaster relief.

The panorama of bioethics

Bioethics is confronted with a wide range of issues. Some of these have been on the agenda for a long time, but others are new. Over the last 50 years, bioethics has been concerned with the ethical analysis of abortion, euthanasia, assisted reproduction and genetic testing. These topics are also discussed in the public media. Citizens like the customs officer will easily recognize them, even if they don't always associate them with bioethics. More recently, bioethical debate has substantially broadened. Not only are more issues coming onto the agenda, but the more traditional topics have often obtained a wider dimension due to the globalization of the world. The following examples demonstrate that bioethics today has moved beyond the concerns that traditionally dominated its agenda.

BRAIN-DEAD PREGNANCY

In November 2013 Marlise Muñoz, 33 years old, was admitted to a Texan hospital after she collapsed at home. She was diagnosed as brain dead. Her husband and family wanted her removed from life support following her previous wishes. Life support was continued, however, as she was 14 weeks' pregnant. The physicians argued that the law in Texas prohibits withholding care from a pregnant woman so that the life of the foetus will be protected. Two months later a judge ruled that the law did not apply in this case since the patient was dead. Marlise was disconnected from life support.

Issues that concern bioethics are illustrated in this case: end-of-life treatment, definition of death, care for pregnant women, the right to life of the foetus, abortion, but also decision-making in the hospital and the relationship between ethics and law. Modern technology and science make it possible to keep people alive, even if prospects for recovery are grim. Bioethical debate has focused on the conditions for interventions, weighing the benefits and harms, and clarifying who ultimately should decide: the patient, the family or the physicians? Life support can help patients to overcome a life-threatening situation. The example of Marlise is different because she had been diagnosed as dead. In that case, the idea of treatment makes no sense; at least for her, but what about the foetus? The state has an interest in protecting unborn life; how is this weighted against the interest of the woman and her family? And if intervention is continued, the woman's body is used to gestate the foetus. At the same time, there are cases where 'life' support is provided if people are dead, for example when they have donated their organs for transplantation. The case therefore raises issues about the limits of technological interventions, as well as the protection of unborn life. But there are also more fundamental queries concerning basic concepts such as life, death and the human body. Finally, it is clear these cases cannot occur everywhere. If emergency services and intensive care are not available, if transportation is deficient, if diagnostic equipment is absent, the patient would have died without medical interference, which is the situation in many poor countries. Even in countries with more resources, these cases are exceptional. But they occur from time to time because the available technology provides the possibility.

COMMERCIAL MOTHERHOOD

Rhonda and Gerry Wile in Arizona could not have children. In vitro fertilization was not an option because Rhonda's uterus was abnormal. They went to India where a growing number of clinics and services specialize in surrogate motherhood. They now have three children conceived with Gerry's sperm and an Indian egg donor. Two Indian women carried the pregnancies in return for $6,000 each. Surrogate motherhood has been legal in India since 2002. The surrogacy industry is growing fast with currently over 1,000 clinics. The overwhelming majority of clients come from outside the country. India has become the largest provider of babies to infertile couples in Western countries.

This case highlights the global phenomenon of medical tourism. Patients, usually from richer countries, travel to private clinics in poorer countries to receive treatment and intervention. This phenomenon has led to new debates and concerns in bioethics. It is not merely the technology as such that creates moral issues (like in the previous case) but its different use across the world. Countries such as China and France have banned surrogacy. But with the internet, citizens can obtain medical services that are not allowed in their own country. A global world raises questions about the application of a legal framework that has been the outcome of ethical debates within particular countries while other countries have different regulations or no legal framework at all. In some countries surrogacy is allowed as long as it is not commercial. Paying women to carry a child for other people produces specific ethical concerns. It is estimated that every year 10,000 foreign couples visit India for reproductive services. The majority of surrogate mothers are very poor and from marginalized communities. They are facing the risks of pregnancy without adequate benefits since most of the money paid goes to clinics and brokers. Pregnancy is outsourced to wombs for rent. It is argued that this practice leads to exploitation and depreciation of women as human incubators, within a paternalistic society that is already discriminatory and disadvantageous for women. Particularly in India, surrogates are stigmatized; they keep their surrogacy secret from their community and parents. Commercial surrogacy also changes the concept of parenthood. There can be people who provide the gametes, others who nurture the child during pregnancy, and people who raise the child after birth, possibly all in other countries. Is the commercial surrogate the mother or simply a contracted worker, reduced to a womb under continuous surveillance in order to guarantee a good product? Recently, India introduced new visa rules to limit commercial surrogacy to couples who have been married for at least two years and are living in countries that do not prohibit surrogacy. The new rules also determine that single people and gay couples can no longer use surrogacy services. The fundamental ethical issues are not addressed within these rules; instead they have led to new debates. Furthermore, it is unclear how they will be enforced in a vast continent where corruption is widespread.

TISSUE TRADE

In February 2012, police in the Ukraine searched a minibus that happened to be loaded with human bones and tissues. Documents indicated that the remains of dead Ukrainians were destined for a factory in Germany that was processing human body parts for implantation in human beings. The factory belonged to RTI Biologics, a Florida-based medical products company. Bone, teeth and other body parts illegally recovered from corpses in Ukrainian morgues were sold on the international market.

In many countries tissues such as corneas, skin, bones, teeth and heart valves are voluntarily donated after death. Like organ donation, this is an altruistic act to help other people. Donated corneas, for example, are transplanted to restore vision. Bones are used to produce paste for orthopaedic operations, and skin materials for cosmetic surgery. But tissue donation, unlike organ donation, is not well regulated. Tissue banks that receive donated materials often cooperate with for-profit processing companies. The United States is the largest producer and exporter of tissue products. Due to global interconnections, tissues can be donated in one country, processed in another, and exported to yet another. The global tissue trade is an enormous market. Each year, in the US alone, 2 million products are derived from human tissue and sold. Recycling corpses is big business. One single body is worth between $80,000 and $200,000 in tissue products. Procurement of body parts is therefore attractive. Hospitals, mortuaries, funeral homes and morgues in many countries are contracted to 'harvest' tissues. Families who altruistically donate tissues do not know that these tissues are processed and sold by commercial companies. In some places families are not even told that tissues are removed from the body of their loved ones. Recipients, on the other hand, are not always informed that processed tissues from a corpse are being implanted. It is often unknown to physicians where the human tissue is coming from. Not only is it impossible to assess the safety of products but lack of traceability prevents public health responses in case of infections. Experts claim that we are more careful with cereals than with human tissues since cereals have barcodes enabling recall if necessary. It has been known for decades that Tutogen, the German medical products company in the case, has been obtaining tissues from Eastern Europe. The products seized in the Ukraine were labelled 'Made in Germany'.

DISASTER ETHICS

On Tuesday 12 January 2010, Port-au-Prince, the capital of the Republic of Haiti was struck by a catastrophic earthquake. More than 220,000 people were killed and 300,000 injured. Humanitarian aid flooded the country. Especially in the first few weeks, relief workers were confronted with a horror show. Operating rooms were not functioning and equipment was defective or missing. Because of infected limb fractures 4,000 people had amputations. Although lives have been saved, many disaster survivors are facing a difficult future in one of the poorest countries in the world.

Each year disasters occur that have a major impact on populations and countries. Everybody will remember the 2004 Indian Ocean tsunami or Hurricane Katrina in 2005. A total of 905 natural disasters were registered in 2012: hurricanes, droughts, earthquakes, volcanic eruptions and inundations. Loss of life is greatest in low-income countries. Especially in Haiti the damage was enormous. It is the poorest country in the Western hemisphere, characterized by political instability and rampant corruption. What would therefore be the best way to help the earthquake victims? Since disasters nowadays are highly visible, they immediately call for international solidarity and compassion. Images of suffering fellow human beings make disasters a paradigm case for humanitarian aid. It is ethics in action. Many foreign relief workers went to Haiti to help. During disasters ethical issues arise, such as who should be treated first. With so many injured people at the same time, difficult choices have to be made. Relief workers know what to do and how to do it, but the necessary tools are not available. They have to practise 'improvised medicine'. Also problematic is determining what kind of treatment would be most beneficial. Amputations may save lives but what will be the long-term quality of life when there are no rehabilitation centres, orthopaedic devices and adequate infrastructure? The relief workers return home but the injured and traumatized stay behind. Years later, many of them continue to live in precarious conditions. Humanitarian assistance can also generate negative phenomena. For example, many children in Haiti became orphans and were in bad circumstances. International adoption agencies came to their rescue. Adoption procedures were expedited. But there were also scandals of abduction since normal safeguards for protecting children were removed. Another example that good humanitarian intentions may have bad consequences was the cholera outbreak a few months after the earthquake, which killed thousands of Haitians over the following two years. The source of the outbreak was United Nations peacekeepers from Nepal who brought a virulent strain of cholera from Southeast Asia into Haiti, a country that had never before had a cholera outbreak.

GENE HUNTING

'Three centuries ago they came for sandalwood. Today the bastards are after our genes!' The Director of the Tonga Human Rights and Democracy Movement did not mince his words during the Australasian Bioethics Association Conference in 2001. A few months earlier, Autogen, an Australian biotechnology company, had announced a deal with the Ministry of Health of Tonga, a small kingdom of 170 islands in the South Pacific. The agreement, brokered in secrecy, would give Autogen the right to collect genetic materials and create a genetic database, in return for annual research funding and royalties. Tonga's population is relatively homogeneous and isolated, and therefore attractive for identifying genetic patterns of common diseases. In the kingdom itself, the announcement produced public outcry. The population had not been informed or consulted. But making human biological materials into commercial property was also against the indigenous belief that human blood and genes are sanctified as owned by God. There were fears that in a small community such as Tonga, genetic information would be readily known. Genetically affected individuals would therefore have difficulties with employment, insurance, bank loans and even marriage.

Tonga, like other Pacific nations has a real health problem. More and more people are affected by diabetes and obesity. Research could help to find causes, cures and preventive strategies. For these reasons, Autogen did not anticipate opposition. They relied on the existing autocratic mechanisms of politics rather than public discussion. When the deal became known, churches and pro-democracy groups argued that collecting genes is disrespectful of indigenous traditions. Obtaining materials after individual informed consent does not take into account the extended family structure in Tonga. They also argued that prospecting genetic materials that are part of God's creation are a form of bio-piracy. Furthermore, the benefits promised were insignificant and only available if, in the future, products can be marketed. Because of the opposition, the project was dropped later in 2001.

An expanding agenda

Textbooks about bioethics will immediately clarify its subjects. They are arranged from before birth (abortion), reproduction (IVF, surrogate motherhood, prenatal screening), genetics (genetic screening, gene therapy), to death (killing and letting die, brain death, advance directives). There are usually some issues between the beginning and the end of life, such as resource allocation, medical research and organ donation. Most textbooks have a similar structure. Some may have a more theoretical focus but the list of relevant subjects has been more or less the same over a long period of time.

The examples in the previous paragraph show how present-day bioethics has moved beyond its traditional scope. Topics such as medical tourism, humanitarian relief, or trafficking have not previously figured on the bioethics agenda. At the same time, traditional topics continue to engage bioethical debate, as the case of Marlise Muñoz demonstrates. While admitting that there is a wider range of topics, the 'newness' of such topics can be contested. It is argued that phenomena such as corruption and exploitation have always existed. Vulnerability is also not a new consideration since human beings as such have always been vulnerable. Disasters have haunted humanity since its beginning. Is there really something new going on in bioethics?

Answering this question requires an examination of the history. Why did bioethics emerge during the 1960s and 1970s? Medicine has, since its origins, been connected with medical ethics. This question will be explored in the following chapters. But a quick answer refers to the progress of medical science and technology. Many of the cases that provoked debate on the ethics of medicine and healthcare were related to the use of technologies that substantially influenced human life. Renal dialysis, heart transplantation, resuscitation technologies, in vitro fertilization, prenatal diagnosis – these are all new technologies that generated debates beyond the traditional bounds of professional medical ethics. In response, bioethics emerged as a new discipline, and has been consolidated during the last 50 years. What has changed recently? The above examples have one characteristic in common: the global dimension. Medicine and healthcare have become international activities. Clinical research is outsourced to developing countries. Human tissues are trafficked across borders. Genetic information is collected in one country and processed into products in another. If surrogate motherhood is not allowed, people can find through the internet other places and opportunities to satisfy the desire to have children. However, it is not only the case that there are new subjects of ethical debate. The global dimension of present-day healthcare has also made existing ethical approaches problematic. New topics are added but the debate itself transforms. For example, the moral ideal that human bodies and their parts can only be exchanged as voluntary gifts and not as paid commodities is increasingly difficult to uphold now that they can be donated in one country and sold in another. One population may have ethical objections to using women as paid baby carriers while for others it is a justified source of income to counter poverty. Globalization has therefore expanded the agenda of bioethics, adding new subjects of ethical concern but also provides a broader scope to traditional subjects, calling into question how to assess these subjects across the world. Is there an ethical framework that can take into account the values of all populations?

A broader theoretical framework

Global bioethics implies the quest for an encompassing ethical framework that applies globally. Since bioethics has emerged and subsequently developed in many countries, the dominant ethical framework has been elaborated within a specific cultural, political and economic context. For example, in the Western context, personal autonomy is highly appreciated and individual patients want to be informed about their care, and want to decide about possible treatment and intervention. This focus on the individual is less crucial in other cultures. In Tonga, for instance, the extended family is important. Families, rather than individuals, are involved in decision-making. Since the extended family is relatively small, private information is difficult to protect. Furthermore, ideas of property are different. Genetic information and material cannot be somebody's property since they are God's creation. This example underlines two points. First, fundamental ethical notions (such as self-determination and individual ownership) differ according to cultural settings. Second, it is problematic to apply the current ethical framework of bioethics in these settings.

On the other hand, not applying the ethical principles of bioethics in other settings implies double standards. It opens the door to exploitation and abuse. If informed consent to remove body parts is required in Western countries, why is this norm not used in other countries? Why are Ukrainian families not entitled to know what happens to the bodies of their loved ones? Similar worries arise about surrogacy in India. Are the women really free to decide? Is using their services the expression of respect for different cultural values or is it the result of asymmetrical relationships where the power of money drives the practice of surrogacy?

The globalization of medicine and healthcare therefore introduces questions concerning the appropriate ethical framework. There are two approaches in global bioethics.

The first recognizes the limits of current frameworks. They are all bound to the cultural settings in which they have emerged. Doing bioethics in another country requires insight into the ethical notions and principles that are typical for this country. Global bioethics is primarily the label for a variety of ethical approaches. It is encompassing in the sense that it includes various types of bioethics such as Chinese bioethics, African bioethics, and even Mediterranean bioethics, but also Jewish and Islamic bioethics. If there is an overriding ethical framework it is basically characterized by the ethical principle of respect. All perspectives are interesting since one can learn how similar problems are addressed in different settings.

The second approach is articulating the need to develop a truly global ethical framework. It acknowledges the ethical concerns of other cultures and value systems but underlines that human beings have the same dignity, needs and interests so that similar rights, principles and values should apply everywhere for everyone. The development of such a framework will not be an easy task. One cannot simply impose the ethical principles that are fundamental in bioethics because they have been accepted within a specific culture. But, on the other hand, one cannot simply leave human beings at the mercy of a cultural setting which can clearly be unjust, unequal and exploitative. The role of bioethics is not to justify the conditions that affect people's health, diseases and disabilities. Rather, bioethics should help to improve these conditions on the basis of ethical arguments and practices that apply to *all* human beings. Why do we care about what is happening in other countries like Haiti? Obviously many people in fact do care, as the surge of humanitarian aid exemplifies. Many physicians and nurses travelled to Haiti to provide hands-on assistance. They felt solidarity with suffering human beings. Global bioethics makes a normative point: We *should* care because there is an encompassing framework of ethical principles that motivate, and even oblige us to do so. This framework refers to a moral order that is higher than the specific cultural setting or value system in which individuals are living. We now live in a global moral community where fundamental principles are shared by everyone. Global bioethics in this sense is the new language of humanitarianism, emphasizing that we are citizens of the world who have responsibilities to each other. Distance and borders are morally irrelevant.

Global bioethics

The global dimension of bioethical issues has produced a new stage, or a new kind of bioethics. The aim of this book is to clarify and explain what global bioethics is. It has a broader agenda and theoretical framework than bioethics as it has developed in the last half century (what will be called 'mainstream bioethics'). This is the result of two features. First, global bioethics has become a *worldwide* discipline since it attends to the ethical concerns of humanity, no longer limited to a country or region of the world, or a particular part of the world population. Second, global bioethics is *encompassing* since it takes into account the ethical values and principles of various populations without assuming that one specific set of values and principles is dominant. The emergence of global bioethics and its characteristics will be examined in the following chapters. It will be important to examine the phenomenon of globalization and its impact on bioethics. There are two views. While bioethics originated in some countries because the development of science and technology created ethical problems in healthcare practice and research, globalization of science and technology will generate similar ethical problems, but now for almost all countries. In this view, the source of ethical problems is still the same (scientific and technological power). The other view, taken in this book, is that globalization itself has become a source of ethical problems (due to economic power). It is not the scale but the type of ethical problems that is different due to particular processes of globalization that are fundamentally changing the social, cultural and economic conditions in which people across the world are living. For example, in many countries the benefits of scientific and technological progress are simply not available for the majority of the population. The ethical problems are the result of social inequality, injustice, violence and poverty. The changing social context negatively impacts human health and well-being. Generally, globalization, up to now, led to more private and commercial healthcare services and less social security and governmental protection. This has made healthcare more accessible for the wealthier members of societies while other groups became more vulnerable. The economic context of science and healthcare is furthermore associated with corruption, trafficking of organs and body parts, and scientific misconduct. If this type of globalization produces ethical problems, global bioethics will not be a different stage but a new kind of bioethics.

CHAPTER SUMMARY

- Bioethics in Western countries has developed since the 1960s and 1970s in response to the power of scientific and technological progress in medicine and healthcare.
- This specific origin is reflected in the agenda of bioethics, which traditionally includes topics from the beginning to the end of individual human life.
- Due to the processes of globalization, bioethics nowadays is confronted with a broader range of challenges because healthcare and medicine has spread around the globe.
- Globalization not only introduces new topics of debate but also questions the existing ethical frameworks of bioethics.
- The result is a new stage or a new kind of bioethics: global bioethics. This will be explored in this book.

2

FROM MEDICAL ETHICS TO BIOETHICS

Although the expression 'medical ethics' was used for the first time in the nineteenth century, many scholars assume that medical practice has always been associated with medical ethics. Health and disease, treatment and care must have engendered ethical questions from the origin of medicine as a specialized activity of healing. Medical practitioners wanted to distinguish themselves by a commitment to high moral standards so that patients could trust them. But in fact, we do not know whether the ethical concerns of the past are similar to the ones of later times when the new term 'medical ethics' was coined. Many earlier publications, as well as writings from other cultures, do not conform to the current notion of medical ethics. They diverge in advocating virtues, conduct or duties while coincide in emphasizing the personal qualities of the physician. Medical ethics was the discourse of medical practitioners. This emphasis was satisfactory for a very long time, but it became problematic after the Second World War.

The good doctor

In the West, Hippocrates (fourth century BC) is known as 'the father of medicine'. He was a contemporary of the famous Greek philosophers Socrates and Plato. In his view, medicine should be emancipated from mythical and magical thinking about illness and suffering. Physicians should act on the basis of experience and rational reasoning. Hippocrates argued that one can no longer assume that diseases have a supernatural cause. The sources of illness are not miraculous but can be found in nature. Physicians should make accurate observations and conduct experiments to identify what pathological processes are going on and how they can be remediated. Hippocrates thought this scientific methodology of observation and analysis should be combined with an ethical approach. A good physician is competent and skilful but also responsible and responsive; he will follow certain ethical rules (as formulated in various codes).

Ancient Greek medicine was not unique in its connection to ethics. Healing activities are as old as humankind. Ancient Mesopotamia was famous for its level of medical expertise. The Code of Hammurabi (king of Babylon in the eighteenth century BC) is applauded as the first attempt to protect patients from incompetent practitioners. Egyptian doctors regarded Imhotep (twenty-seventh century BC) as the founder of medicine. The same role was ascribed to Sushruta and Charaka in the ancient Indian medicine of Ayurveda. They built on an older tradition in which Hindu physicians took so-called Vaidya's Oath requesting them to give absolute priority to the care of their patients. The father of traditional Chinese medicine, Sun Si Miao, formulated ethical prescriptions, similar to the Hippocratic Oath. A good doctor should be selfless, quiet and determined, showing compassion and an 'open heart'. In different cultures, therefore, medicine as a human activity has been connected to concerns about good and reliable practices, either by emphasizing the virtues of the individual practitioner or external standards for professional behaviour.

SUN SI MIAO: *ON THE ABSOLUTE SINCERITY OF GREAT PHYSICIANS*

'A Great Physician should not pay attention to status, wealth or age; neither should he question whether the particular person is attractive or unattractive, whether he is an enemy or friend, whether he is a Chinese or a foreigner, or finally, whether he is uneducated or educated. He should meet everyone on equal grounds. He should always act as if he were thinking of his close relatives.'[1]

Virtues

Many of the ancient texts on medicine and medical ethics are more likely to be the product of schools than works of individuals. The texts illustrate that there were groups of practitioners with a particular vision of medicine, combining scientific discipline with moral requirements; this is what distinguishes them from other types of healers. The significance of this vision is that it explains that medicine has specific ethical implications for its practitioners: they have to commit themselves to a particular set of moral rules; they have to manifest certain virtues, for example compassion, integrity, honesty, self-control and prudence. In order to act in a competent manner, the physician needs to be a virtuous person.

The role of virtues is important since the doctor–patient relationship is asymmetric. The ill person in need of assistance is always the weaker party. The agent is the doctor and the patient is passive. Virtues direct the physician to the best interests of the patient; they help to fulfil his obligations. These ethical dispositions need to be nurtured, trained and developed. The education of physicians therefore implies more than manual and technical competencies; it is a long process of transforming a person into a good professional.

Codes of conduct

Another feature of medical ethics is codification, i.e. the statement of codes of conduct expressing rules and prescriptions for the behaviour of professionals. Though codes, like Hammurabi's, have existed since ancient times, the formulation of explicit rules and norms by the professionals themselves became fashionable in the eighteenth and nineteenth century. At that time, the growth of medicine, the establishment of hospitals, rapid commercialization, and the rising demand for medical treatment contributed to the perception that the usual ethics of the virtuous professional were no longer sufficient. There was, for example, growing competition and rivalry among doctors that could not be solved with appeals on the moral sensitivity of individual physicians. Such problems could only be addressed if collective standards were created for the medical profession as a whole. The English doctor Thomas Percival (1740–1804) is usually given credit for this transition from individual virtue ethics to professional ethics. He encouraged professional collaboration and argued that when doctors have disputes, they need to be regulated collectively, in the same way as they, as a profession, determine what a reliable treatment is, how scientific experiments are done, and what counts as objective evidence or quality care. If physicians as a professional body can demonstrate such self-regulation they will in return obtain patients' respect and social trust; they will also be granted collective autonomy. Percival published his rules in 1803 under the title *Medical Ethics*. This was the first time that the term 'medical ethics' was used in print.

Percival's approach to medical ethics became influential when professional associations of doctors were established. In 1847, the American Medical Association (AMA) adopted, as one of its first activities, a code of ethics based on his book. With this code, a new vision of medical ethics was introduced that emphasized professional responsibilities rather than individual virtues.

The purpose of ethics

The fact that medicine and ethics have converged in many different cultures suggests that moral issues have always been regarded as elemental in medical practice. But the emphasis on ethics was not disinterested. In early Greece, when the Hippocratic doctors were active, everybody could claim to be a healer and offer medical services. There was no professional identity; standards of care or practice did not exist and ill people were supposed to find their way among a multitude of competing healers. In this medical marketplace, Hippocratic doctors tried to distinguish themselves as practitioners who worked with rigorous empirical methods and followed ethical rules; they were not eyeing people's money.

Percival's ethics was a response to the growth of new medical institutions as well as medical commerce. Particularly in the new hospitals, physicians, surgeons and apothecaries needed to cooperate. Individual virtues, important in solo private practice, would not suffice to overcome rivalries and competition in this new setting. Percival therefore emphasized the social responsibility of professionals to society that gives privileges. Instead of personal virtue ethics, they needed a professional ethics based on the ideal of collaboration. In more recent times, codes of ethics adopted by medical associations have been regarded with suspicion since ethics is used as leverage to claim a monopoly for a specific category of physicians.

Perhaps economic self-interest has been a driving force in the development of medical ethics, but there was at the same time a genuine concern about the possible negative impact of economic interests on medical practice. The older medical ethics texts in different cultures emphasized that the virtuous doctor should not be motivated by money. The physician's first priority should be the interest of the patient; that is what separated him from other practitioners who were primarily driven by earning money or selling drugs. The later efforts of codification can be regarded from the same perspective. The AMA Code was adopted in a strongly commercialized environment but was in fact an attempt to correct market imperfections, for example by prohibiting advertising and by making sure that practitioners were reliable through licensing. The AMA also proposed an 'ethical' policy regarding drugs by advocating that patent medicines of secret composition should no longer be sold directly to the public.

Professional ethics

Today, the AMA Code is celebrated as the first modern professional code of medical ethics. For the first time physicians dared to break away from traditional virtue ethics, a morality based on the personal qualities of the practitioner, and they accepted the need for formal standards and obligations in a document voluntarily adopted by the profession as a whole. This was indeed a radical transformation of medical ethics into professional ethics. But the influence of the AMA Code outside of the United States was limited.

Many European countries took another approach: 'medical deontology'. This term first appeared in 1834 as the title of a book by Jeremy Bentham, the English philosopher and founder of the ethics of utilitarianism. Deontology is the practical part of ethics ('morality made easy' as Bentham wrote[2]); it is concerned with the distribution of obligations. For Bentham, duty and interest are closely connected, and both are related to virtues. Being good means doing good. Both are in the interest of the person himself or herself and of other persons at the same time. Bentham's ideas were influential in France. Maxime Simon published a well-known book on medical deontology in 1845, stating that the profession of medicine imposes a strict morality on its members.[3] Medicine is presented as a 'noble profession' that requires its practitioners to combine the brain and the heart. Simon systematically discusses three types of duties: (a) duties of physicians towards themselves and towards science; (b) duties of physicians towards patients; and (c) duties of physicians towards society. The epicentre of medical ethics for Simon was within the individual doctor. If we want to improve or change medicine, we need to focus on improving the physician.

This emphasis on deontology as medical duties connected with individual virtues rather than semi-legal rules of conduct standardized in codes, was prevalent in Europe, at least until the mid-twentieth century. One reason is that professional associations were established rather late compared to the US, and were initially not emphasizing medical ethics. In the UK, the British Medical Association (founded under another name in 1832) never succeeded in adopting a code of ethics. In France, since 1845 many medical associations (or unions) have been established at local and regional levels. A General Association at the national level was formed in 1858 as well as a national union of medical syndicates in 1881. Neither national organization ever adopted a code of ethics, although individual doctors published about medical ethical issues and local syndicates developed deontological statutes. The general sentiment of German doctors was expressed by the famous medical scientist, Rudolf Virchow. In an official speech for the Berlin Medical Society in 1885, he declared himself proud that in this organization it has not been necessary to make a code of ethics. Virchow proudly explained that it was not necessary to write down the duties of doctors in an external code since they all had them internalized.

The divergent development of professional ethics had different backgrounds. Improving medical education was the initial goal of the AMA. Education was very diverse, its quality inconsistent, and doctors were trained in heterogeneous ways. Because of this diversity in training and education, medical practice was chaotic. There was an obvious need for uniform standards of behaviour and rules for good practice, in order to create a professional community, especially in times when medical science was rapidly advancing. In Europe the same urgency did not exist. Medical ethics continued to emphasize the importance of virtuous practitioners and underscore their duties. At the same time, emerging insurance companies, increasing state interference and patient activism created challenges that enlarged the notion of medical ethics. In countries such as France and Germany, doctors were increasingly confronted with social and welfare legislation as well as mutual aid societies, with new issues such as work injuries and medical prognostication. These phenomena illustrated that individual doctors had obligations to society. In this context of social change, codification was re-evaluated as an instrument to create professional solidarity and to articulate a professional ethics to resist growing state influence. The French Medical Deontology Code was eventually adopted in 1947 as joint effort of medical association and government. It introduced a section on 'duties of brotherhood': the physician has duties towards his colleagues; he also has an obligation to provide 'moral assistance' to fellow members of his profession. The same idea was expressed previously by Percival, emphasizing ethics as an 'Esprit de Corps' (a common spirit of comradeship among the members). Medical ethics is the professional ethics shared among colleagues.

In retrospect it seems that the efforts of codification in medical ethics are relatively recent. For a long time, and in many countries, medical ethics continued to be regarded as a personal commitment, through either taking an oath or accepting a deontology. However, over time this personal commitment became included in a professional ethics. It was no longer sufficient that certain virtues and duties were internalized by its practitioners, it was also necessary, given the changing social conditions of medical practice, that obligations for professional conduct were externalized in codes of conduct. The underlying idea, however, has been the same. Medicine is not just a job. It is a special kind of occupation, i.e. a profession that requires an ethical framework. The term 'profession' comes from the Latin *professio*: an avowal or promise; it refers to an act of publicly declaring to be a member of a profession and to have special ethical commitments. Since it has a particular body of knowledge and skills, medicine requires long formal training. But medicine is also focused on important social values such as health and preservation of life. Its expertise is therefore valued by society, which recognizes the authority of professionals. Members of a profession enjoy a high degree of autonomy. It is their expertise to make practical judgements concerning diagnosis, prognosis and treatment. They determine how they practice as well as the circumstances in which they practice. It is up to professionals to decide what the benefits and harms of interventions are. A profession therefore determines the substance of its own work and regulates in the sense that it is licensing new members and is using collegial discipline. These privileges are warranted because professionals have accepted a set of ethical standards; they are devoted to the ideal of service to others and have special obligations, often expressed in a code of ethics.

COMMON FEATURES OF PROFESSIONAL ETHICS

- Particular expertise required to practice.
- Extensive and long formal training.
- Focus on important social values.
- Authority of professionals recognized by society.
- Professional autonomy.
- Self-regulation.
- Ideal of service to others.
- Special obligations (code of ethics).

Medical ethics under pressure

The traditional concept of medical ethics with its emphasis on the virtues, conduct and duties of professionals became increasingly problematic in the decades after the Second World War. Three developments put the concept under pressure.

1. Criticism of the medical profession

Since the 1960s, professions were scrutinized for their political and cultural influence. They were regarded as monopolistic institutions primarily engaged in protecting the privileges and status of their members. They were also criticized because of their power. Rather than serving others, professions were increasingly considered as mechanisms to serve their own interests. Especially the medical profession caused discontent. It was not only argued that the role of medicine in promoting health was overestimated but even that it was itself endangering the health of populations and individuals. In daily practice, the ethics of professionals is driven by self-interest; they only want to expand their power through 'medicalizing' ever more areas of ordinary life and behaviour. The medical profession has become a major institution of social control. It is responsible for new burdens of disease, increase of disabling dependence, and undermining the ability of individuals to cope with illness and suffering.

MEDICALIZATION

'The medical establishment has become a major threat to health. Dependence on professional health care affects all social relations ... A professional and physician-based health care system which has grown beyond tolerable bounds is sickening for three reasons: it must produce clinical damages which outweigh its potential benefits; it cannot but obscure the political conditions which render society unhealthy; and it tends to expropriate the power of the individual to heal himself and to shape his or her environment.'[4]

---

2. Power of science and technology

The 1950s and 1960s saw unprecedented advances in medical science and practice. New diagnostic technologies such as fibre-glass endoscopy and coronary contrast radiology were introduced. Innovative surgery brought artificial lens implantation, hip prostheses and pacemakers. Medication such as oral contraceptives and corticosteroids became available, following the introduction of penicillin during the war, the first effective antibacterial drug. These new interventions led to drastic changes in medical practice. But they also raised ethical issues. In the 1950s, artificial respirators were built to treat patients with poliomyelitis, leading to the establishment of intensive care units. Life-supporting technologies generated new questions: when exactly is a person dead; when is critical care indicated; and can it be withdrawn if the result is that the patient expires? In 1960, kidney dialysis was first applied to save the life of a renal patient. However, there were few machines and too many patients so the question was who would be allowed to live and who would be left to die? In 1967, the first heart transplantation was performed. This intervention led to rethinking of definitions of death. The traditional ethics of doing no harm and promoting the interest of the individual patient was no longer sufficient when care for one patient is terminated in order to save another. The boundaries between life and death became blurred, as did the duties of physicians.

Simultaneously, significant changes were taking place in medical science. Clinical research expanded rapidly with more and more new medication tested in various categories of human subjects. Important advances were made in the basic sciences. In 1953 Watson and Crick discovered the structure of DNA; this opened the door to the revolutionary development of genetics. Increasing knowledge of the bio-molecular processes important for the origin of life and mechanisms of disease created the possibility that human life itself could be manipulated and changed.

3. Social change

Critique of the medical profession and concerns with the growing power of science and technology occurred within a changing social environment. The asymmetric doctor–patient relationship of traditional medical ethics in which the doctor is the authority and the patient is passive and obedient, was no longer accepted and medical professionals started to be criticized for their paternalism. There is also the more fundamental critique that medicine has become impersonal. Medical knowledge is expanding but medical care is deteriorating. Health professionals have more interest in diseases and interventions than in patients. In the words of Mexican philosopher Ivan Illich: 'the patient is reduced to an object being repaired; he is no longer a subject being helped to heal.'[5] In this climate, a new type of patient is emerging, using the language of patients' rights and demanding new mechanisms of public control. Patients are emancipating. They emphasize their rights rather than the virtues and duties of physicians. Medical ethics is blamed for continuing the dominance and authority of professionals while present-day citizens are self-determining persons. Since patients are the interested party, the ones who are suffering, they should be in control. In daily practice there is a gap between the ethical ideals and the actual behaviour of health professionals. Doctors are focused on research, driven by scientific knowledge and technology but without any feelings of empathy for patients.

Continuity and discontinuity

Although Percival introduced the term 'medical ethics' in 1803, it is not clear when the history of medical ethics began. There is a tendency to assume that there has been continuity with similar ethical concerns from the beginning of medicine itself. Similar challenges occur if we want to determine when medical ethics was transformed into bioethics. Is bioethics really new or simply a new disguise for older issues? Is it dealing with the standard set of ethical concerns that have preoccupied medicine since the beginning? It is clear, however, that in the 1960s and 1970s a transition took place from the traditional concept of medical ethics to a new concept of ethics, though it is difficult to pinpoint a particular moment in time when this new concept emerged. It is also clear that this new concept differs substantially from the traditional one.

Broadening ethics

Questioning authority and power of medical professionals is associated with a decline of trust in physicians. At the same time, technological and scientific innovations introduce many new possibilities for treatment; it also puts ethical questions on the agenda that are beyond the scope of professional ethics. New developments in medical research and transplantation also show that the interests of individual patients do not always prevail over scientific and social interests. Decisions concerning the possible use of these innovations are too often left to doctors alone. At the same time, a new type of patient is emerging who wants to be in charge of his or her own health and life. This patient rejects the depersonalization and dehumanization of healthcare executed by paternalistic physicians, and claims personal care and respect.

Against this backdrop, the notion of professional ethics is extended in various directions:

a   *Inclusiveness*
Ethics of healthcare can no longer exclusively focus on medical practitioners. The nature of ethical challenges demands the involvement of patients, and in fact everyone, sick or well. It also engages other healthcare practitioners, in particular nurses. It furthermore needs the active participation of other professionals in law, social sciences, humanities, philosophy, theology, political science, anthropology and history. Ethics should be the language of many voices besides the medical one.

b   *Reflection*
Traditional medical ethics is static. It is primarily transferred from one professional generation to another. It is learned by example and role modelling, watching senior practitioners. There is usually no need for explicit teaching. The new ethics discourse requires analysis, debate and reflection upon values and principles. There are no easy and ready-made answers. Since ethics is a matter of rational argumentation rather than authority, there is a need for moral dialogue and deliberation among different actors.

c   *Holistic approach*
The new ethics discourse takes into account that health depends on many factors that are not medical: nutrition, housing, work conditions, lifestyle and hygiene. The human person is to be considered within the larger context of society, culture and environment. Fragmented, specialized and de-personalized care is no longer sufficient to promote individual health.

d   *Human values*
Birth, suffering and death are not merely medical facts but have meanings depending on values. Ever more scientific and technological innovations are

available in healthcare but the ethical question of whether they should be applied depends on these values. Now that life and human nature themselves have become scientific projects, human beings have to determine how and for which purposes these innovations will be used. Otherwise science and technology, rather than being instruments to be shaped by human beings, will determine how humans will be shaped. There is a need to bridge the gap between the world of science and the world of human values.

The transition

Different times and occasions have been mentioned for the transformation of medical ethics into bioethics. Significant moments are often related to disturbing experiences:

a   *Scandals of medical research*
    The publication of Henry Beecher's whistle-blowing article in 1966 is for some scholars the defining moment for the birth of bioethics.[6] Beecher analysed 22 cases of clearly unethical clinical research, all published in leading medical journals. Some human experiments clearly violated the rights of research subjects, jeopardized their health and lives, and sacrificed patients for the sake of science. Traditional medical ethics did not prevent these ethical transgressions. It showed that professional self-regulation was inadequate and that a new ethical approach was needed.
    For other scholars, the defining moment was earlier. Self-regulation and reliance on duties and virtues of professionals was discredited by medical experimentation during the war. The Nuremberg Medical Trial in fact condemned the German medical profession for atrocities committed in the name of science. The 1947 Nuremberg Code was the first international document to protect the rights of research subjects. It demonstrated that the phase of traditional medical ethics was over. A new ethical framework based on human rights should replace it.

b   *Challenges of medical technology*
    The ethical queries connected to the use of new medical technologies are often mentioned as being responsible for the birth of bioethics: artificial resuscitation, organ transplantation and intensive care. The year 1960 is a significant moment. The invention of the arterio-venous shunt enabled chronic dialysis and saved the life of the first patient with renal failure. But the number of dialysis machines was limited so that only few patients could be helped. To select patients a special committee was established with non-physicians. This captured enormous media attention, and brought the moral problem of allocation of scarce resources to the centre of public debate. The case is the start of bioethics since it showed the limits of the traditional approach to medical ethics. For the first time, physicians delegated the moral issue of selecting patients to live or to die to a committee of laypersons. The ethical

challenge of new technology also stimulated public debate and scholarly reflection. Finally, the case posed a problem that medical ethics has not faced before: allocating scarce resources cannot be resolved within the context of the doctor–patient relationship; it requires considerations of justice, i.e. balancing the individual patient's interests against those of others in the same population of chronic patients.

Bioethics emerged from reflection on the power of medical science and technology. But the emergence was gradual: a slow transition from the prevailing approach of medical ethics to a new and broader ethical discourse. Bioethics had in fact many births. Edmund Pellegrino, one of the founders of bioethics, has called the transition phase 'proto-bioethics'.[7] In the 1960s and 1970s, the language of human values was dominant, driven by concerns over the 'dehumanization' of medicine. In several European countries, these were also the concerns of advocates of so-called 'anthropological' medicine. They rejected the demarcation between body and mind in contemporary medicine. In their view, the methodology of the natural sciences was insufficient to understand the human person; medicine is a science of the human person and should therefore use a comprehensive understanding of life, disease and suffering. Refocusing medical attention on the subjectivity of the patient paved the way for a new understanding of the moral dimensions of healthcare.

CHAPTER SUMMARY

- The term 'medical ethics' was first used in the nineteenth century, though the general assumption is that medicine and ethics have been connected from the beginning.
- Central in the tradition of medical ethics is the practitioner, with emphasis on virtues, conduct or duties.
- With the establishment of professional organizations in the nineteenth century, medical ethics was interpreted as professional ethics.
- Traditional medical ethics became problematic in the 1950s and 1960s because of: (a) critical attitudes towards professions; (b) the growing power of medical science and technology; and (c) social change with the rise of a new type of patient.
- A new and broader ethical discourse gradually emerged, emphasizing:
  - Inclusiveness: a patient-centred and multidisciplinary approach.
  - Reflection: using rational argument and moral deliberation.
  - Holistic approach with a broader view of health and healthcare.
  - Human values.

Notes

1 Hans-Martin Sass (2005) Emergency management in public health ethics: Triage, epidemics, biomedical terror and warfare. *Eubios Journal of Asian and International Bioethics*: 161–166 (quote page 162).
2 Jeremy Bentham (1983) *Deontology: or Morality made easy* (edited by Amnon Goldworth) In: J.R. Dinwiddy (ed.) *The collected works of Jeremy Bentham*. Clarendon Press: Oxford, pp. 117–281.
3 Maxime Simon (1845) *Deontologie medicale: ou des devoirs et des droits des medecins dans l'état actuel de civilisation* [Medical deontology: or the duties and rights of physicians in present-day civilisation]. J. B. Baillière: Paris.
4 Ivan Illich (1975) *Medical Nemesis. The expropriation of health.* Calder & Boyars: London, p. 11.
5 This critique of the medical profession is from: Ivan Illich (1975) *Medical Nemesis. The expropriation of health.* Calder & Boyars: London, p. 70.
6 Henry K. Beecher (1966) Ethics and clinical research. *The New England Journal of Medicine*, 274(24): 1354–1360.
7 Edmund Pellegrino (1999) The origins and evolution of bioethics: Some personal reflections. *Kennedy Institute of Ethics Journal*, 9(1): 73–88 (quote page 74).

3

FROM BIOETHICS TO GLOBAL BIOETHICS

The term 'bioethics' was coined by Van Rensselaer Potter.[1] In order to deal with the fundamental problems of humankind, it was necessary, according to Potter, to develop a new discipline. It needed to be broader than the usual medical ethics, and combine the knowledge of the sciences, particularly the life sciences, with the expertise of philosophy and ethics. The new term was an immediate success. Evidently it was an appropriate label to epitomize the critique and need for change formulated in the previous decades. But the new discipline did not develop in the way Potter had envisioned, so he renamed it in 1988 as 'global bioethics'.

Potter's priority problems

Van Rensselaer Potter (1911–2001) was educated in chemistry and biology. He spent nearly all of his professional life at the University of Wisconsin-Madison, where he received his Ph.D. in biochemistry in 1938. Two years later he was appointed as staff member at the new McArdle Laboratory for Cancer Research. Potter was an enthusiastic researcher. In the 1960s he started to publish on issues outside the initial scope of cancer research, such as the concept of human progress, the interrelation between science and society, and the role of the individual in modern society. He became interested in broader issues because of the challenges of the research in which he was engaged. Cancer is a complex phenomenon that requires interdisciplinary collaboration. Scientists cannot merely focus on individual and medical perspectives. Cancer is related to lifestyle and individual behaviour, for example smoking, but also to environmental pollution with carcinogenic substances. As long as medical research is focused on the individual level, it can bring limited progress, for example with new chemotherapies that can alleviate suffering and prolong life expectancy, or with new surgical interventions. Much more progress can be accomplished with preventive programmes educating people to live more wisely. His long years of cancer research convinced Potter that a broader approach beyond the individual and medical perspective was necessary. At the same time he regretted that his long-term preoccupation with cancer had prevented him from addressing more important issues. Potter summarized these, what he calls priority problems of our time, as the six Ps:

- population;
- peace;
- pollution;
- poverty;
- politics; and
- progress.

According to Potter, if we do not address these major problems, it will not matter whether medical science succeeds in prolonging the average lifespan by another ten to twenty years because humanity as such will not survive. Population growth is a problem since the world's population is increasing faster than the resources available to sustain it are. Peace itself is not a problem but rather our inability to realize and maintain it. War and violence are endangering the survival of the human species, especially in Potter's time when nuclear warfare was a real threat. Pollution is a major challenge since it is causing the environment to deteriorate. Poverty leaves millions of people in miserable conditions. Politics is problematic since policy decisions are usually focused on short-term effects. In democratic political systems with changing governments long-term perspectives are generally neglected. Politicians are more concerned with their re-election than with goals that attend to the survival of the human species. Finally, progress is on Potter's list because it is always assumed that things will get better. But improvement will depend on how and in what direction 'progress' is made – more is not always better.

In Potter's analysis, the basic question is how we can make sure that there will be a future for our children and grandchildren. If we do not address the above major problems, future life will be unbearable and humankind will not continue to exist. What we need is a science of survival.

BIOETHICS ACCORDING TO POTTER

'Mankind is urgently in need of new wisdom that will provide the 'knowledge of how to use knowledge' for man's survival and for improvement in the quality of life. This concept of wisdom as a guide for action ... might be called *Science of Survival* ... A science of survival must be more than science alone, and I therefore propose the term *Bioethics* in order to emphasize the two most important ingredients in achieving the new wisdom that is so desperately needed: biological knowledge and human values.'[2]

A new approach: bioethics

For Potter, it was obvious that a radical departure from traditional medical ethics was necessary. In order to be able to deal with the priority problems of humankind we need an innovative approach in ethics that combines the science of living systems, or biological knowledge (*bio*), with the knowledge of human value systems and philosophy (*ethics*). This approach demands that moral traditions are re-examined in the light of growing knowledge. But it also requires overcoming the tendency to take issues apart, analyse and specialize rather than to combine, synthesize and generalize.

The first characteristic of bioethics in Potter's view is its orientation towards the future. This is exemplified in the title of his first book: *Bioethics – Bridge to the future*. Bioethics should be a bridge between the present and the future because, for the survival of humankind, it is vital to focus on long-term interests and goals. In order to avoid disasters such as nuclear warfare or ecological catastrophes, we need to develop positive visions of the future. Such visions can only be obtained in a scientific manner, making assessments on the basis of adequate information and knowledge but also using knowledge about what is possible and what is probable. Determining future possibilities therefore requires the combination of knowledge and methods from the sciences and the humanities. For Potter, the ultimate goal of bioethics is long-term global human survival. This goal can only be reached by forging compromises between 'sanctity of life' and 'quality of life', between individual interests and the social good, and between the quality of the environment and commercial exploitation (or what Potter calls the 'sanctity of the dollar').

The second characteristic of Potter's notion of bioethics is interdisciplinarity. The problems of humankind are multidimensional. Addressing them requires combining all categories of knowledge from disciplines as different as basic biology, social sciences and humanities. Proceeding as usual with each expert in his own specialty will not yield any solutions. We do not need more technological or specialized knowledge. What should be created, according to Potter, is a new type of scholarship combining the knowledge of new science with old wisdom. Interdisciplinary groups should exchange new ideas and examine old ones in the light of new scientific knowledge. Such approaches can generate the wisdom that is fundamental for the overarching long-term goal of human survival. Ideas and wisdom will only be generated if we can bridge two gaps that are typical for modern times: the divide between science and ethics, and the gap between nature and culture. In Potter's analysis, one of the reasons why the future is in danger is that the sciences and the humanities are not communicating. There are two separate domains that have no common vision of the problems that humankind is facing; the discourse of facts is far apart from the discourse of values. Another reason is that we do not use our knowledge of biological evolution to guide and direct cultural evolution. We cannot be sure that our species will continue to exist. Natural selection can lead to extinction because it is focused on self-preservation and reproduction in the immediate present. At the same time, our species is the only one that is conscious of the process of evolution and can take steps to guarantee survival. Human beings can and should use their knowledge of nature and evolutionary processes to bring real progress in culture and society. Instead of separating nature and culture, human beings should build a culture that has survival and development as its goal.

The third characteristic of bioethics is that human beings are part of nature. We cannot continue to degrade and destroy the environment. Bioethics should widen its scope and focus on the question of how to preserve, in Potter's words, 'the fragile web of nonhuman life that sustains human society'.[3] In the 1960s concern for the environment increased. Rachel Carson published her book on the deleterious impact of pesticides in 1962. The supertanker *Torrey Canyon* shipwrecked on the west coast of England in 1967 causing the first major oil spill. In 1970, American environmental activists organized a nationwide Earth Day to raise awareness about environmental issues. In the same year, the US government established the Environmental Protection Agency. And in 1971 the United Nations proclaimed the annual celebration of an international Earth Day. In his environmental concerns Potter was influenced by Aldo Leopold, one of the founders of environmental ethics. Human beings, in Leopold's view, are part of the ecosystem that includes soils, waters, plants and animals. Potter dedicated his first book on bioethics to Leopold in the strong belief that bioethics should include environmental concerns.

Bioethics as a bridge

Bioethics as advocated by Potter is best characterized as a bridge. Since its main purpose is the creation of connections, a bridge is only an instrument to facilitate movements from one area to another. It is always 'between', directing attention to what it connects. As a metaphor, the bridge is a symbol of communication; it refers to allowing passage, reaching across gaps, overcoming divides, separations and obstacles, and creating spatial coherence. Most often, bridges are human constructions; they have to be made if we want to cross them. They are also expressions of power and symbols of culture (like the aqueducts of Roman times, or the bridge in Mostar). Bioethics is no different. Rather than the insular focus of traditional medical ethics, it must reach out in different directions and bring together what is usually separated. For Potter, there is a need to make four bridges at the same time. To address contemporary problems, the new discipline must bridge the gaps between present and future, science and values, nature and culture, man and nature. Only this broader outreach will produce a really different approach. Bioethics should be the final stage of the development of ethics over time, already predicted by Leopold. The first stage is dealing with relations between individuals while the second is focusing on the relations between individuals and society. The third stage should have a broader scope, i.e. the relations between human beings and the environment. Bioethics, in Potter's view, should be the realization of this final stage.

BIOETHICS AS FOUR BRIDGES ACCORDING TO POTTER

1   *Bridge between present and future*
    Bioethics is a new approach focused on long-term interests and goals that safeguard the survival of humanity.
2   *Bridge between science and values*
    Bioethics is a new discipline combining biological knowledge with a knowledge of human value systems.
3   *Bridge between nature and culture*
    Bioethics is responsible for the future, applying scientific knowledge of biological realities and the nature of human beings in order to accomplish cultural evolution.
4   *Bridge between man and nature*
    Bioethics is a new ethics taking into account the new science of ecology and regarding human beings as interrelated with their environment.

The surge of bioethics

Bioethics has developed rapidly since the 1970s. Potter himself was surprised to see how quickly the new term 'bioethics' was used in the scholarly and public debate. Starting in the United States, specialized institutes were established as well as the first professional association and the first academic journal. An important event was the creation of the National Commission for the Protection of Human Subjects of Biomedical and Behavioral Research in 1974. It can be regarded as the first bioethics committee at the national level. As a consequence of legislation aimed at regulating the field of human experimentation, it demonstrated that bioethics had not only expanded as an academic discipline but also as a public and policy concern. The growth of bioethics in the United States was followed with similar developments in other countries.

MILESTONES IN THE EARLY HISTORY OF BIOETHICS

1969   USA: Institute of Society, Ethics and the Life Science (Hastings Center)
1970   USA: Society of Health and Human Values
1971   USA: Joseph and Rose Kennedy Institute for the Study of Human Reproduction and Bioethics (at Georgetown University)
1971   USA: First issue of journal *Hastings Center Report*
1972   Argentina: Institute for Medical Humanities
1974   USA: National Commission for the Protection of Human Subjects of Biomedical and Behavioral Research
1974   Netherlands: Department of Healthcare Ethics, Maastricht

1974	Belgium: Establishment of an ethics committee at the Medical School Louvain
1975	Spain: Institut Borja de Bioetica, Barcelona
1975	UK: First issue of *Journal of Medical Ethics*
1976	Canada: Bioethics Centre in Montreal
1978	USA: *Encyclopedia of Bioethics*
1983	France: National Consultative Ethics Committee for Life and Health Sciences
1984	Sweden: National Council on Medical Ethics
1985	European Association of Centres of Medical Ethics

Institutional achievements were fuelled by high profile cases. In 1972, newspapers revealed the Tuskegee study. Since 1932, poor black men with syphilis were enrolled in a government-sponsored study but they were never informed that they were research subjects. They were also never told that effective treatment with penicillin had become available. The public outcry about this unethical research led to the creation of a national commission setting ethical standards and recommending policies for medical research. The Tuskegee case was a public sign that professional self-regulation was insufficient and that strict oversight of medical research was necessary. A few years later another case questioned professional authority in clinical medicine. Karen Ann Quinlan was in a vegetative state and on life support. Her parents requested the artificial ventilation be discontinued so that Karen would be allowed to die. The physicians and the hospital refused. The New Jersey Supreme Court decided in 1976 that the wishes of the parents, as Karen's surrogates, should be respected. Similar cases occurred elsewhere. In 1973, the legal verdict in the Postma case stating that the patient's death in certain specified circumstances may be justified was the start of an intense public debate on euthanasia in the Netherlands. In 1978, the birth of Louise Brown in the United Kingdom as the result of in vitro fertilization provoked a worldwide ethical debate. The new reproductive technologies and the possibilities of the biosciences to influence and even create human life motivated France in 1983 to be the first country to establish a national bioethics committee with a wider mandate than medical research.

A more comprehensive scope

Debates on ethical questions connected to the growth of medical research and technology demonstrated two changes in medical ethics. First, the ethics discussions were no longer focused on the behaviour of professionals. Many ethical issues went beyond the usual orientation on good conduct, duties and virtues. New ethical problems have emerged related to death and dying, continuing or foregoing treatment, reproductive technology, and allocation of scarce resources. The scope of medical ethics therefore has substantially enlarged. Second, the ethical debate is no longer in the hands of medical experts. The media, policy-makers, lawyers and health administrators are involved, but first of all citizens became aware of the significance of ethical issues. Cases like Tuskegee and Quinlan affirmed that professional self-regulation needed to be replaced by emphasis on patients' rights and reviewed by third parties, particularly courts and ethics committees.

This broadening of medical ethics took place in the late 1960s and early 1970s. A leading role was played by a new institute at Georgetown University in Washington, DC. At the instigation of André Hellegers, an obstetrician, the Kennedy Institute for the Study of Human Reproduction and Bioethics was founded in 1971. It was the first university institute focused specifically on bioethics. The basic idea was to create an interdisciplinary setting combining science and ethics to study the new problems emerging in medical science and healthcare. It was this 'Georgetown model' that would set the tone for the further development of the field of bioethics. Just three years later, the term 'bioethics' was in widespread use.

Discipline

In a relatively short period of time bioethics, initially conceived as a vision, has become a separate discipline. Teaching programmes have come into existence in many schools. Networks of ethics committees and ethics consultation services in healthcare facilities have been established, as well as flourishing research programmes, and scholarly journals, textbooks, conferences and associations. New concepts were introduced (for example, autonomy, justice and informed consent). Specific methodologies and theories were elaborated (based for instance on the principles of justice or of respect for personal autonomy). In its first 20 years, philosophical inquiry and language dominated the field. Bioethics is now profiling itself as a branch of applied ethics. The new discipline is governed by the paradigm of 'principlism', the conviction that its ethical framework is principle based. This view is expressed in the definition given in the *Encyclopedia of Bioethics*, published in 1978. It is canonized in Beauchamp and Childress' *Principles of Biomedical Ethics*, one of the most influential textbooks of the new discipline.

THE PRINCIPLE-BASED PARADIGM OF BIOETHICS

Bioethics is 'the systematic study of human conduct in the area of the life sciences and health care, in so far as this conduct is examined in the light of moral values and principles.'[4]

Biomedical ethics is 'the application of general ethical theories, principles, and rules to problems of therapeutic practice, health care delivery, and medical and biological research.'[5]

In this conception, ethics is performing four tasks: clarifying concepts; analysing and structuring arguments; weighing alternatives; and advising a preferable course of action. These tasks can be applied in research, in the clinical setting, and in policy-making. Since the focus is on concrete dilemmas, bioethics can connect philosophical theory with practical analysis of cases and with the provision of directions for policy.

The principle-based approach was demanded in the early days of bioethics. The National Commission was mandated to identify the basic ethical principles underlying the conduct of research involving human subjects. In its Belmont Report (1978) three principles were distinguished, i.e. respect for persons (or autonomy), beneficence, and justice.[6] Beauchamp and Childress proposed four principles, adding non-maleficence to the other three. Although disagreements arose over the relative importance of principles, and other scholars were elaborating theories based on fewer or more principles, the approach was attractive. Principles provide a source of moral knowledge that is open to reason and experience. The medical profession used to claim that the ethical norms for practicing medicine can only be identified by health professionals themselves. The emphasis on principles shows that this claim is wrong. Principles are commonly shared and accessible for everyone with reason and experience. Furthermore, principles are attractive for normative ethics since they have a double meaning: they refer to the starting point for moral justification (as in the Latin term *principium*) but they also formulate the first, most significant directives for action (as in the Latin term *princeps*).

Controversies around terms and origins

In two decades of rapid development, bioethics firmly established itself as a discipline as well as a profession, with specialized areas such as clinical ethics, research ethics, public health ethics and policy advice. The paradigm of principlism, however, became increasingly criticized. Other methodologies and theoretical approaches were elaborated, such as phenomenological ethics, hermeneutic ethics, narrative ethics, casuistry, virtue ethics and care ethics. Anthropologists and sociologists studied the social and cultural context of the bioethical discourse showing that bioethics in fact was not a universal and objective approach but deeply dependent on a specific value system. Historical analyses present bioethics as a typical American invention. It not only originated there, but it is also the expression of its ethos that is characterized by individualism, technological optimism and pragmatism. It has ingrained the belief that the future can always be made better, and that there is an answer to every problem.

These characteristics became problematic when in the 1990s bioethics advanced in other parts of the world. The need for an expansive view is shown in two, at first sight, minor controversies. The first concerns the terminology. The word 'bioethics' was not uniformly accepted. Even in the US many scholars continued to speak about 'medical ethics' but in a broader sense, no longer referring to physician ethics. Others used the notion 'biomedical ethics'. In other countries, 'healthcare ethics' was a more common term. This is more than a linguistic battle. It reflects concerns as to whether bioethics is really a new approach or just another name for a continuation, in an updated form, of traditional medical ethics. It also questions the proper role of bioethics discourse. In France, for example, the pragmatism of bioethics is not appreciated. Intellectuals, especially philosophers, argue that bioethics is not a discipline, and that it does not require any special expertise. It is primarily a public discourse about health, disease, medicine and life sciences in which every citizen can participate. It is dangerous to establish expert bodies of specialists in charge of ethics. They will result in catechisms of moral dos and don'ts, suggesting that ethics is the practical rule of individual life rather than society's reflection upon the progress of science. Similar, but more radical points of view, were defended in Germany in the 1990s. Here, bioethics itself is regarded as a suspect activity. It is an academic scheme to justify questionable practices such as infanticide of handicapped new-borns or controversial research, reminding people of the immoral science during the Nazi period. Moreover, bioethics is criticized as a facilitator of commercial interests, representing especially pharmaceutical businesses from the US. It is a subtle, soft repressive tool used by powerful interests groups to make practices acceptable and palatable for reluctant populations. For some time, bioethics conferences in Germany mobilized more protestors than participants.

The second controversy concerns the origin of bioethics. Although Potter was the first to use the term 'bioethics' in a publication in autumn 1970, his priority claim is diluted by the argument that the word was already in use around the same time by the founders of the Kennedy Institute. Proposing a 'bilocal' birth therefore endows the same seniority to different conceptions of bioethics. The story is further complicated by the claim that bioethics is a European innovation, and that the term was in fact coined long before the emergence of bioethics as a movement and discipline. The German pastor Fritz Jahr introduced the new German word 'Bio-Ethik' in a publication in 1926. His concept of bioethics is broad, based on respect for both human beings as well as other living organisms in the universe, similar to the respect for life advocated by his contemporary Albert Schweitzer. Whatever the claims, the story of the birth of bioethics shows that dissatisfaction with the narrow scope of medical ethics and the need for a new interdisciplinary approach was not a sudden event. Behind the disputes about the term and its origin, however, is a larger question: how to characterize the movements and disciplines that are labelled as bioethics? What kind of discipline should bioethics be?

BIOETHICS ACCORDING TO JAHR

Bioethics is '… the assumption of moral obligations not only towards humans, but towards all forms of life. In reality, bio-ethics is not just a discovery of modern times. […] the guiding rule for our actions may be the bio-ethical demand: '*Respect every living being on principle as an end in itself and treat it, if possible, as such!*'[7]

Just another medical ethics?

For Potter the answer was clear. In 1975 he pointed out that the word bioethics had become fashionable.[8] But he was disappointed. It was only a new word for old business. The broad vision he had in mind was restricted to medical issues and medical technology. The Georgetown interpretation of bioethics is in essence 'medical ethics redefined'; it does not produce a new approach but only applies the traditional approaches to new sets of problems. What is called bioethics is for Potter 'an outgrowth of medical ethics'. For this reason he prefers to label it 'medical bioethics' to demarcate the difference with his own broader vision. First, medical bioethics is primarily concerned with the perspective of individual patients: how can their lives be enhanced, maintained and prolonged through the application of medical technologies? The basic problem, in Potter's view, is that medical bioethics continues to elaborate an ethics of individuals and relations between individuals; it is not really a new ethical approach. Second, medical bioethics is exclusively interested in the short-term consequences of medical and technological interventions as well as the prolongation of our current individual existence. Third, it is unrelated to social, cultural, political, and environmental determinants of human life. Finally, it is not interdisciplinary: it brings in philosophers and theologians, but does not recognize the crucial role of scientists, particularly biologists.

Potter concedes that medical bioethics has a somewhat broader approach than traditional medical ethics. It focuses, for example, on new technologies, particularly in the field of reproductive medicine, which generates intricate ethical questions. But it is still too narrow to address what are, in his view, the basic and urgent ethical problems today that are threatening the survival of humankind. A much broader vision is necessary to cope with these problems. Now that the term 'bioethics' is used in the conventional medical way, it does no longer evoke the need for a more inclusive approach, new perspectives and new syntheses. Potter wants to re-emphasize the concern for the future of the human species by qualifying the terminology. Medical bioethics needs to be combined with ecological bioethics, and other forms of ethics related to human life such as agricultural ethics. All these approaches in bioethics should be merged in a new synthetic and interdisciplinary approach that Potter now calls 'global bioethics'.

POTTER'S CRITIQUE OF BIOETHICS

- It is medical ethics under a new name; it is restricted to medical applications; it is focused on individual survival; it is concerned with short-term views and solutions.
- It emphasizes individual autonomy, not social good.
- It is specialized, not presenting a general perspective.
- It is applied ethics, not a new interdisciplinary approach.

- It has no global perspective; its focus is on problems specific for developed countries, ignoring health problems in others parts of the world.
- It has no interest in environmental ethics, agricultural ethics, and social ethics.

Expanding bioethics

To transform bioethics into more than a new name, the field needs to expand in various directions. Bioethics has now a somewhat broader range than traditional medical ethics, including other persons than health professionals, covering areas of research, and providing regulation and oversight. But it is not broad enough; its issues and concerns are rather limited. Bioethics has demarcated its own territory; it has become an entity in itself and has lost its function as bridge. It has no interest in environmental ethics; it does not regard human beings as responsible for non-human life as well as the conservation and preservation of the biosphere. It has no interest in agricultural ethics; it is not addressing the issue of sustainable food production and healthy consumption. It has no interest in social ethics; it does not examine problems generated by the corporate drive for continuous growth, market expansion and maximum profits. Furthermore, it is primarily focused on problems that are specific for rich and developed countries, ignoring health problems in other parts of the world. It also assumes that the bioethical discourse as born and matured in these countries can simply be exported as a universal framework that applies to all countries.

The concept of bioethics as a bridge has two additional implications. First, it postulates that human beings are not isolated, self-ruling monads but essentially connected and connecting. They are bridge builders, reaching out to others. This view of humans as relational beings presents a perspective that differs from the one usually prevailing in bioethics, emphasizing individual autonomy rather than social interests, social responsibilities and the common good. Second, it is dynamic. Concepts are also like bridges; they do not primarily represent the world but they lead to something; they bring us from one experience to another. For ethics, philosophical analysis will not suffice. Reflection therefore should be complemented with activism.

Global bioethics

The notion of 'global bioethics' is introduced by Potter in a second book, published in 1988. It articulated the new vision that we need an ethics with a better balance between the human and the natural world, and with a broader scope relating medical concerns to social, cultural and environmental ones. The adjective 'global' demonstrates what should be new; it means 'worldwide in scope' as well as 'unified and comprehensive'.

> ## GLOBAL BIOETHICS
>
> 'The time has come to recognize that we can no longer examine medical options without considering ecological science and the larger problems of society on a global scale ...' Global bioethics therefore is 'a unification of medical bioethics and ecological bioethics.' [...] 'The two branches need to be harmonized and unified to a consensual point of view that may well be termed global bioethics, stressing the two meanings of the word global. A system of ethics is global, on the one hand, if it is unified and comprehensive, and in the more usual sense, if it is worldwide in scope.'[9]

The fact that bioethics is a worldwide ethics can have two meanings: international or planetary. Bioethical issues and concerns transcend national boundaries. But global bioethics is more than international bioethics; it is not merely a matter of crossing borders, it concerns the planet as a whole. Bioethics nowadays is relevant to all countries and takes into account the concerns of all human beings wherever they are and whatever their religious or cultural beliefs. While bioethics has emerged in Western countries, it is expanding globally. There is new social space, not simply a collection of countries, regions and continents that engages bioethical discourse. This new space has emerged since ethical problems today are global. An important source of inspiration for Potter at this point was the work of Pierre Teilhard de Chardin, French philosopher and geologist. Writing in the 1940s and 1950s Teilhard anticipated what we now call 'globalization'. He argued that humanity will develop into a global community. Due to the processes of 'planetary compression' (intensified communication, travel, exchanges through economic networks) and 'psychic interpenetration' (increased interconnectedness and a growing sense of universal solidarity) humankind will be involved in an irresistible process of unification. Human beings are becoming increasingly aware of their interdependency and their common destiny. The world population is growing while the surface of the earth remains the same; therefore, people are obliged to cooperate even more intensely.

Potter's second meaning of 'global' refers to bioethics as more encompassing and comprehensive, combining traditional professional (medical and nursing) ethics with ecological concerns and the larger problems of society and culture. Events in his time, such as the disasters of Seveso in Italy in 1976 (thousands of people and animals were contaminated with the chemical dioxin) and Bhopal in 1984 in India (an industrial accident causing the death of up to 20,000 people due to toxic gases) convinced him of the relationship between health and the environment. For Potter, global bioethics is the mainstream into which medical and ecological bioethics eventually must merge. Taking global bioethics seriously will imply a further evolution of ethics as predicted by Leopold: from a focus on relations between individuals, to relations between individuals and society, and ultimately to relations between human beings and their environment. The evolution of ethics in the context of healthcare reflects this pattern: developing from medical ethics into bioethics, healthcare ethics or biomedical ethics, we are witnessing today the emergence of global bioethics.

CHAPTER SUMMARY

- The word 'bioethics' as a broader approach to medical ethics was introduced in the scientific literature by Van Rensselaer Potter in 1970.
- Fundamental problems such as pollution and poverty threaten the survival of humanity. To cope with these problems, it is necessary to combine life sciences and ethics.
- For Potter, bioethics is a new and interdisciplinary approach; a bridge between present and future, science and values, nature and culture, humans and nature.
- Bioethics developed rapidly since the 1970s, first in the US, then in other countries. It is institutionalized as a separate discipline. As a branch of applied ethics it used a principle-based methodology to address specific biomedical problems.
- For Potter, bioethics as it has developed is just medical ethics under another name, not really a new and broader approach; it continues to emphasize medical, individual, and short-term concerns; it neglects social and environmental issues; its scope and agenda are limited.
- To overcome its limitations, in 1988 Potter introduced the notion of 'global bioethics'. It has two main features:
  - worldwide scope, and
  - comprehensive approach.

Notes

1 The two main publications of Van Rensselaer Potter are: *Bioethics: Bridge to the future* (1971) Prentice Hall: Englewood Cliffs, NJ; and *Global Bioethics: Building on the Leopold legacy* (1988) Michigan State University Press: East Lansing.
2 Potter (1971) *Bioethics: Bridge to the future.* Prentice Hall: Englewood Cliffs, NJ, pp. 1–2.
3 This reference is from Potter's article: Biocybernetics and survival. *Zygon* 1970 5(3): 229–246 (quotation on page 243).
4 Warren Reich (ed.) (1978) *Encyclopedia of Bioethics.* Free Press: New York, p. xix.
5 Tom L. Beauchamp and James F. Childress (1983) *Principles of biomedical ethics.* Oxford University Press, New York/Oxford, pp. ix–x.
6 National Commission for the Protection of Human Subjects of Biomedical and Behavioral Research (1979) The Belmont Report: Ethical principles and guidelines for the protection of human subjects of research. *Federal Register* 44(76): 23191–7.
7 Fritz Jahr (1927) Bio-Ethik: eine Umschau über die ethischen Beziehungen des Menschen zu Tier und Pflanze (Bio-ethics: a panorama of ethical relations of man toward the animal and the plant) *Kosmos*, 24 (quotations on page 2 and 4).

8 Van Rensselaer Potter (1975) Humility with responsibility – A bioethic for oncologists: Presidential address. *Cancer Research* 35: 2297–2306.
9 Van Rensselaer Potter (1988) *Global bioethics*, pp. 2, 76, 78.

4

GLOBALIZATION OF BIOETHICS

For a long time, Potter's ideas were not influential. His publications were hardly read and he was not recognized by the bioethics community. For example, Potter's role was not acknowledged in the first edition of the *Encyclopedia of Bioethics*. This started to change in the 1990s. His work became known especially outside of the United States, in various countries such as Colombia, Croatia, Italy and Japan. In 1988, the journal *Global Bioethics* was established by Brunetto Chiarelli, professor of anthropology at the University of Florence, Italy; one year earlier he had founded the Italian Association of Bioethics. Aiming at the integration of biological sciences and humanistic understanding, the journal was initially published in Italian but since 1994 all articles have appeared in English. In 2000, Potter was awarded the first Bioethics Prize of the International Society of Bioethics, convening in Gijon, Spain. This chapter will show how bioethics has developed as a global activity. The central question is: How has a broader approach to bioethics gradually emerged, using Potter's new label of 'global bioethics'?

Globalization

The brief answer to this question is that the context of bioethics has significantly changed, transforming bioethics itself. The keyword for these changes is 'globalization'. This is a complex phenomenon that has been significantly altering human existence during the past two decades. There is no agreement among scholars how exactly to describe, define or interpret this phenomenon. But it is certain that communication patterns have changed with the advent of new technologies. Computers, mobile telephones, internet, email and social media facilitate human interaction and create worldwide interconnectedness. Greater interdependence across the globe is also promoted by activities that transcend geographical boundaries, for example those of news media, transnational corporations and international research organizations. Global institutions such as the United Nations (UN) and Doctors without Borders (MSF) have become more important. Globalization is not a single process but can best be understood as a set of processes with multiple dimensions.

GLOBALIZATION

'Globalization refers to a multidimensional set of social processes that create, multiply, stretch, and intensify worldwide social interdependencies and exchanges while at the same time fostering in people a growing awareness of deepening connections between the local and the distant.'[1]

Dimensions of globalization

The main dimensions of globalization are as follows:

1   *Economical*: globalization is associated with the emergence of a new economic order that regards the world as a single market. To promote free trade, existing trade barriers have been eliminated. New forms of commerce and a new financial infrastructure have emerged with transnational corporations more powerful than many nation states.
2   *Political*: globalization is a political project in which the nation state, politics and governance are increasingly 'deterritorialized'. The flow of people, money and technology has made the nation state less powerful. Intergovernmental organizations play an increasing role. At the same time, economic globalization requires a lot of political interventions to facilitate free trade.
3   *Environmental*: globalization is driven by the values of consumerism; it allows the accumulation of material possessions and increasing economic welfare. At the same time, continuous growth endangers the ecosystems of the planet. The global interdependence implies that environmental degradation will have impacts beyond borders. Pollution, destruction of biodiversity and global warming are now worldwide phenomena.
4   *Cultural*: globalization is a process in which cultures are exchanging. Products of one culture are almost instantaneously available in other cultures. This may lead to better appreciation for the diversity of cultures but also to fears that one culture will impose itself. For example, in scientific publications and internet communication, the English language has become dominant. Many currently existing languages are disappearing.
5   *Ideological*: globalization is possible in different ways. However, it is often guided by what is called 'globalisms': specific ideas, norms and values that are taken for granted. The dominant globalism, at least in the earlier stages of globalization, is neoliberalism; this assumes that the market is a self-regulating mechanism; the goal is to remove any constraints on free competition.

These dimensions show that processes of globalization have positive and negative aspects. They create enormous possibilities for communication but at the same time risks of homogenization of language and culture. They make more economic goods available but at the risk of environmental degradation. Increasing worldwide interconnectedness in healthcare and medical science will also produce new opportunities and challenges that will be reflected in bioethics.

Globalizing bioethics

The transformation of bioethics into global bioethics due to the changing context of globalization has been a gradual process. Four stages can be distinguished.

1. Broader scope

In the first stage, the dominant paradigm of bioethics is increasingly criticized. The focus is on the concept of individual autonomy since this implies a relative neglect of notions such as the common good, public interest and community. The individualism of bioethics discourse makes it hard to examine issues such as resource allocation, technology assessment, the aims of healthcare, and justice. Daniel Callahan, the founder of the Hastings Center, has since 1981 repeatedly criticized the reigning approach as 'minimalist ethics'.[2] Its main concern is that actions are freely chosen and that harm to others is avoided. Further moral judgement is not possible. As long as decisions are freely made by autonomous individuals, the substance of their decisions cannot be morally assessed. This thin ethics has two consequences. First, public morality is separated from private morality; it only exists on the basis of voluntary contracts and engagements. The public interest is the aggregate total of individual interests. Moral vocabulary therefore is transparent but also lean. Second, the agenda of bioethics is limited. The primacy of moral autonomy turns many choices into private, not moral, choices. Questions such as what is good for us as a society or what are the proper goals of medical progress can no longer be asked. Sociologist Renée Fox supports this critique: bioethics is centred on the value complex of individual rights, self-determination and privacy, at the expense of social responsibility and social justice.[3] Since the 1990s, many more voices would argue for a stronger social perspective. The thin ethics of individual autonomy is traditionally concerned with the patient problems of clinical medicine and medical technology, but cannot adequately address the social and institutional context of medical choices. Bioethics should therefore broaden its agenda in light of growing knowledge that health is also determined by socio-economic factors rather than just healthcare. It should become global in the sense of more encompassing.

MINIMALIST ETHICS

'... the sole text of the morality of an action, or of a whole way of life, is whether it avoids harm to others. If that minimal standard can be met, then there is no further basis for judging personal or communal moral goods and goals, for praising or blaming others, or for educating others about higher moral obligations to self or community.'[4]

2. Global issues

The next stage is the confrontation of bioethics with a new set of problems associated with globalization. The recognition of HIV/AIDS as a new and deadly disease in the early 1980s made bioethics aware of the limitations of its current ethical framework. It was generally assumed that infectious diseases were no longer a major health threat. In 1979, the WHO officially declared that smallpox, once one of the most fatal infections, had been eradicated. The emergence of the HIV/AIDS pandemic accentuated the importance of public health and the common good. The pandemic demonstrated the significance of the socio-economic context for the dissemination of the disease. It also brought to light the role of social inequalities and poverty in making some groups more vulnerable than others. Particularly resource-poor African countries were hit exceptionally hard. The context itself could significantly worsen the conditions of affected people through social phenomena such as discrimination, marginalization and stigmatization. Furthermore, HIV/AIDS impressed as a global problem. Effective prevention and treatment programmes required worldwide implementation and coordination. The UN recognized that the disease was a global emergency, a threat to the survival of humanity. But mechanisms for global governance were weak. The growing awareness that problems associated with globalization could not be addressed by individual countries is reflected in new approaches and ways of thinking in bioethics. An example is the increasing emphasis on human rights. Another is the debate on global justice, universal access to medication, and the need to assist resource-poor countries in their struggle with catastrophic diseases. This all contributed to a gradual broadening of the bioethical debate. The earlier established boundaries of bioethics needed to be extended. In light of public health problems, a new vision was required, going beyond bioethics' individualistic orientation, its focus on individual medical care, and sophisticated interventions and technologies. In the 1990s, other global problems would enter the bioethical agenda: organ trade, brain drain of healthcare workers, and the conduct of transnational companies. These moral issues reiterated Potter's point that bioethics can no longer be solely focused on relations between individuals.

3. Global expansion: internationalization and cross-cultural studies

The third stage of transforming bioethics into a global endeavour is the proliferation of international activities and collaborations. The 1990s were the decade in which bioethics became visible as a global activity. In all regions of the world, initiatives were taken to establish professional associations and platforms for cooperation, to create new journals, and to organize conferences. Intergovernmental organizations such as UNESCO and WHO started formal programmes and activities, showing that bioethics had become a global concern. A major impetus for international cooperation was the Human Genome Project. Starting in 1990, 5 per cent of its annual budget was allocated to research into the ethical, legal and social issues of human genomics. In 1991, the European Union (EU) initiated a biomedical and health research programme that included bioethics as one of the research areas. A prerequisite for funding was international cooperation. The programme included medical or biotechnology with, for example, concerns about confidentiality, and the impact of research on society.

INTERNATIONAL ACTIVITIES IN GLOBAL BIOETHICS (START DATE)

1987	European Society for Philosophy of Medicine and Healthcare
1991	Latin American Association of Bioethics Institutions
1991	Group of Advisors to the European Commission on the Ethical Implications of Biotechnology
1992	International Association of Bioethics
1992	International Bioethics Committee, UNESCO
1992	Steering Committee on Bioethics, Council of Europe
1993	Bioethics Unit of UNESCO
1994	Pan American Health Organization's Regional Program on Bioethics
1996	International Society of Bioethics
1997	Asian Bioethics Association
2001	Pan African Bioethics Initiative
2002	Ethics and Health Initiative of WHO
2003	Arab Committee on Bioethics and Biotechnology

This was also the decade that witnessed an explosion of cross-cultural studies in bioethics. A growing number of publications emphasized the specific bioethical approaches of a country, region, culture or religion. Proposals were launched for typically Asian, Catholic or Mediterranean bioethics. Comparative studies flourished, contrasting Western bioethics with, among others, Japanese or Filipino bioethics. This emergent focus on cultural diversity and pluralism was inspired by two intellectual sources. One is the philosophical debate on multiculturalism. Philosophers such as Charles Taylor and Will Kymlicka argued that respect for cultural differences implies recognition and sometimes special protection rather than mere toleration.[5] In liberal societies, all individuals have similar basic rights and needs. But some have different cultural identities based on ethnicity, race, gender or religion; they are often marginalized and disadvantaged; how can they be recognized as equals in a pluralistic society? Bioethics has emerged as a universal discourse, emphasizing common needs and interests of human beings, and thus principles that apply equally to all of them. How can respect for difference and recognition of specific moral views connected with particular cultural identities be reconciled with such discourse? The awareness of otherness, and the discrepancy between what is common and taken for granted, and what is strange and unfamiliar was introduced in bioethics from a second source: the social sciences, particularly medical anthropology. Comparative research on ethical issues in different cultures provided extensive knowledge about similarities in approaches and views. But, more often, the moral landscape was presented as diversified and heterogeneous, not only showing that problems are different across cultures, but even more that moral visions and perspectives may substantially diverge. For example, in Japan, the role of family members in medical decision-making is much more important than in the United States. Informing patients of a terminal cancer diagnosis is usually not done. According to the Ubuntu worldview in many African countries (see Chapter 8), human beings are interdependent; persons only exist through relationships and community with other persons. In such worldviews, an autonomous individual is an alien notion.

4. Global theory: elaborating universal frameworks

Finally, the recognition of global diversity of bioethical approaches raises the question whether there can be any shared or common ethical principles and values. Ultimately, processes of globalization confront humankind with similar problems, that are not confined to particular cultures, and that can only be adequately addressed through cooperation. Cross-cultural studies can provide descriptive analyses and interpretations of different bioethical visions but in the end the question is what should be done to find answers to global problems such as poverty, pandemics and climate change that pose serious risks to humanity. The fourth stage therefore poses a new challenge. So far, mainstream bioethics, as it has developed since its inception in the 1970s, faces internal criticism that it operates with a limited paradigm and centres on a small set of ethical principles, giving priority to individual autonomy. It now also faces external criticism that its paradigm and set of principles is typical for Western cultures and not shared in many other cultures (at least not in the same priority order). If bioethics wants to address the moral problems generated in processes of globalization, it cannot proceed as usual and apply the principles it has developed to other cultures. It should recognize that it has emerged within a specific cultural setting and that the moral approaches that are appropriate in this setting cannot simply be transferred to another. In order to be global, bioethics will not only need a broader scope, taking into account the type of issues and problems produced by globalization; it will also need a broader ethical framework. This is the multicultural challenge. Is it possible to frame a broader approach so that differences can be appreciated but at the same time commonalities expressed? Can divergence be respected while convergence is promoted? These questions form the background of several efforts to articulate a broader framework for global bioethics. The European Convention on Human Rights and Biomedicine, adopted by the Council of Europe in 1997 (also called the Oviedo Convention), and now signed by 35 European states was a major step in bioethics. It inspired the drafting of similar global policy documents. The Convention situates itself in the tradition of international human rights law, and therefore links global bioethics, biomedicine and human rights. If diverse European countries could agree on a common framework for bioethics, why not try to negotiate a similar consensus on basic bioethical principles for the entire world? This must have been the rationale of member states of UNESCO when they mandated the organization to draw up a declaration of fundamental principles in the field of bioethics. In 2005, member states unanimously adopted the Universal Declaration on Bioethics and Human Rights (UDBHR). It is the first document of international law that formulates a *global* framework for bioethics.

Maturing of global bioethics

Although Potter introduced the name in 1988, it took time for 'global bioethics' to mature. The same was true for bioethics itself since the term was coined in 1970. For Edmund Pellegrino the era of bioethics as philosophical ethics was over in 1985, when the present era of global bioethics began. But in this sense 'global' is used primarily as 'encompassing'. Global bioethics got beyond philosophical bioethics: it includes a range of professional and clinical issues, as well as social policy, organizational, sociological and economic concerns, and legal and religious questions. In the 1990s, 'global' increasingly came to refer to 'worldwide'. With the HIV/AIDS pandemic, global issues entered the bioethics agenda. This global scope is reflected in the revised edition of the *Encyclopedia of Bioethics* (1995): more attention was paid to the international and intercultural dimensions of bioethics. The argument was made that second generation bioethics should embrace social, environmental and global issues; it cannot merely be a broader conceived medical ethics. The 'bio' in bioethics should no longer be restricted to biomedicine and human beings but should acknowledge all forms of life. There now is a need for a substantially different approach. Analysing varying ethical perspectives across the world and recognizing the differences in bioethics globally, the possibility emerges of a comprehensive framework for bioethics that articulates similar concerns, values and principles for all humanity. In this sense, 'global' is referring to 'unified', i.e. commonly shared by everyone on the planet. Global bioethics in this sense was created in 2005 with the UNESCO Declaration.

The process of maturing of global bioethics between 1988 and 2005 is highlighted in several significant cases. Like bioethics was born and sustained in the

1970s through a series of research scandals and controversial clinical cases, the discourse on global bioethics was nourished by recurrent issues that elicited intense debate. One emblematic case is female genital mutilation (FGM, see Chapter 11). It is a ritual traditionally practiced in many countries for a variety of reasons. Because of the injuries and medical complications, the practice came to be regarded as a public health issue in most Western countries, and some countries such as the US adopted laws to prohibit it. Female cutting also was considered as a violation of human rights. In 1997, WHO together with other UN agencies issued a statement arguing for its prevention and eradication.[6] On the other hand, anthropologists have argued that cultural practices should be respected. On what basis can outsiders condemn these practices that are rooted in ancient traditions and different historical and cultural settings, without imposing the norms of their own culture?

An even more acrimonious debate emerged in research ethics in 1997 regarding the use of placebos in clinical trials in developing countries. The standard of care in developed countries is to compare the new drug with currently available medication. In HIV/AIDS trials in Africa and Asia, sponsored by the US government, placebo controls were used. The argument was that medication was too expensive in these regions of the world, so that the standard of care was no treatment. This argument was criticized since it introduces double standards: one higher and more restricted standard in developed countries and a less stringent one in other countries. How can research that is deemed unethical in some countries be executed in other countries? The standard of care debate clearly demonstrated that medical research had become a global enterprise. It also put the question on the bioethics agenda: what should be the ethical framework for such global activity?

The third paradigmatic case occurred in Nigeria, involving one of the world's largest pharmaceutical companies. A governmental committee investigated the trial and concluded that it was illegal and unethical. Because of the emergency situation and the desperation of the parents it was easy to enrol patients, suggesting free treatment for a serious disease. The committee report, however, was never released. In 2002, Nigerian families sued Pfizer in New York because the untested drug had caused grave injuries (11 children died and 200 were permanently disabled) and informed consent procedures had not been followed. The lawsuit was dismissed since the events in Nigeria were outside US jurisdiction. In 2006, the *Washington Post* broke the story after the Nigerian report was leaked: international rules were violated and African children were used as guinea pigs. The publication created international outrage.

Following the publication, a new Nigerian expert committee examined the trial. It appeared that the trial had never been approved by an ethics committee and that the letter of approval was falsified. Several state and federal authorities in Nigeria filed lawsuits against Pfizer that were finally settled in 2009. In the same year, the United States Court of Appeals reversed the earlier dismissal. The Court stated that the requirement of informed consent constitutes a universally accepted norm of customary international law.

THE TROVAN CASE

Kano, the second largest city in Nigeria, was struck in early 1996 by an epidemic of meningitis. While thousands of children were treated in an ill-equipped hospital facility, assisted by MSF, pharmaceutical company Pfizer came in to test a new antibiotics drug Trovafloxacin. The drug had never before been administered to children orally. Parents were often not aware that their children were included in a clinical trial. In many cases no permission was asked to test the drug. Pfizer argued that informed consent could not be obtained from parents because they were illiterate.

The Trovan case is an important milestone in the development of global bioethics, for three reasons. First, it resulted in the acknowledgment that a global ethical framework is developing; at least informed consent is sufficiently accepted in international human rights law that it can be considered a universal norm. Second, it has focused attention on relatively new dimensions of healthcare such as exploitation and vulnerability that are exacerbated through globalization. Third, the case shows that even if there is agreement on a global ethical framework, major efforts should be directed at application and implementation, especially in countries where bioethical infrastructure (ethics committees, ethically relevant legislation, ethics education) is deficient. Finally, differential ethical approaches can have adverse effects. The mistrust created by the case in Nigeria led to boycotts of vaccination campaigns with Muslim leaders arguing that it was a Western complot to poison the population. The programme had to be suspended until vaccines could be imported from Indonesia.

Different versions of global bioethics

There is agreement that bioethics nowadays is subjected to globalization and that it operates within a broader context. But opinions differ as to the impact of globalization upon bioethics itself. Conceding that there are other issues on the current agenda due to processes of globalization, it does not follow that global bioethics exists. It might be only convenient shorthand for the globalization of bioethics. Some argue that if global bioethics exists at all, it is the sub-discipline of bioethics that focuses on international comparisons, like there are specialized areas such as clinical bioethics, research bioethics and public health ethics. Some would even argue that there is no need for a new name. It is misleading since globalization is not anything new; there are merely new formulations of old problems. What the term 'global bioethics' really signifies is not clear: is it an indicator that the context of bioethics is enlarging or is it a proclamation of another kind of bioethics? In fact, the answers vary since there is a spectre of visions ranging from thin to thick versions of global bioethics.

a. Thin versions

These versions agree that the term 'global bioethics' can be correctly used to refer to new developments. But they reject the idea that it signifies a different kind of bioethics. At least four versions can be distinguished.

The first stresses that the moral geography of relevant issues has substantially changed. It means that bioethics today is confronted with a range of new topics, as demonstrated by the examples in Chapter 1. These topics are on the agenda because of increasing interconnectedness. International exchanges between medical schools and health professional training programmes have increased enormously, like international migration of health professionals. International cooperation in research and healthcare nowadays is unavoidable. Health resources such as drugs and devices are produced in many countries, like most goods in the global era. Globalization makes it easy to move products and people around the world. This has positive and negative effects. It also generates ethical questions that need to be addressed in bioethics. In this version, talking about 'global bioethics' is nothing more than referring to this broader agenda.

Another version of global bioethics emphasizes that the scope of bioethics has widened. Due to international exchange and cooperation there are not only more issues to consider but their relevancy is different. The current bioethics debate is focusing on glamorous and sophisticated issues for the relatively healthy, worrying well people, mostly in Western countries; they care about issues such as cloning or enhancement, while for the majority of people in the world other daily concerns will be urgent, such as access to medication, water, adequate nutrition or basic public health. Global bioethics in this version means that priority should be given to certain issues on the agenda, thus rendering bioethics more relevant for more people. It should become 'everyday bioethics' (instead of 'frontier bioethics') or 'bioethics from below'. But still, this changing emphasis does not imply a really new or different kind of bioethics.

The third version argues that contemporary bioethics is encompassing so that its methods are more inclusive. It is global because it incorporates values, concepts and methods that are relevant for as many settings as possible. Now that the world is growing together and borders are irrelevant one can better compare various ethical systems and worldviews. One can learn from Mediterranean, Chinese or Islamic bioethics, and analyse the differences and commonalities between these ethical approaches. Cultural competence is required to be sensitive to ethical views that are different. Global bioethics is a convenient label that brings all these varieties in ethical worldviews together, but again, not essentially new.

The fourth thin version of global bioethics emphasizes discursive activity. Cross-cultural dialogue and debate is the only way to progress towards an ethical framework that is relevant globally. Such a framework does not exist but through dialogue one learns not only what distinguishes other perspectives, but also what is typical for one's own perspective. Global bioethics therefore celebrates moral pluralism. It recognizes that the dominant paradigm of principlism itself is the expression of a particular cultural setting, and that it cannot impose this paradigm to other settings with other ethical worldviews. However, it has not presented an alternative perspective.

b. Thick versions

For other scholars, global bioethics is more than a container term for new issues or methods, and more than a procedural discourse. It is a substantive and comprehensive bioethics that articulates ethical perspectives that are relevant worldwide. Thin versions are wrong since a shared moral language to address global issues exists. There is not simply a need for common values or principles, or a hope that they will emerge, but they actually are available, although there can be disagreement about which values or principles are predominant. Thin versions are also insufficient because the global nature of contemporary bioethical problems requests global answers. We live in one world, not many. If today's moral challenges are not addressed within a global ethical framework, bioethics will be a marginal discourse that only reiterates and reinforces the social, economic and political powers at work in globalization. Global bioethics therefore is a new discourse that emphasizes global values and global responsibilities. There are several thick versions of global bioethics.

The first assumes the strength and infallibility of one approach in bioethics and takes it to have universal relevancy. This approach of assimilation used to be significant in the heydays of principlism. Other ethical views ultimately will have to accept the values and principles of the dominant approach. Nowadays, not many scholars in bioethics are defending it; it is in fact more typical for religious or political fundamentalism. At the same time, this version is often used by critics of global bioethics to suggest that ethical approaches are imposed.

More common is the second thick version which includes different types of cosmopolitanism. They proceed from the idea that there is a global moral community; all human beings are citizens of the world and members of this community, sharing common values and responsibilities. In global bioethics, at least four influential cosmopolitan theories can be distinguished. All emphasize that humans share the capacity to reason. Global bioethics should therefore be based on rational, normative argument.

- *Utilitarian theories* assume that there is only one ethical standard: what will have the best consequences for everyone is the right thing to do. For Peter Singer only a global ethics can provide answers to problems that affect the whole planet such as insecurity, poverty and climate change.[7] Because there is a clear ethical standard, moral relativism should be rejected. Respect for other cultures should not imply relativism while at the same time we should recognize that Western culture has no monopoly on wisdom. Singer argues that we should use rational arguments that are independent of any culture, and that go beyond the borders of our own culture.

- The *capabilities approach* advanced by Amartya Sen and Martha Nussbaum argues that what is necessary for human life and flourishing is the same everywhere: food, clothing, shelter, health and education.[8] Global justice will only be achieved when people have substantial freedoms or opportunities to choose and to act so that they can realize their capabilities. Whether they will be able to do this depends on individual characteristics but also on political, social and economic conditions. Capabilities are options; they provide a zone of freedom to individuals but what will be chosen (a particular functioning) can vary. According to Nussbaum there are central capabilities (such as bodily health and bodily integrity) that are indispensable for a life worthy of human dignity. All individuals should have these core opportunities. The needs for human flourishing are the same across the globe, so that the same standards should be applied everywhere.

CAPABILITIES

'It holds that the key question to ask ... is 'What is each person able to do and to be?' In other words, the approach takes *each person as an end*, asking not just about the total or average well-being but about the opportunities available to each person. It is *focused on choice or freedom*, holding that the crucial good societies should be promoting for their people a set of opportunities, or substantial freedoms, which people then may or may not exercise in action: the choice is theirs ... The approach is resolutely *pluralist about value*: it holds that the capability achievements that are central for people are different in quality, not just in quantity ...'[9]

- *Human rights based approaches* argue that all human beings have certain universal rights because of their inherent dignity and equality. Human rights therefore provide a common language to solve global bioethical problems. This language focuses on the societal preconditions of health and human flourishing as well as on the individual interactions between patients and professional practitioners. It is an ideal global discourse that relates medical concerns with social and environmental concerns. It addresses individuals, communities, populations and governments. Human rights and bioethics were first connected in the 1947 Nuremberg Code resulting from the trial of physicians who performed criminal experiments with prisoners in Nazi concentration camps. Human rights based approaches were particularly articulated in the context of the HIV/AIDS pandemic by Jonathan Mann, the first Director of WHO's Global Program on AIDS. He argued that a global policy required the explicit connection between medicine, human rights, ethics and health.[10]

- *Contractarian theories* focus on the social rules and arrangements, particularly the global institutions within which global problems arise. These institutions should afford human beings access to basic necessities. Confronted with pervasive inequalities with many people living in poverty, hunger, inadequate shelter and without basic healthcare, while affluence, health and life expectancy in high-income countries is only increasing, the question is how global justice can be accomplished. While there is so much progress in science, technology, economy and also in moral norms, why does misery at a global level continue to exist? Thomas Pogge answers this question by critically analysing global institutional arrangements.[11] Citizens and governments of wealthy societies fail to prevent global poverty; they could do more. But the main failure is that they assume that they are not morally responsible for this global condition. Pogge argues that they are in fact actively causing global poverty because they are responsible for the global institutional order that is effectively harming the global poor. Globalization produces interdependencies that impact the living conditions of people. The global order that perpetuates poverty and inequality for many is benefiting people in wealthy countries. Institutional arrangements need to be assessed in terms of a universal criterion of global justice that is fair to everybody.

A GLOBAL MORAL ORDER

'In the contemporary world, human lives are profoundly affected by non-domestic social institutions ... About such global institutions, at least, we cannot agree to disagree, as they can at any time be structured in only one way. If it is to be possible to justify them to persons in all parts of the world and also to reach agreement on how they should be adjusted and reformed in the light of the new experience or changed circumstances, then we must aspire to a *single, universal* criterion of justice which all persons and people can accept as the basis for moral judgments about the global order and about other social institutions with substantial international causal effects.'[12]

---

c Intermediate versions

Thick theories of global bioethics are criticized from two perspectives.

Libertarianism argues that there is no way to overcome moral pluralism. We are all moral strangers. People do not even share the same moral concepts. While in the West, bioethics is a conceptual system, in Asia it is more regarded as a way of life; family and community are morally more important than individual autonomy. There simply is no common foundation to build a global bioethics. Thick versions are efforts to generalize one's own particular value system in the rest of the world.

Communitarianism emphasizes that ethical values are always related to specific communities that share values, history and tradition. The idea of a global community is an oxymoron since there is no sense of belonging, identification or solidarity at a global level. In fact there are many kinds of community. All communities are bounded. Beyond a community's borders there are no commonalities. Thick versions of global bioethics that assume universality and individualism as basic values are the expression of Western communities.

In response to these criticisms, intermediate versions of global bioethics have been elaborated. They do not give up the idea of cosmopolitanism in response to the challenges of globalization but they underline that global bioethics is not a finished product but a project that has not yet resulted in a unified normative approach, comparable to principlism in mainstream bioethics. Intermediate versions have two suppositions in common: convergence and recognition of differences.

- In a world of diversity there is *convergence* towards commonly shared values. Although it is admitted that currently global bioethics is not a cosmopolitan ethics, there is a development towards such ethics, precisely as an effect of processes of globalization. Because specific bioethical approaches are globalized, they are scrutinized, analysed, debated, applied, modified and reinterpreted. They are not imposed on the rest of the world but transformed. Bioethics is not a product that can be imported and used regardless of the local culture. Because it is itself part of culture, exchange means adaptation and modification, and sometimes rejection. In this process of multifarious cultural exchange, a consensus will gradually emerge on a comprehensive approach. Globalization implies accommodation rather than assimilation. Global responsibilities and universal values will be articulated that, although not universally accepted, are applicable to all human beings wherever they are, because they are justifiable on the basis of reason and common interests.

- The second common notion is *recognition of differences*. One can disagree on the existence of a global moral community. Perhaps it is only a metaphor. But growing global connectedness is cultivating a global community in many dimensions of life. Facing global threats such as climate change and pandemics reinforces global consciousness and fosters the search for common approaches. It is not unreasonable to assume that also in bioethics, many values, norms and principles are shared. Exactly the awareness that the dominant paradigm and Western origin of bioethics faces limits in other cultures encourages the necessity to take into account more perspectives and develop a richer and more comprehensive ethical framework. The emergence of such a framework, however, should not lead to a bioethical monoculture. Thick versions of global bioethics should not emphasize adaptation to or integration in a dominant framework so that differences in the end will disappear. Nor should they argue that a new overriding perspective will eliminate different approaches. The challenge is how to distinguish among acceptable and unacceptable differences while at the same time an ethical framework of global bioethics is emerging.

Intermediate versions argue that this challenge can be addressed by combining convergence and divergence. Criticisms of global bioethics often presuppose simplistic views of globalization. While worldwide interconnectedness bridges the gap between distance and proximity, multiculturalism assumes a radical contrast between moral strangers and friends or family. But it is not correct to say that globalization produces either uniformity or multiplicity; it does both. Contemporary people are part of multiple cultures. It is not clear where their roots exactly are. They consider themselves at the same time Dutch, European and citizens of the world. The same is true for the notion of culture itself. No culture today is monolithic and pure. All cultural traditions are dynamic; they have changed and are changeable; they are necessarily a mélange of different components. Differences do not exclude that there is a common core. The term 'interculturality' is therefore more appropriate since it acknowledges diversity while at the same time insisting on universal values (see Chapter 8). While multiculturalism emphasizes respect for diversity, individual freedom, equal treatment, interculturality introduces a moral vocabulary of interaction, dialogue, participation and cooperation. A common ground needs to be cultivated through interaction and communication. Convergence is not given but the result of ongoing activity.

Global bioethics in an intermediate version is finally characterized by a dual perspective. It is global in the sense that it assumes a universal ethical framework (as the result of intercultural dialogue and consensus) and at the same time local in the sense that this framework necessarily has to be applied in diverse cultural settings. This duality is unavoidable. If there are bioethical values and principles that are universal in scope, their meaning has to be specified in particular contexts before they can be applied to the issues and problems arising there. What is true for a contemporary human being who is a world citizen in the global world and simultaneously a fellow citizen within a specific world, is also true for bioethics as a moral discourse that combines universality and particularity.

The need for a global bioethics

To properly deal with global issues in healthcare, life sciences and research, more than a thin version of global bioethics will be required. The reason is found in the nature of these issues. It is certainly true that bioethics continues to be confronted with problems that are associated with scientific and technological advancement. The Muñoz case discussed in Chapter 1 illustrates this point. Nonetheless, many problems today are different, as the other examples demonstrate. They are on the bioethics agenda as consequences of processes of globalization. They are the result of the dominant ideology of neoliberalism. The power of money and commercial interests, rather than the power of science and technology produce many of today's bioethical challenges.

Mainstream bioethics as it has developed since the 1970s is criticized as 'rich man's ethics'.[13] It is often a handmaiden to scientific progress without asking critical questions about the medical and scientific enterprise itself. It is more focused on pleasing the scientific and business communities than protecting the rights of the weak and powerless. It is easily perceived as a way to make high-tech medicine more acceptable to the public and to policy-makers. It is primarily concerned with the value implications of medical progress, but hardly questions progress itself. Against this backdrop, global bioethics cannot be an extension of bioethics as thin versions propose. It needs to be different. It must be able to critically expose the effects of one-sided globalization, not only within healthcare, but on a wider scale in regard to the environment, social justice, equality, scientific research and democratic participation. Global bioethics should scrutinize the policies of global institutions and transnational companies that give priority to economic growth rather than health and social well-being, and to reduction of government expenditure rather than protection of vulnerable populations. It should side with the powerless and the oppressed. The conclusion is that globalization requires more than a reorientation or broadening of bioethics. Mainstream bioethics 'reborn' will not deliver a satisfactory normative discourse to address global issues. The call is for a different kind of bioethics. It should not be so encompassing that it comes to include almost everything. Global bioethics has a focus on 'bio'; it is operating at the intersection of ethics, health, life and science, and on the problems arising at this specific intersection. Thick versions that employ general ethical theories often make bioethics congruent with global ethics in general. Global bioethics should combine the cosmopolitan ideal with practical applications in connection to health and life sciences. An intermediate version that takes into account individual, social and environmental concerns, and that unites universal and particular perspectives is therefore preferable.

The intermediate version of global bioethics presented in this book does not, unlike thick versions, consider global bioethics as a finished product with elaborated theories that are ready to be applied in different settings. Unlike thin versions, it does not regard global bioethics as merely a label for a variety of diverging approaches, or as utopian expectation that perhaps one day will be realized. On the contrary, global bioethics is dynamic. It is imagined as an ongoing activity; it is under construction while it is developing in continuous dialogue among a growing number of stakeholders across the world, gradually converging on shared basic values and general principles, while diverging on many specific issues.

CHAPTER SUMMARY

- Economic, political, environmental, cultural and ideological processes of globalization have significantly changed the context of bioethics.
- Bioethics is globalized in four stages:
  - Broader scope

- – Global issues on the agenda
- – Expansion due to internationalization and cross-cultural studies
- – Global theory.
- Potter introduced the term 'global bioethics' in 1988; three emblematic cases showed the maturation of the field in the 1990s: female genital mutilation, placebos in clinical trials in developing countries, and the Trovan case in Nigeria.
- It is controversial whether globalization of bioethics resulted in a new kind of bioethics. Three versions of global bioethics are distinguished:
  - – Thin versions
    - ☐ Global bioethics is the name for a range of new topics
    - ☐ Global bioethics is an indicator of a wider scope
    - ☐ Global bioethics is a label for encompassing methods covering a variety of ethical worldviews
    - ☐ Global bioethics is a discursive activity that recognizes moral pluralism.
  - – Thick versions
    - ☐ Global bioethics is assimilation to a dominant framework
    - ☐ Global bioethics is a cosmopolitan theory
      - ■ Utilitarian approaches
      - ■ Capabilities approaches
      - ■ Human rights approaches
      - ■ Contractarian approaches.
  - – Intermediate versions emphasize convergence and recognition of differences.
- There is a need for intermediate versions of global bioethics because the social, economic and environmental effects of globalization require critical analysis, combining universal and particular perspectives.

Notes

1 Manfred Steger (2003) *Globalization, A very short introduction*. Oxford University Press: Oxford/New York, p. 13.
2 See: Daniel Callahan (1981) Minimalist ethics. On the pacification of morality, in Arthur L. Caplan and Daniel Callahan (eds) *Ethics in hard times*. Plenum Press: New York and London, pp. 261–281.
3 Renée C. Fox (1989) *The sociology of medicine: A participant observer's view*. Prentice Hall: Englewood Cliffs, NJ.
4 Daniel Callahan (1981) *Minimalist ethics*, p. 265.
5 See: Charles Taylor (1992) *The ethics of authenticity*. Harvard University Press: Boston; Will Kymlicka (1996) *Multicultural citizenship: A liberal theory of minority rights*. Clarendon Press: Oxford.

6 For the 1997 WHO statement on FGM, see: www.un.org/womenwatch/daw/csw/csw52/statements_missions/Interagency_Statement_on_Eliminating_FGM.pdf (accessed 5 August 2015).

7 Peter Singer (2003) *One world: The ethics of globalization*. Yale University Press: New Haven & London.

8 Martha C. Nussbaum (2011) *Creating capabilities: The human development approach*. The Belknap Press of Harvard University Press: Cambridge (MA) and London (UK); Amartya Sen (1999) *Commodities and capabilities*. Oxford University Press: Oxford.

9 Martha Nussbaum (2011) *Creating capabilities. The human development approach*. The Belknap Press of Harvard University Press: Cambridge (MA) and London (UK), pp. 18–19.

10 Jonathan Mann (1997) Medicine and public health, ethics and human rights. *Hastings Center Report* 37(3): 6–13.

11 Thomas Pogge (2013) *World poverty and human rights: Cosmopolitan responsibilities and reforms*. Polity Press: Cambridge (UK) and Malden (MA), 2nd edition.

12 Thomas Pogge (2008) *World poverty and human rights*, p. 39.

13 Erich Loewy (2002) Bioethics: Past, present, and an open future. *Cambridge Quarterly of Healthcare Ethics* 11: 388–397 (quotation on p. 396).

5

GLOBAL BIOETHICAL PROBLEMS

The panorama of bioethics has nowadays significantly expanded as examples in Chapter 1 illustrate. Traditional bioethical problems related to scientific and technological advances in healthcare are still there, but new and different issues have emerged due to the processes of globalization. Global bioethics is arguably developing in response to the theoretical and practical challenges of these processes. Such was the argument of Potter: a new approach is needed because of a new type of problem. In order to better understand global bioethics, it is necessary to examine the nature of these challenges.

Global problems

Phenomena related to globalization are not identical to global problems. Not all issues are problematic, and not all issues are global. Talking about the subject of global warming is different from exposing the global problem of rising temperatures across the world. A similar difference exists between global health and the global problem of health inequalities. In discussing global bioethical problems, two questions need to be differentiated: what makes an issue a bioethical problem, and what makes a problem a global problem? Let us start with the second question.

What makes a problem a global problem?

'International' or 'transnational' events assume the central role of nation states; they are often touching one or more countries, or refer to cross-border phenomena. Migration, for example, is considered a problem for some countries since people move from one area to another. 'Global' events on the other hand are different since they no longer refer to nations as the basic units in the world. Globalization is a complex set of processes with multiple dimensions (Chapter 4). It has transformed the notions of time and space. 'Global' means that we can no longer assume a two-dimensional space with centres and peripheries, as well as clear boundaries. The term points to an unbounded hyperspace with shifting sub-spaces. The keyword is 'deterritorialization'. Global spaces such as airports, amusement parks and hospitals are detached from local references. Nothing reminds us of Singapore, Atlanta or Amsterdam when we deplane after a long flight; perhaps until we see signs or hear language but even that will no longer be helpful since in the business of travel (like entertainment and medicine) the common language is most often English.

The global nature of a problem is determined by the following features:

1 *Worldwide scale.* The problem is not geographically located in a specific space or place. Migration as a global rather than transnational problem means that it is a phenomenon that no longer concerns only a limited number of countries; it is disseminated all over the globe, and therefore has effects that are not specifically located.

2 *Interconnectedness.* One global issue is often associated with other issues. Population growth is linked to high infant mortality, shortages of food, environmental degradation and migration. Otherwise, there are disconnections between impact and origin of problems. Global problems are manifested in certain areas while they are caused in other areas. Rising temperatures across the globe are mostly the result of affluent and polluting lifestyles in the developed world; they result in rising sea levels that risk inundating countries far away, endangering the lives of people who are generally poor. Individuals are affected at micro-level while global problems are created at macro-level. That problems are interconnected means that solving one problem will be difficult without addressing other problems and sometimes focusing on only one problem will exacerbate another.

3 *Persistence.* Global problems have evolved over time and will not easily disappear; they often have a systemic character. Addressing them requires a long-term perspective, as advocated by Potter. Since issues are interconnected, and since there is not one overriding authority that can address them, this type of problem will require sustained cooperation to develop global policies.

4 *General scope.* A global problem is unbounded. It is not a problem for somebody or a limited number of persons but for everyone. This is a difference with mainstream bioethics that focuses on challenges of new technologies that are relevant for a comparatively small group of physicians, patients and policy-makers in a small number of countries.

5 *Need for global action.* Problems are global if they cannot be solved through separate bilateral action; one state or organization cannot effectively solve a global problem. There is a need for collaboration. Problems also go beyond the potency of individual actors; they can only be addressed through collective action. This kind of problem requires a new mindset, since labelling them as 'global' implies that they present a common threat that can only be countered by unbounded responses that are driven by a sense of commonality and solidarity. Global cooperation will only succeed if there is at least a basis of mutual respect and a set of shared values.

A LISTING OF GLOBAL BIOETHICAL PROBLEMS

- Biodiversity loss
- Biological and toxic weapons
- Bio-piracy
- Brain drain and care drain; migration of health workers
- Climate change
- Commercialization of research, medicine and ethical review
- Corruption
- Dual use; bio-terrorism, bio-security
- Exploitation of vulnerable populations
- Food safety and security
- Health disparities (10/90 gap of WHO)
- Health tourism
- Humanitarian assistance and disaster relief
- Inequitable access to treatment and care
- Integrity; conflicts of interest
- Intellectual property rights regime
- Pandemics, and emerging infectious diseases
- Poverty
- Publication ethics, fraud, ghost writing
- Refugees, displacement
- Trafficking (organ, tissues, body parts; humans)
- Wars and violence, repression
- Water shortages

What makes an issue a bioethical problem?

The previous section discusses aspects that transform an issue into a global one. But if an issue is identified as global, it does not necessarily imply that it is a problem. Tourism nowadays is a global phenomenon but generally not regarded as a problem. It becomes problematic if travellers bring back home infectious micro-organisms producing a pandemic, or when patients travel abroad to buy organs from poor vendors. Outsourcing clinical trials to developing countries can speed up the research process and therefore possible approval of new medication but it becomes problematic if it targets vulnerable populations that do not benefit or are possibly harmed since different ethical standards are applied. These examples show that from a bioethical perspective an issue morphs into a problem if it has specific relevance and poses a normative challenge.

1   *Specific relevance.* Climate change was for a long time not regarded as a relevant problem for bioethics. That changed when data increasingly showed the impact of rising temperatures on health and healthcare. Since 2008, the World Health Organization has had a specific work plan on climate change and human health, organizing global conferences on the topic since 2014. Therefore, when a global issue is negatively impacting health and human life it becomes problematic. Being relevant also implies that addressing the problem requires contributions from the life sciences, healthcare, health research and biotechnologies. The first criterion for being a bioethical problem therefore is that the issue is related to health and human life. However, this identifies primarily the bio-dimension, and not the ethical aspect.

2. *Normative challenge.* A global issue is problematic when it evokes a moral sense of indignation or is regarded as a violation of moral principles, values or rights. For example, removing body parts from deceased people in the Ukraine without informing their families and for commercial processing in other countries is an instance of a global bioethical problem related to tissue trade. Or, doing research with children in Nigeria without the same respect for patients' rights as would be required in the United States shows that research ethics is problematic if it does not use the same normative standards globally. These examples present bioethical problems since they involve injustice, unequal treatment and exploitation. They also motivate action; they present a challenge to do something about them. These global issues are not just a matter of description, analysis and explanation, though important for understanding what the issue involves. But as specifically *bioethical* problems they refer to events that are not acceptable, at least prima facie; they call for normative analyses and interventions. Of course, the assumption of a global problem as a normative challenge is that global bioethics has a normative framework at its disposal and can engage it to address this type of problem.

However, it is still not clear what characterizes a *problem*. The two criteria mentioned explain why global problems are bioethical problems. They do not clarify what makes these issues and concerns problems in the first place (see Figure 5.1).

What are problems?

Philosophers have often analysed the specific qualities of what it means to be confronted with problems. Three characteristics of problems can help to further clarify the point of global bioethics problems.

a   *Ambiguity.* A problem is characterized by doubt, uncertainty or puzzlement. It concerns an issue on which opinions differ, on which people disagree or on which there is no opinion at all. This ambiguous, puzzling nature presents what Aristotle has called 'aporia'. It is not clear what the nature and cause of

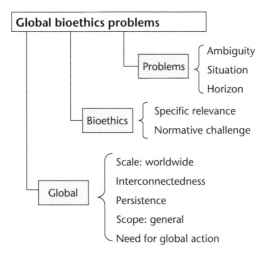

FIGURE 5.1 Global bioethical problems

the problem is, nor what type of solution or course of action is appropriate since different values and interpretations are at stake. But because of this, a problem is the beginning of reasoning and discussing; it triggers an inquiring process.

b   *Situation.* People do not agree on problems. Drug abuse, for example, is a legal problem for many bioethicists in countries like the US, not an ethical one, while in several European countries it is primarily regarded as an ethical problem. Similarly for lack of access to healthcare: many regard this as an economic or policy issue rather than a bioethical problem. This basic disagreement indicates that problems are not simply an external reality that can be detected, discovered or noticed. Problems arise within a particular context as a result of active interplay between subject and object. The American philosopher John Dewey has used the term 'situation' to refer to this central feature of problems. Rather than being isolated singular objects or events, problems are always parts or aspects of what Dewey calls, 'the environing world'.[1] Problems are not simply out there, waiting for us to be addressed. The knowing subject is not a passive spectator who identifies problems. But he is challenged to be active since the situation itself is troubled, confused and indeterminate. It initiates reflection, deliberation, hypothesizing, intervention, manipulation and experimentation. All advances in knowing are the result of activity instigated by a problematic situation. Activity is focused on transforming the problem into a resolved situation. The emphasis on a problem as an 'indeterminate situation' not only connects subject and object but also knowing and acting.[2] For Dewey, a problem is forward-looking; it is defined by its consequences. For example, in bioethics, problems refer to normative action based on what should happen. If drug abuse is defined as a legal problem, the response will be repression and criminalization. But in a global perspective such response is inadequate (since legal systems differ). It also seems to amplify the problem (making drug trade more attractive and profitable). These consequences will trigger other definitions of the problem. Therefore, problems lead to knowledge and action because we want to move from a problematic situation to a cleared-up situation. The challenge for ethics is not different. Problems are part of moral situations that are characterized by uncertainty and conflict. It is not clear what the right and just approach is. Moral principles, in Dewey's perspective, are tools for analysing a moral situation.

c   *Horizon*. The temporal space within which problems are situated is not only forward-looking. Problems are also based on 'precedents' or 'antecedents'. Without background knowledge, experiences and values it would not be possible to consider a particular phenomenon as problematic. Phenomenological philosophers have clarified this aspect of problems with the notion 'horizon'.[3] Prior experiences provide the background that determines whether certain issues in the foreground will be perceived and interpreted as problems. This antecedent general framework of sense is a pre-given structure of knowledge, values and experiences that provides the horizon within which some issues are conceptualized as problematic. Problems, therefore, are not only connected to possible consequences but also to antecedents. Because of these connections to situation and horizon, identifying problems is a dynamic process. Available knowledge and experience determine what will be regarded as a problem, while the problematic situation itself will generate new knowledge and experience so that the horizon will change and be adapted in order to accommodate future problems. In order to explain what issues are interpreted as global problems it is necessary to understand the cognitive and value structure of global bioethics.

THE NOTION OF HORIZON

The 'horizon' in phenomenology has three dimensions:

a   it is a general framework that allows phenomena to manifest themselves and in which phenomena obtain their meaning;
b   it is a limit that is versatile but cannot be surpassed;
c   it can be modified and enlarged since it is relative to our situatedness.

'One could say that the horizon embraces what one is conscious of in a non-thematic way. Itself remaining non-thematic, the horizon keeps the space open for the emergence of each and every theme. The horizon is a structure of determination that predelineates the purview within which each and every phenomenon appears.'[4]

The horizon of bioethics

Potter has argued that a comprehensive approach is needed since bioethics is confronted with new types of problems that are not primarily relevant to individuals but to the collective of all living beings because they endanger the survival of humankind. Furthermore, these problems are not produced by the application of science and technology; rather, scientific knowledge and technological innovation may provide ethics with possible new ways to address the problems. These observations of Potter give some clues to clarify the horizon within which problematic situations animate bioethical reflection and action.

Why did certain issues become problematic for mainstream bioethics? The sources of moral problems during the first few decades of the new discipline are twofold: first, powerful challenges of scientific and technological advancement; second, professional power manifested in prevailing medical paternalism. From the beginning, the dominant paradigm of bioethics is individualistic, so that the horizon in which the progress of science and technology as well as the conduct of healthcare professionals may generate problems is determined by a focus on individual rights and values, self-determination and privacy. Issues, events, activities and interventions transform into bioethical problems because they conflict, at least primarily, with the value of individual autonomy and patients' rights. The focus of mainstream bioethics therefore is on problems arising in the context of clinical medicine and medical research where new medical technology and healthcare knowledge is applied within the relationship between healthcare providers and patients. This is demonstrated in the case of Marlise Muñoz (Chapter 1). The case provoked intense debates on the rights of the mother, the family and the foetus. The physicians, the hospital and the state were blamed for defying the family's wishes. The ethical controversy concentrated on the right of individuals to decline life-sustaining treatment versus the interest of the foetus. The value of individual autonomy determined the horizon in which the case emerged as problematic. Another aspect is the availability of sophisticated medical technology, necessary to determine brain death. Until recently, it was impossible to maintain a brain-dead pregnant woman on 'life support'. Prolonged critical care management is needed to maintain the patient's vital functions as well as to support the foetus in order to deliver a viable and healthy child. Specialists from neonatology, intensive care medicine, obstetrics, neurosurgery and anaesthesiology need to cooperate to guarantee a successful outcome. Given these preconditions, hardly more than 30 cases in the entire world have been reported in the scientific literature since 1982. Only 12 viable infants have been born, mostly in a small number of countries with the technical capacity required. The extraordinary media attention for the Muñoz case is therefore not reflecting the prevalence of the problem but rather its symbolic status: demonstrating the potential of medical technology while at the same time highlighting the right of individuals in the face of medical and state interference. The fact that this case became a significant ethical problem in the public and professional debate articulates the horizon of mainstream bioethics. Almost no attention was given to reports that in 2012 globally 19,000 children under the age of five died every day; two-thirds of them because of infectious diseases, nearly all preventable without sophisticated technology.

What is the horizon of global bioethics? Two features stand out as already articulated by Potter. One is that the focus is not merely on the individual person but on the relatedness of persons to each other, the community, nature, other forms of life, the environment. This refers to the earlier mentioned aspects of interconnectedness and global scope. The second is that the challenges are not first of all produced by scientific and technological advances but are the result of social, economic and political powers at work in globalization. Bioethical issues therefore do not emerge as problems because there is a lack of individual autonomy (as in mainstream bioethics) but because the social conditions are unjust, stigmatizing, exploitative and inhumane. Many diseases are the result of poverty and its consequences such as lack of sanitation, poor nutrition and environmental pollution. They can also be the result of economic and policy processes. An example is the 10/90 gap in global health research.

THE 10/90 GAP

Expenditure on research in global health has increased rapidly. However, in 2000 the Global Forum for Health Research estimated that less than 10 per cent of the $55 billion global spending on health research is devoted to diseases or conditions that account for 90 per cent of the global burden of disease. For example, pneumonia, diarrhoea, tuberculosis and malaria together account for 20 per cent of the disease burden in the world, receive less than 1 per cent of the public and private funds for health research. This disparity is the result of economic as well as policy decisions. It is not profitable to develop new drugs for poor populations that cannot afford them. There also is no urgency since these populations usually cannot put any pressure on policy-makers.

Limited access to treatment and care is a global bioethical problem because effective medication is not available due to priorities in research. Even when they are available, entire populations are deprived from necessary interventions. This is not the result of individual interactions but the consequence of the economic structure of pharmaceutical research, as Thomas Pogge argues.[5] The current regime of patent rules that gives inventor companies a temporary monopoly on their inventions makes new drugs too expensive for many populations, particularly in the developing world. The rules of the world economy deprive especially poor people from treatment for diseases that can be cured, such as malaria, tuberculosis and pneumonia. Consequently, millions of people die each year from curable medical conditions. Problems of course are manifested in individual persons but created in the broader context in which they live. Another example is suicide. The suicide rate in India is among the highest in the world; one fifth of all global suicides take place there. The most common method of suicide is ingestion of pesticides. In rural areas the rates are double those in urban areas, especially among marginal farmers with small landholdings and heavy debts. This public health problem could be prevented, or at least mitigated by economic policies and land reforms. But people are abandoned by domestic and international policies in which respect for life and dignity as well as social justice do not figure prominently.[6]

These two features of the horizon of global bioethics affirm that the global perspective is not simply characterized by scale and scope. It is not just a matter of being worldwide and encompassing, involving all countries and all people. If this was the case then problems would be globalized but not really global. For example, the case of commercial surrogate motherhood presented in Chapter 1 is not a problem in India (where it is legally allowed); it is a moral problem in France and other countries (where it is prohibited). From a global perspective, commercial surrogate motherhood is not the same challenge everywhere; as a problem it is bounded to a specific ethical framework limited to a particular territory; the only thing one can do is to compare these frameworks, but there is no sense in speaking of a global problem. In short, a bioethical problem does not become a global problem by simply moving from a local or national to a global scale, nor by simply shifting in scope and becoming more encompassing. In order to grasp global bioethical problems it is necessary to explore two other specific characteristics of globalization.

The global situation

Dewey's idea that problems are always part of a context ('situated') can help to clarify the specificity of the global situation. Earlier in this chapter, interconnectedness was mentioned as typical feature of a global problem. It refers to two related dimensions of globalization: mobility and interdependency:

1   *Mobility* is one of the defining qualities of processes of globalization. This is obvious in the domain of healthcare. Health students and teachers participate increasingly in international exchanges. The International Federation of Medical Students' Associations claims that each year 10,000 medical students around the world participate in exchanges.[7] In another way, distance in medical education is eliminated: more and more programmes include online teaching courses. Health professionals are migrating. Around 25 per cent of physicians practicing in the US have been trained abroad. In countries like New Zealand and the United Kingdom more than a third of all doctors are educated in other countries. Especially, health professionals in developing countries move to the more developed world. For example, more than half of the physicians trained in Liberia, Angola and Tanzania have migrated. Patients are migrating, seeking treatment abroad. This phenomenon of health tourism

is actively promoted by some countries, offering wealthy patients from developed countries a package of medical interventions. There are also specialized forms of tourism: transplantation, reproductive, or stem cell tourism. Medical research is migrating. Currently between 40 and 65 per cent of clinical trials are conducted outside of the United States. Health resources such as drugs and devices have become mobile. India is now the largest producer of generic medication. Drugs are bought there by Western charities and NGOs, then exported to countries in Africa.

HEALTH TOURISM

Thailand, Singapore and India promote themselves as medical tourism destinations. Talking about 'tourism' instead of 'medical travel' or 'health-related travel' is not neutral since medical need rather than leisure is concerned. The phenomenon is the result of industrial policy: commercial five-star hospitals are aggressively marketing services to wealthy clientele across borders. Patients are travelling because treatments are not available at home, because the costs are five to ten times higher, or because there are long waiting lists for the treatment they need. Health tourism is not a minor phenomenon: the five private hospitals in Thailand treated over 104,000 medical tourists in 2010, generating 180 million USD in medical revenue. At the same time, the high-tech care offered to tourists is often not available for the majority of the population in the country itself.

Movement as a trademark of globalization implies that there is not only mobility of people, services and goods, but also of ideas, culture and values. Furthermore, threats and opportunities, benefits and harms are moving. What is an advantage in one place may be a disadvantage in another. This global situation means that territory or space is no longer distinctive. Problems are not located but dynamic, not fixed but evolving and transforming, not isolated but interrelated. They can only be adequately addressed through a global approach. Finally, the mobility of global problems necessitates an active ethical response. It is not sufficient to observe these flows. Global bioethics must be a dynamic combination of reflection and action.

2   *Interdependency* as a fundamental dimension of globalization is manifested in various ways. People are increasingly interrelated. It is not merely that internet and international travel facilitate global connections but people today are more aware that they are embedded within a network of relatedness. This experience of interdependency may give rise to a more relational perspective on human beings. The same is true for the dependency between human beings and environment. Global phenomena such as climate change, environmental degradation, disasters and the emergence of new infectious diseases have created a sense of mutual vulnerability. They show that human behaviour is

intimately connected to the surrounding nature and animals, and to the diversity of the biosphere. It makes human beings aware that if they continue to disregard harmonious relationships with other living beings and with the environment, the survival of humankind itself may be jeopardized. This experience of interdependence may also give rise to a different ethical vision that takes into account future generations and protection of the biosphere, beyond the limited concerns of individual autonomy. Globalization makes people aware that they share the same fate since there is only one globe.

The experiences of interdependency will be important for the way we deal with global problems, as the next chapter will discuss. But they also caution against a simplistic view of globalization. Sometimes 'global' is opposed to 'local'. Processes of globalization are then regarded as threats to local cultures and traditions, engulfing specific customs within a wider, amorphous pattern that is the same everywhere. The critique that global bioethics is imposed on other countries ('moral colonialism') expresses similar fears. Earlier in this chapter it was argued that territory and space have become less distinctive. 'Global' is often considered as free of context, 'de-contextualized'; global phenomena go across diverse social and cultural conditions, and are not bound by particular contexts. At the same time, all human experience and existence is local; we live within a specific locality; our body as physical substance is located. In everyday life, there is no opposition between global and local. The global is manifested within the local, and is often produced at the local level. This connection is aptly expressed in the subtitle of a recent book on HIV/AIDS: *Global disease – local pain.*[8] Global phenomena are localized; local attributes are globalized. Global processes can transform local conditions, so that one can speak, for example, about 'global cities'. In other words, the global and the local are not opposed, but they are intimately connected and interacting. Globalization is never an abstract set of processes but always grounded; it is produced as well as contested within local settings. This interrelationship of global and local has several implications for our view of globalization.

One is that new geographies may arise that transcend traditional national boundaries; new spaces are emerging for the operation of transnational actors and agencies but also for new legal regimes (for example, the regime of intellectual property rights that is now globally imposed, see Chapter 8). Globalization creates new networks that are placeless (as the internet, the financial system, and surveillance systems demonstrate). New movements arise beyond national territories, such as the international human rights movement and global environmentalism. Nonetheless, the actors are always localized, so that they can be identified and held accountable. Globalization is not an anonymous system beyond any space and place.

The second implication is that binary images are not sufficient. For example, the distinction between centre and periphery is disappearing. Processes of globalization are polycentric; there are multiple centres of activity and they are continuously shifting. Global bioethics therefore cannot be the diffusion of mainstream bioethics from a centre into the periphery. This interpretation would suffice in an international or transnational perspective where there is a hegemonic centre of activity. A global perspective, however, assumes a bioethical hyperspace while activities develop in various localities. Other binary distinctions become more complex too; there are many intermediary categories, for example between stranger and friend, citizen and alien, and distant and close people.

The third implication is that emphasis is shifting from culture to identity. Substantial numbers of people live outside their country of origin; they often do not share the same culture with other people in their neighbourhood. Cultures themselves have become interconnected and hybrid. Many people have partial, overlapping identities.

Finally, the interrelationship of global and local implies that the notion of border is diversified. 'Global' as 'beyond borders' refers not simply to the borders of an area, territory or nation; in fact there are multiple boundaries that are crossed. This illuminates Potter's suggestion that various types of bridges will be required.

Sources of global problems

Why is the global situation in which problems arise troubling? Why are such problems a concern for bioethics? The short answer is: because mobility and interdependency are not equally balanced. Globalization in principle has the potential to benefit everybody. But in practice it is associated with rising inequality and exclusion. There is often asymmetry of movement. Labour and natural resources are flowing from less developed to more developed countries. Doctors and nurses are trained in developing countries and then migrate to more developed ones. Wealthy patients travel to poor countries while organs and body parts flow in the reverse direction. The same is true for interdependency. Greenhouse gases produced in industrialized countries contribute to climate change so that sea levels are rising, causing serious problems in developing countries that have contributed almost nothing to the basic problem but nonetheless feel most of the impact. New medication is often tested in vulnerable populations in resource-poor countries who usually have no access to healthcare. They are the subjects that might be harmed in medical research while the benefits often go to other people in resource-rich countries with efficient healthcare systems.

In order to understand global bioethical problems it is important to examine how these problems are produced. If they are associated with uneven developments in the global situation, it will be necessary to analyse the source of the problems in more detail. In previous chapters it has been argued that the source of the problems in global bioethics is different from that in mainstream bioethics.

Metaphor of the market

This source is not simply globalization. It is rather a particular, one-sided interpretation that has been driving the processes of globalization since the 1980s. Earlier, it was argued that globalization as a very broad and complex phenomenon has several dimensions (Chapter 4). But in dominant policies and practices, it is often regarded as a primarily economic process, based on the vision that the world has become one single global market. However, the notion of 'market' is not just economic. It was often used, especially by political scientist Friedrich von Hayek, philosopher Ayn Rand, and economist Milton Friedman as the utopian vision.[9] They used 'market' as a metaphor for the organization of social life. Of all forms of social organization, the market is the most fair and efficient one. It is also considered as the only framework within which individual liberty and freedom can flourish. As a self-regulating force, the market will give room to self-actualizing individuals whose productivity and creativity will work for the benefit of all. There is no need for protection or regulation. Everything should be transformed into a commodity or service and transacted in a market. Competition is the core virtue. Each individual is responsible and accountable for his or her action, including care. The free market, therefore, is a recipe for the problems of the world. The other dimensions of globalization are dwarfed by this utopian vision of the free market.

COMPETITION AS THE PRINCIPLE OF SOCIAL ORGANIZATION

'The liberal argument is in favor of making the best possible use of the forces of competition as a means of co-ordinating human efforts, not as an argument for leaving things just as they are. It is based on the conviction that, where effective competition can be created, it is a better way of guiding individual efforts than any other.

It was men's submission to the impersonal forces of the market that in the past has made possible the growth of a civilization which without this could not have developed ...'[10]

Politics of neoliberalism

The utopia of the market has engendered a specific discourse and set of practices that have dominated processes of globalization since the 1980s. These are often summarized under the label 'neoliberalism'. This label covers a set of economic and political views, as well as policy practices that have a pervasive influence on politics, social relations and everyday life. It is not a coherent and uniform philosophy. At the same time, it is regarded as an ideology, a missionary faith, or a socio-cultural logic that drives many of the developments of globalization, often taken for granted as a self-evident normative framework, and not leaving much room for criticism.

Neoliberalism puts emphasis on the removal of constraints on free market competition, and encourages privatization, deregulation, reduction of public expenditure, tax reform and protection of property rights. Globalization in this ideology basically is a synonym of liberalization. When global markets are free, this will foster individual liberty and human well-being. The role of the state should be limited; its primary task is to create the institutional framework to secure free trade and private property rights. The power of governments should be used to deregulate and remove constraints and social policies that curtail the flow of commodities. The state should withdraw from social provision and protection because that impedes the proper functioning of markets. Public utilities and institutions, as well as social welfare provisions, should be privatized. Every domain of human life should be open for market transactions so that individual citizens are free to choose what they want. Genetic tests and preventive as well as therapeutic interventions are consumables. Healthcare is a business that will flourish in a climate of competitiveness and efficiency. Medical research can thrive if it operates in a global market. Only then will it be able to provide individuals with a range of choices concerning drugs and interventions, broader than ever before. Another claim of neoliberalism is that globalization is inevitable. The dissemination of free market principles is like a natural force. Furthermore, nobody is in charge. Processes of globalization do not have main agents or leaders who are accountable. They are driven by what the Finnish philosopher Georg Henrik von Wright has called 'anonymous forces' and 'invisible actors'[11] Finally, the claim is that everyone benefits, at least in the long run. Benefits will 'trickle down'. Inequalities and negative impacts on vulnerable populations will only be transitional and temporary. Economic liberalization will in the end free individuals from the frailties of human existence.

NEOLIBERALISM

'Neoliberalism is … a theory of political economic practices that proposes that human well-being can best be advanced by liberating individual entrepreneurial freedoms and skills with an institutional framework characterized by strong private property rights, free markets, and free trade … Furthermore, if markets do not exist (in areas such as land, water, education, health care, social security) then they must be created, by state action if necessary. But beyond these tasks the state should not venture.'[12]

The negative effects of this ideology are now increasingly recognized. It has multiplied vulnerabilities at a global scale. It has increased social inequalities. It has caused the deterioration of basic services such as public healthcare in most countries. It has only benefited the top 1 per cent of people; for the majority of populations existence has become more precarious and fragile. Jobs have been undermined and made temporary. Social security is broken down. Existential insecurity has increased. The environment is neglected and degraded. Globalization processes are connected with growing injustices, social disintegration and progressive exclusion. According to the market thinking of neoliberal globalization, the human person is primarily *homo economicus*; a rational self-interested individual motivated by minimizing costs and maximizing gains for himself. He is primarily encouraged to act by incentives for his self-interest. He only relates to others through market exchanges. This view is based on the individual choice and the community is absent. The market logic therefore separates economic activities from social relationships. Competition rather than cooperation is the preferred mode of social interaction. The pervasive influences of neoliberal policies over the last few decades have created transformations beyond rising inequality, poverty and government debt. Today we are confronted with irreversible destruction and degradation; vast areas of land and water are dead or intoxicated for centuries. Tropical and subtropical forests are rapidly disappearing; fisheries are depleted. Simultaneously, the numbers of displaced people are staggering, and rates of incarceration rising while growing populations even in the richer countries are expelled from jobs as well as basic services. Human lives everywhere are impacted by a dynamics of exploitation, extraction and expulsion. Sociologist Saskia Sassen sees at work 'predatory formations' that are only focused on 'liberated profit seeking and indifference to the environment'.[13] Shrinking and transforming the social context of human lives has exactly been the purpose of the neoliberal ideology, assuming that it will liberate the individual good.

RATIONAL EGOISM

'The basic *social* principle ... is that just as life is an end in itself, so every living human being is an end in himself, not the means to the ends or the welfare of others – and, therefore, that man must live for his own sake, neither sacrificing himself to others nor sacrificing others to himself.

The principle of *trade* is the only rational ethical principle for all human relationships, personal and social, private and public, spiritual and material. It is the principle of *justice.*'[14]

It is clear that the current domination of neoliberal ideology has been facilitated by politics and law. Liberalization of trade, deregulation of society, and restriction of the centralized power of government has not been accomplished by free market dynamics but by rather heavy political control. Instead of the invisible hand of market forces it is often the visible hand of governments and international organizations (the World Bank, the World Trade Organization [WTO] and IMF) that are directing the processes of globalization. Markets are shaped by laws, regulations and institutions, as economist Joseph Stiglitz argues.[15] Neoliberalism implies increasing regulation rather than laissez-faire. This is obvious in the enormous growth of bureaucracy, particularly in the European Union. What once started as an idealistic project based on notions of solidarity and community has now become a hard-core neoliberal mechanism for privatization and so-called deregulation. Free markets are created through intervention and interference, often through concerted political action. Similar concerted action has disseminated the norms, rules, procedures and formalities from business administration in all dimensions of present-day society (where 'targets' and 'benchmarks' determine daily life). Education, research, healthcare, culture, environmental protection, safety and defence are all submitted to the overarching framework of market logic, not because market ideology is naturally expanding but because it is deliberately promoted to dismantle social structures of welfare and protection. Politics and law therefore have created the conditions in which globalization, in particular neoliberal market policies, could flourish. These policies have exposed more people worldwide to more threats and hazards, and have decreased their capacities to cope. These policies are based on the assumption that human beings are self-interested, rational individuals. In fact, over the last few decades, domestic and international policies have systematically promoted a particular normative framework influencing the lives of people around the globe.

The impact of neoliberalism

Global bioethics has emerged as a response to the ethical problems produced by neoliberal policies. This response originates from the moral concern that everyone's health needs should be addressed and that all persons, not just those in an advantaged position, should benefit from the progress of science and technology. It shows the desire to refocus on the well-being of human beings that is often jeopardized by damaging and unjust structures and policies. It also expresses the view that health is not the same as economic welfare, and is dependent on socio-cultural and environmental circumstances. Many of the problems on the agenda of global bioethics are the results of one-sided, ideologically driven processes of globalization.

The example of health tourism illustrates the impact of neoliberal policies.[16] Pressured by international bodies, countries like India and Thailand have aggressively promoted private healthcare as a commodity in the global medical market since the 1990s. Medical tourism is in fact a building stone for 'bio-economy'. The argument is that market-driven healthcare will stimulate economic growth, generate foreign exchange, raise the standard of healthcare and increase equity in access to care within the country. The 'trickle down benefits', however, are overshadowed by serious negative effects. Public expenditures for health have decreased and the social welfare infrastructure is reduced. The overall effect is that the quality and provision for healthcare services for the majority of the population has diminished while expensive private care is available for the elite. Furthermore, privatization of healthcare also created an internal brain drain: doctors trained in public institutions move into private settings where salaries are higher. India currently has one of the most highly privatized healthcare systems in the world. At the same time, almost 25 per cent of the population does not receive any medical treatment due to indebtedness or poverty. While 80 per cent of the population lives in rural areas, over 75 per cent of the physicians and 70 per cent of publicly funded hospital beds are in urban centres. Neoliberal policies therefore lead to distortions of priorities. The widening gap between private and public health services reiterates the divide between the rich and the poor. A two-tiered healthcare system has emerged with excellent care for the wealthy and low-quality public-funded care for the poor majority. Neoliberal policies in healthcare have therefore reinforced injustice. Since public funds are transferred to private care, the limited resources of a country like India are used to subsidize the costs of treating patients from developed countries. Deficiencies in the healthcare provision in the latter countries, for example the long waiting lists due to chronic understaffing of medical services in the United Kingdom, motivates patients to seek care elsewhere. That another approach is possible is illustrated by Cuba, one of the first countries to promote health tourism. Advertising 'sea, sun and surgery', the country attracts medical tourists to pay for the system of free, public healthcare for its citizens. Medical tourism is not an advantage for the elite but benefits the population at large.

The most damaging effect of neoliberal policies is the breakdown of the healthcare system in many developing countries since the 1980s.[17] Reduction of government expenditures for health and social services, privatization of health services, reduced salaries of health workers, and introduction of user fees have had dramatic negative effects on healthcare in many countries. Not only was access to healthcare declining for the majority of populations, but also many health indicators worsened. For example, in Madagascar the infant mortality rate increased with 53.5 per cent between 1980 and 1985; in Ghana the majority of doctors working in the public health sector had left the country by 1987; life expectancy in Tanzania decreased from 50.1 years in 1992 to 43.1 years in 2002. In Latin America neoliberal health reforms did not improve quality of care but increased inequity and inefficiency. The principal beneficiaries of reforms were not patients or health professionals but hospital corporations, transnational private insurance firms, and consultancy agencies.

Implications for global bioethics

Understanding the characteristics of global bioethical problems and their emergence in the context of neoliberal globalization determines how these problems can best be addressed (see Chapter 6). The implications of this understanding for global bioethics will be elaborated in the remainder of this book.

So far, the argument has been as follows. Mainstream bioethics has originated because of the ill effects of the power of science and technology. Contemporary global bioethics in its turn is fuelled by the adverse effects of neoliberal policies and practices. It is not merely the case that bioethics today is situated in the context of globalization, which can have positive as well as negative consequences. Rather, it is a one-sided dominant process of globalization that is the breeding ground for bioethical problems today. This process is guided by the utopian vision of individuals and societies as determined by the free market. It presents itself as an inescapable and uncontrollable combination of politics, philosophy and practice. The radical implications of the diagnosis that the sources of global bioethical problems are within the neoliberal ideology of globalization rather than globalization in itself are often not recognized.

First, bioethics should engage in a fundamental analysis of the context in which problems emerge, are sustained or aggravated. This will require a different bioethical discourse. The ethical framework of mainstream bioethics with its emphasis on individual autonomy, rational decision-making, informed consent, ownership of the body, and personal responsibility mimics the main tenets of neoliberal ideology, and applies them within the setting of healthcare. For example, similar basic assumptions are used when it is argued that vulnerability of individuals and populations in research can be reduced through protecting and empowering individual decision-makers; that exploitation of research subjects is not wrong as long as it renders them better off; that individuals should have the freedom to sell parts of their body as long as the choice is voluntary and free; or that health tourism is laudable because it enhances the range of options for individual well-being. The same ideas of the rational self-interested individual as well as trade as the primary principle of human interaction as in neoliberal discourse are at work here within bioethical discourse. The point is that as long as bioethics is modelled on the neoliberal framework it will never be able to address the sources of contemporary bioethical problems. Using an individual focus abstracted from the social dimensions of human existence, and neglecting the impact of market mechanisms on social life will not allow bioethics to scrutinize the conditions and contexts that produce global bioethical problems. It will, for example, continue to regard vulnerability as a deficit of personal autonomy and will not focus on the circumstances that produce vulnerability, not only for individuals but for entire groups of people. It will not be able to recognize that organ vendors do not really have a choice when they live in dire conditions of poverty and indebtedness, or that the choices for wealthy medical tourists depend on deteriorated health services and inequalities for the majority of populations in countries that are offering these private services. The argument is not simply that bioethical discourse necessarily will remain superficial in the sense that it does not address the root causes of problems because of its concentration on the symptoms, ignoring the basic mechanisms. The similarities between neoliberal and bioethical discourse may engender the risk that bioethics itself comes to play an ideological role by assuming that the underlying conditions and background circumstances of many problems are outside the scope of its discourse (see Figure 5.2).

Second, bioethics should examine remedies and alternatives to the dominant ethical framework if it really wants to address the global problems of today. Expanding or applying the principlism or other theoretical approaches of mainstream bioethics to global problems will not be sufficient. A different type of bioethics is needed, with new concepts, methods and practices. For example, since global problems are interconnected, bioethics itself should make connections. This will require a broader interdisciplinary approach, not only engaging life sciences and philosophy but also social sciences, political sciences, international law, global studies, and comparative disciplines. It also requires going beyond interdisciplinarity through developing a comprehensive perspective that brings together knowledge and practice from many areas, inside and outside academia, coping with global

Neoliberalism

Bioethics

Homo economicus:

- rational individual motivated by minimizing costs and maximizing gain for himself

- relates to others through market exchanges and transactions

- primacy of personal responsibility

- society and community do not exist or are irrelevant

Autonomous individual:

- rational decision-maker

- care is individual affair

- ownership of body

- informed consent as transaction

- no responsibility for social, economic and political conditions

FIGURE 5.2 Neoliberalism and bioethics

issues. The metaphor of the bridge, introduced by Potter, will be more appropriate than ever. Global bioethics will furthermore need to develop its own perspective beyond borders, in order to be able to deal with problems that are present in a broader social and cultural space. It has to address the question whether there can be a global moral order or community that enables critique of global phenomena. At the same time, global bioethics needs independency. Its discourse should not be co-opted or dominated by a more powerful discourse or ideology. It is important to maintain an independent voice in regard to medicine and the life science, but also in regard to politics and economics. Critical analysis and reflection are demanded. Scrutinizing the dominant normative framework will demand a focus on power relationships, not merely, as in mainstream bioethics, within healthcare, but now also within the context of medicine, care and societies, thus obliterating the usual distinction between bioethics and biopolitics. Global bioethics will furthermore continue to be a practical activity. It will engage academic research, but in the awareness that research nowadays is often intimately entangled in the neoliberal ideology, and 'commissioned' by powerful actors. Global bioethics will, more often than mainstream bioethics, engage in policy-making, public debate, advocacy and social activism. However, a distinction must be made between a practical and strategic focus.[18] The first operates within existing structures and will promote the interests of individuals as much as possible within the broader context in which they live. The strategic focus on the other hand will explicitly question the existing order with the aim of exploring how structures and social relations can be transformed. The attention of global bioethics will move towards this strategic focus while continuing to have a theoretical and practical focus. Finally, a major concept in global bioethics is cooperation. Unless processes of globalization are controlled, problems will multiply, and threats to the survival of humankind will increase. But control necessarily requires cooperation of as many actors as possible. Cooperation is only feasible on the basis of mutual respect and shared values. It will not be the result of application of ethical principles but of negotiation about what principles will be shared. To face global threats a collective response will be necessary. But then areas of commonality will have to be determined. How can this be accomplished? The main concepts and tools of global bioethics will be elaborated in the forthcoming chapters.

CHAPTER SUMMARY

- This chapter clarifies global bioethics problems in three steps:
  - Problems are global because of the following characteristics: 1) worldwide scale; 2) interconnectedness; 3) persistence; 4) general scope; and 5) need for global action.
  - Problems are bioethical if: 1) they have specific relevance for health and human life; and 2) pose a normative challenge.
  - Problems in general have three characteristics:
    - ☐ ambiguity
    - ☐ situation
    - ☐ horizon.
- To explain why certain issues have emerged as global bioethics problems, the horizon as well as situation of global bioethics are explored:
  - The horizon of global bioethics has two features:
    - ☐ Focus on the relatedness of individuals
    - ☐ Taking into account the significance of social, political and economic powers.
  - The situation of global bioethics has two dimensions:
    - ☐ mobility
    - ☐ interdependency.
- The sources of global bioethical problems are related to the ideology of the free market and the politics of neoliberalism that has been dominating the processes of globalization since the 1980s.
- Understanding how and why global bioethical problems arise has implications for bioethics. Formulating adequate responses will require a global bioethics with new concepts, methods and practices.

Notes

1 See: John Dewey (1981) *The later works, 1925–1953. Volume One, 1925: Experience and Nature.* Edited by Jo Ann Boydston. Southern Illinois University Press: Carbondale, p. 184.
2 The quotation about the problematic situation is from: Larry A. Hickman and Thomas M. Alexander (eds) (1998) *The essential Dewey. Volume 2: Ethics, Logics, Psychology.* Indiana University Press: Bloomington and Indianapolis, p. 140.
3 Saulius Geniusas (2012) *The origins of the horizon in Husserl's phenomenology.* Springer: Dordrecht.

4 Geniusas (2012) *The origins of the horizon in Husserl's phenomenology*, p. 7.

5 Thomas Pogge (2013) *World poverty and human rights: Cosmopolitan responsibilities and reforms*. Polity Press: Cambridge (UK) and Malden (MA), 2nd edition.

6 Jonathan Kennedy and Lawrence King (2014) The political economy of farmers' suicides in India: Indebted cash-crop farmers with marginal landholdings explain state-level variation in suicide rates. *Globalization and Health* 2014; 10:16; doi: 10.1186/1744-8603-10-16.

7 See: www.amsa.org/members/career/international-exchanges/ (accessed 5 August 2015).

8 Hakan Seckinelgin (2008) *International politics of HIV/AIDS: Global disease – local pain*. Routledge: Abingdon (UK).

9 David Harvey (2005) *A brief history of neoliberalism*. Oxford University Press: Oxford, New York.

10 Friedrich Hayek (1944) *The road to serfdom*. University of Chicago Press: Chicago, pp. 36 and 204.

11 Von Wright is quoted by Zygmunt Bauman (1998) *Globalization: The human consequences*. Columbia University Press: New York, p. 57.

12 David Harvey (2005) *A brief history of neoliberalism*, p. 2.

13 Saskia Sasssen (2014) *Expulsions: Brutality and complexity in the global economy*. The Belknap Press of Harvard University Press: Cambridge (Mass) and London (England), p. 215.

14 Ayn Rand (1964) *The virtue of selfishness: A new concept of egoism*. Signet/Penguin: New York, pp. 27, 31 and 80.

15 Joseph Stiglitz (2012) *The price of inequality: How today's divided society endangers our future*. W.W.Norton & Company: London/New York.

16 See, for example, Chen, Y.Y. Brandon and Flood, Colleen M. (2013) Medical tourism's impact on health care equity and access in low- and middle-income countries: Making the case for regulation. *Journal of Law, Medicine & Ethics* 41(1): 286–300; Smith, Kristen (2012) The problematization of medical tourism: A critique of neoliberalism. *Developing World Bioethics* 12(1): 1–8.

17 For the negative impact of neoliberal policies on healthcare, see: Sara E. Davies (2010) *Global politics of health*. Polity Press: Cambridge (UK) and Malden (USA).

18 See Maxine Molyneux (1985) Mobilization without emancipation? Women's interests, the state, and revolution in Nicaragua. *Feminist Studies* 11(2): 227–254.

6

GLOBAL RESPONSES

Global bioethics develops in response to processes of globalization that are producing specific and new types of problems. What kind of responses can global bioethics provide? The analysis in the previous chapter highlighted that responses should at least have three qualities. First, they should target the scale and scope of the problems. Bioethics can only appropriately address global problems if it has a worldwide and comprehensive perspective. Second, the source of the problems needs to be targeted. Bioethics should scrutinize the neoliberal logic that drives everyday life and political decision-making in our global era. This logic operates on the basis of a pervasive, often implicit normative framework of competition, efficiency, self-interested rationality, and individual freedom from social and cultural constraints. Otherwise, it cannot be understood how bioethical problems today arise and flourish. Third, since the global and local are not opposed but interconnected, time and space become less relevant. Global responses are always local; they can only be applied when localized. At the same time they are dynamic; once in place, they move to other spaces and become globalized. Finally, they are polymorphic; lacking a dominant paradigm manifested in one prestigious centre or organization, a multi-centric range of activities is employed by multifarious networks. Against this backdrop, global bioethics itself is not just a new phase in time, as the latest new discipline. Rather, it has the character of a new stage, a 'hyperspace' with qualities and approaches that are not just an extension of earlier approaches.

However, global bioethics is contested, and thus, its potential to provide any answers at all. Some argue that it is merely a label to bring together various ethical approaches across the world. It cannot and should not provide answers that are global. This chapter begins with addressing these objections. They often presuppose a narrow or one-sided view of globalization. The chapter will argue that it is possible, even necessary, to develop global responses, at least if one wants to escape from the dominant neoliberal ideology and not to acquiesce in the unavoidability of global problems. These responses are possible because global bioethics presupposes, as discussed previously, a different horizon that puts in focus a perspective of human existence beyond individual self-actualizing competition. Finally, the chapter will argue that global bioethics is able to provide four kinds of response to global bioethical problems: a) a global ethical framework as an alternative to the dominant one; b) different ways of governance for global problems; c) inclusive global practices; and d) independent critical discourse and strategic practice. These will be further elaborated and explained in subsequent chapters.

Global bioethics without answers

The idea that global bioethics has the potential to provide responses to global bioethical problems is contested with various arguments.

- **Nothing new**. Global bioethics in this empirical view is the 'old' bioethics applied on a wider scale. There is in fact nothing new. Rather than talking about 'global bioethics', one should talk about 'globalizing bioethics'. It just means that specifically Western bioethics has spread around the globe. This is illustrated by the fact that English-speaking countries dominate the leading international journals in bioethics so that the agenda of bioethical debate is clearly determined by geography. This thin version of global bioethics either implies that answers are there (from mainstream bioethics) or that answers are provided within the local setting. The problem with this view is that it does not acknowledge the fundamental impact of globalization. It assumes that centre and periphery are separated so that mainstream bioethics can gradually disseminate from the centre (the West). This assumption has become obsolete due to processes of globalization. The dynamics and interconnectedness of these processes, as well as the emergence of new global problems necessarily transform bioethics into an approach or discipline that transcends its Western roots, concepts and methods. It is not surprising that publications in leading journals do not reflect such change. It takes time for new journals to develop, and recently several globally orientated ones have started to appear. Also, only 6 per cent of the world population are native English speakers. To assess the status of global bioethics, it is necessary to take into account more parameters than English publications.

- **Not possible**. Global bioethics in this rationalist view is impossible. The human condition is defined by moral diversity. Philosopher Tristram Engelhardt argues that there is disagreement about all ethical issues; not just about particular ones such as abortion and euthanasia but about worldviews and ethics itself. These disagreements have always existed; they are persistent and perennial. Furthermore, there is no possibility to resolve these issues through rational argument since the foundations of morality are controversial.

Thus, global bioethics is an irrational and failed project; there is a plurality of bioethics. Any attempt at a global consensus will be in vain. It is politics rather than ethics. Responding to global problems will elicit, as Engelhardt calls it, a 'cacophony of competing answers'.[1] The only justified way to use the term 'global bioethics' is as an empty frame within which particular approaches to bioethics can peacefully cooperate.

GLOBAL BIOETHICS ACCORDING TO ENGELHARDT

'... a global bioethics can at best provide a thin moral framework, a space within which individuals and moral communities can peaceably pursue divergent understandings of morality and bioethics within limited democracies and within a global market. Such a bioethics cannot provide a content-full understanding of the right, the good, virtue, or human flourishing.'[2]

Engelhardt's argument that global bioethics is impossible is remarkably static. Processes of globalization that have been deeply transforming the human condition for several decades surprisingly have no significant influence on moral debate. There is a multiplication of moral issues but no change in moral views, ideas and arguments. Moral progress does not exist. Rationality rules, not moral imagination. Facing global problems, human beings are empty-handed and morally impotent. Every answer will be particular. One can continue to analyse and discuss them but not to convince others or reach agreement. The only purpose is to voluntarily create procedural mechanisms of cooperation that allow moral strangers to exchange views in a peaceful way, like in the market. Basically, addressing global problems produced by market ideology requires that bioethics itself becomes a marketplace.

Another point of view arguing that bioethics cannot provide answers to global problems emphasizes that it is so dominated by principlism and a focus on technological fixes for individuals that it cannot be reformed. Now that the main challenges refer to global processes of power and inequality, bioethics cannot make the transition to global bioethics; it is doomed to remain an abstract and impotent discourse that can never be globalized. Another normative approach beyond bioethics is necessary: biopolitics. This view builds on the earlier critiques, for example of Dan Callahan, that bioethics is 'an accommodating handmaiden' serving to legitimize problems created by medical technology.[3] But, for Callahan the conclusion is not to reject bioethics but to expand it.

- **Not desirable**. A view often advanced in anthropological and social studies is that globalization in fact is Westernization. Since moral values are always dependent on cultures, they can only be relevant and applicable in a specific cultural setting. Against this backdrop, global bioethics is the imposition of a specific form of local ethics. When global bioethics claims to be universal it is in fact imposing its restricted, Western views on other parts of the world. The critique is that arguing that some moral values are 'universal' and need to be recognized by all rational beings is a more subtle form of colonizing than traditional imperialism. It is subtle because it does not work through domination or power enforcing 'superior' values, but the result is the same.

BIOETHICAL IMPERIALISM

'A so-called global bioethics may borrow some canons of morality from existing bioethics or invent something new. The fact is that Western bioethics is dominant in the world. So, the newly articulated global bioethics may be tainted with a strong color of Western culture, or may just be … another version of Western bioethics within the clothes of global bioethics. When it is imposed on the non-Western communities or heretic communities within Western culture, this constitutes ethical imperialism.'[4]

The claim that bioethics is an American invention is now creating a backlash against the claims of global bioethics; if bioethics is characterized by and specific to a particular culture, it not only excludes its application in other different culture but it highlights the dangers of bioethical imperialism. Engelhardt, for example, considers the search for moral consensus and global declarations as efforts to promote and export a particular bioethics to the rest of the world. Declarations on global bioethics are nothing more than arbitrary agreements between various groups of people. However, it is not clear what this critique actually opposes. Does it reject the idea of global bioethics as such, or rather one type of bioethics that is globalized?

- **Not necessary**. A pragmatic view is that it is not necessary to agree on global bioethics as a common set of values and principles in order to address global problems. Like in clinical ethics, one can agree on how to ethically address problematic cases while agreement on underlying principles is lacking. Resolution of cases can also follow on the basis of agreed moral principles without agreement on the theoretical justification of their application. Much will depend on the circumstances in which these principles are applied. These have to be weighed in careful case deliberation as is usually done in the setting of clinical ethics committees. Moral disagreements can thus be overcome by pragmatic approaches on a deliberative basis. In moral practice, people from different cultures can come together and agree on specific issues. Ethics is not merely theory but praxis in concrete contexts. The problem with this view is that bioethics may have given up global approaches, but economic, social and political institutions have not. Piecemeal and case-based analyses will illuminate trends and movements but not affect them.

- **Hubris**. Sceptical views doubt the potential of global bioethics. Its aspirations are high but they can never be effectuated. One argument is that global bioethics is conceptually overstretched. The notion has become too broad; it nearly includes everything, i.e. all problems of the contemporary world. It is ethics at large, covering politics, social science, economy, ecology, culture, philosophy and theology. It has sometimes lost the fundamental connection to medicine and healthcare. An example is war. It is obvious that war has negative effects on health; medicine itself can be used as an instrument of war (e.g. biological weapons). War is therefore a global bioethics problem. But the problem of war itself is outside the scope of bioethics. Basically, this distinction is not new. In mainstream bioethics many ethical problems originated from developments in science and technology. For example, genetics produced ethical queries but nobody argued that genetics should be integrated into bioethics. Similarly, nowadays bioethics problems are produced by economic, social and political developments. The implication is that global bioethics should broaden its knowledge and expertise. It should become more thoroughly interdisciplinary without expanding itself into a mega-discourse about economy or politics.

Another sceptical argument is impotence. Global problems are simply too big and overwhelming. Global bioethics should be modest; it is a scholarly conversation among bioethicists from around the world. Although the circle of professionals is expanding, the aim is to discuss issues of universal concern with the prospect of consensus, nothing more. One cannot solve the world's problems. Global bioethics is facing an insurmountable challenges. It is more helpful to make a distinction between bioethics and biopolitics, and leave the global issues to the complex work of politics.

New context – different answers

Can global bioethics provide any answers in light of these objections and criticisms? A positive reply assumes that the rise and context of global bioethics is interpreted as a multifaceted and complex phenomenon. Globalization is often feared for 'harmonization', equalizing differences among cultures, traditions and ideas. Concern with homogeneity may explain the emphasis on moral diversity. But it is insufficient to approach and understand globalization with binary thinking. Often, a limited and static conception of the 'global' is assumed to be opposed to the 'local'. The 'global' is considered to be context-free, a decontextualized space, encompassing and moving across diverse circumstances and conditions. In reality, manifestations of the 'global' depend on specific distributions of resources, i.e. scientific expertise and global capital. That the 'global' is articulated through 'local' efforts is demonstrated in the example of health tourism. To be globally visible, this phenomenon must be facilitated by government policies. This is possible in a limited number of countries that have the right ingredients, such as well-educated, English-speaking health professionals and adequate medical institutions. Local actions are needed but they will only be successful if they are linked to a global framework that is shared, and becomes less 'local' in its manifestation. 'Tourists' are assured that the healthcare received will not be specifically Thai or Indian but will meet global standards. In continuous processes of interaction and interconnection 'global' and 'local' themselves are transforming and changing.

The same is true for ethics. Global bioethics is criticized since it can never overcome perennial and persistent disagreement. Even in a dynamic and evolving world we are mired in the opposition between agreement and disagreement. We do not even have the rational possibilities to overcome difference, discord and diversity. This focus on disagreement as the fundamental fact in ethics is one-sided. It unduly rules out the emergence of common visions and ideals, as well as shared normative practices and images. Many scholars have pointed out that incompatibilities between bioethical views are exaggerated. In fact, there are substantial similarities between different approaches to bioethics, for instance Western and non-Western bioethics. The debate on so-called Asian values is a famous illustration.

ASIAN VALUES

In the 1990s, East Asian political leaders articulated 'Asian values' (such as orderly conduct, harmony and discipline) as substantially different from 'Western values' (such as individual liberty and rights). Politicians from China, Malaysia and Singapore rejected the universality of human rights in favour of regional differences. This movement has been criticized by Amartya Sen, himself from Asia. He points out that like science and technology itself, democratic ideas, liberty and public participation in political decision-making are not exclusively Western notions but have been important in all cultures and traditions. Arguments in favour of freedom, tolerance and equality have been expressed in Indian and Chinese traditions. In fact, Asia – where 60 per cent of the world population lives – is characterized by diversity and heterogeneity. Articulating one identity flows from an impoverished understanding of civilizations and their interdependences. Specifying 'Asian values' can easily disguise authoritarian paternalism. Sen concludes that '... so-called Asian values that are invoked to justify authoritarianism are not especially Asian in any significant sense.'[5]

Taking moral diversity seriously is inescapable but human existence is not just determined by controversies, disagreements and diversity. Promoting one singular classification as distinctive (e.g. 'Asian') reduces people to one dimension of their social existence. It does not recognize that people have plural identities. Furthermore, it denies the importance of interactions: cultures and traditions are not homogeneous, stationary and isolated. Finally, it excludes the possibility of normative judgements across cultures.

The criticizing views presuppose a specific conception of ethics as a discourse that is context-free.

First, ethics is primarily taken as theory. It is rationally identifying and analysing principles and norms that can subsequently be applied. Theories come before practice otherwise normative judgements would not be possible. This presupposition ignores that ethical practices are not pre-formed and given but developed and nurtured. Ethical claims are developing not from a theoretical framework but they are arising in practice. Practical experiences lead to ethical reflection and theoretical analysis, encouraging the elaboration of an ethical framework that will become more complex and sophisticated over time. Binary thinking only allows for either a binding universal ethics for all persons or multiple diverse and particular ethics that should be respected. There is no middle ground, no possibility of building on limited agreement and then expanding on areas of overlapping consensus. It is taken for granted that global bioethics can only exist as the rational and deductive application of universal principles in the entire world and accepted by everyone. In this critical view, ethics is not a matter of deliberation, communication and negotiation.

The second presupposition is that ethics is transcendent; it is a discourse above the conditions in which it is applied. It should do more than reiterating the fundamental values that determine its conditions: it should critically examine them. However, in everyday practice and in a non-ideal world, ethics may not be neutral but impregnated with the ideology that is producing its problems. As argued previously, this is often the case with bioethics. Its mainstream discourse repeats and applies the same concepts and ideas that are producing the ethical problems in the first place. It reiterates the logic of neoliberalism by primarily emphasizing the rational choices of free and autonomous individuals so that external command and control are no longer required. Engelhardt's critique, for example, solves the problem of disagreement by appealing to the market as a model for ethics. Human beings can collaborate procedurally on the basis of consent and negotiation. The only moral image that is reasonable is the 'moral trading floor'.[6] This perspective moreover presupposes a specific image of the individual: 'we are separated' since we all have different moral views; we are all moral strangers. The basic unit of ethical discourse is the free and responsible individual who operates in a market-like moral space. The emphasis is on the individual over the power of government, and not embedded in society and culture. The limitations of these presuppositions within the context of globalization have precisely encouraged the development of global bioethics, calling for a new and broader ethical perspective.

Finally, the critique argues that global bioethics is a political instrument used to dominate countries across the globe. Declarations of global principles are the result of strong actors with bargaining power while representatives of most countries do not want to resist the emerging consensus. Ultimately, the resolution of disagreement is political. In this critical view, global bioethics brings into the public debate a political process that simply legitimizes the functioning of the market and the significance of individual moral choices. Bioethics is a political instrument since political decisions have to be justified with an appeal to moral principles. Bioethical concepts and principles can be used to divert or neutralize possible criticism: bioethics can effectively focus the debate on the specific issues of individual consent and decision-making, leaving the social context and political–economic power relations outside of its scope. This view of bioethics underestimates the potential of ethical discourse to influence political processes. It postulates a wrong dichotomy between bioethics as centred on individuals, and biopolitics as addressed to groups, organizations, states and structures (see further Chapter 12). However, global bioethics can inspire groups to ameliorate the living conditions for individuals. Human rights discourse, for example, does not just provide a legal and ethical framework but it animates groups and communities around the world (women, children, immigrants, disabled people) with a new consciousness of their political status, against discrimination, marginalization and oppression by states, organizations and businesses. Referring to a global ethical framework can therefore have a liberating and emancipating role. It evokes or aspires to the possibility of better conditions of human existence and respect. Social scientist Arjun Appadurai gives the example of homeless people in Mumbai.[7] They organized themselves around the idea that housing is not just dwelling and shelter but has human significance, it expresses dignity and intimacy, and is a condition for sociality and citizenship. This example illustrates why the idea of global bioethics is supported not so much by established and mainstream experts but by those who experience the unequal impact of globalization: feminist bioethicists, organizations of disabled people, and representatives of minorities.

Answers are unavoidable and necessary

Some scholars advocating global bioethics make stronger claims. If the existence and urgency of global bioethical problems is acknowledged – which is not always the case – there is no alternative. Global challenges have bioethical implications; they require analysis and examination in order to formulate policies. Global issues cannot be contained within a specific country, culture or community. National and regional laws, policies and regulations are inadequate. Of course, there will be disagreement on how best to draft and apply global responses. But it is implausible to argue that bioethics cannot and should not contribute to global policies. The nature of the bioethical problems of today makes it a practical necessity to have global bioethics. The global impact of problems demands a global approach. Many of these problems, as the previous chapter pointed out, are interconnected. This means that there is 'systemic risk': the entire global system may break down. One cannot address one problem at a time. An encompassing process is needed rather than problem management. Mainstream bioethics will not formulate such approaches. To be able to address global problems, a comprehensive bioethics is needed, and this development is already in progress.

There is more than the argument that policies and regulations are needed to deal with global problems. More important is the challenge to understand the present human condition. Ethics is not simply the application of principles to complex situations. It is not merely a theory to consider in practice. It is more than the effort to distinguish right from wrong, good from bad. Ethics also is a quest to understand what it means to be human. It involves moral experience, moral sensitivity, social concerns and public virtues. For most of its history, philosophy in the West has not only been a doctrine, discourse or theoretical activity but a way of life, an existential choice, an exercise in practical morality, and concern about the world, not unlike in many other philosophical and spiritual traditions in other parts of the world.[8]

Therefore, tension between principles and practice is not a new problem in ethics. Global bioethics reactivates the debate on the nature of ethical enquiry. Is contemporary ethics orientated to rational and discursive activity, a living experience or a way of life, or perhaps all of these? The moral problems of today critically question our taken-for-granted moral values and principles pursued for our own gain when confronted with the misery, injustice and inequality of the 'global other'. This confrontation provokes ethical questions. For example, whether there are any goods that human beings share and that are common to humanity rather than the object of individual choice and appropriation. What are the basic social goods that in every society are essential for human flourishing?

There is also a need to reconceive the idea of cultural diversity. Addressing global problems requires that cultural diversity is not merely accepted or respected. Culture is often regarded as something of the past: heritage, custom, or tradition. It is, however, just as much orientated to the future; it conceives designs for social life, and it expresses collective aspirations. Appadurai characterizes culture as: 'a dialogue between aspirations and sedimented traditions.' Aspirations concerning health and happiness, the good life and dignity exist in all cultures and societies. He suggests using within global discourse the 'capacity to aspire' which is inherent in culture in order to engage and give voice to marginal populations, to insert values in economic analysis, and to produce consensus.[9] For global bioethics, this implies imagining possibilities rather than probabilities, the possibility of different worlds as an ethical horizon within which other human capabilities can be realized. An ethics of possibility will then give rise to a politics of hope.

Finally, there is more to say about the possibility of moral progress in response to the pessimism of the critique of global bioethics.[10] It is true that the history of humankind can be written as a long series of atrocities, cruelties and barbarisms, demonstrating the futility and impotence of ethical discourse. On the other hand, detailed empirical studies show that today we are living in the most peaceful time of human existence. Violence in all its forms (such as murder, rape, torture, civil wars, genocide and terrorism) has substantially declined. Although explanations for these reductions differ, it is clear that they are associated with important changes in moral sensibilities and behaviours: increasing self-control, the emergence of a culture of dignity and cooperation, and growing empathy with fellow human beings. Over time, moral horizons seem to have enlarged so that the perspectives of other persons can be taken into account. Gradually, the circle of moral concerns has expanded, so that one could abstract from direct and immediate experience and develop sympathy for more groups of people. This has not only impacted violence. Also, long-standing phenomena such as slavery, interstate wars, spousal abuse, infanticide and child abuse have become intolerable. Moral progress has been accomplished because the circle of ethics has expanded in the course of history: from family and tribe to nation and state, and to all human beings, and perhaps to animals and nature. This expansion reflects the development of ethics predicted by Potter's colleague Aldo Leopold (see Chapter 3): moving from a focus on individuals, to society, and to the environment, with bioethics, at least in the vision of Potter, as the final stage.

Between theoretical impossibility and practical reality

The ability of global bioethics to provide responses to global problems is contested. On the one hand are those who emphasize irremediable disagreement, thus the impossibility of global bioethics, on the other are those who point out that there is fundamental agreement on at least some basic principles, and that global bioethics therefore is a reality. An intermediate position is proposed in this book. It argues that although there is widespread disagreement there is also limited agreement. And, since ethics is dynamic and evolving, this agreement may grow over time. This intermediate version of global bioethics takes into account several lessons from the above criticism.

- Recognition of the fact of diversity and variability in bioethics matters. Global bioethics can become a possibility if it is accepted that the other is different as well as the same. Recognizing differences and pluralism does not preclude commonalities. Similarly, consensus does not exclude dissent. When a global ethical framework could be accomplished, it can only be applied to issues in particular settings. The 'universality' of the framework always has to be 'localized'. In particular settings disagreements will exist. How to balance or prioritize the various ethical components of the framework? How do ethical concerns regarding vulnerability or equality come into play? Universality therefore does not rule out particularity. On the contrary, both are at stake at the same time, operating and reinforcing each other in complex dialectic interactions.
- Because it is imprinted with the dialectics between universalism and moral diversity global bioethics is not static but dynamic and moving like globalization itself. Global bioethics is not a finished product applicable across the world, but an intercultural process. It is evolving not merely through abstract reasoning and use of principles, but through engagement with concrete, practical issues in 'localities', subsequently reaching out and searching for global ethical orientations. This creates the possibility of convergence towards commonly shared values.
- Recognition of differences and the possibility of convergence determine how global bioethics will develop responses to global problems. It will search for commonality within and through diversity, attempting to reconcile sameness and otherness. It will not deductively apply global principles on the entire world. Articulating commonality in a global ethical framework will result

from a process of accommodation. Hence the importance of global deliberation and intercultural dialogue. Shared values can only be identified through consultation, deliberation and negotiation within an emerging global community, and building on overlapping consensus. It is evident that this will be a long-term process. It will necessarily involve politics. It will not deliver the consistent and clear products of rational reasoning. Many relevant questions will arise. Is there a global community? Who has the authority to make global ethical frameworks? How can global actions be implemented?

Global bioethics is in the making. There are several versions of global bioethics currently operating. Most of them are developing within the dynamics of globalization, but there certainly is not one similar global bioethics approach applied across the world. However, there are approaches, practices and experiences that are providing direction. They need further critical analysis, theoretical exploration and practical examination.

The horizon of global bioethics

How and from what point of view will global bioethics be able to formulate responses to global problems? This question refers back to the issue of horizon discussed in the previous chapter. How can global bioethics expand its horizon beyond the limitations and preoccupations of the commonly accepted horizon of mainstream bioethics? Two critical repertoires scrutinize the myopic deficiencies and distortions of the current horizon: the critique of mainstream bioethics and the critique of neoliberal ideology. These repertoires simultaneously articulate what is missing in a global perspective, and thus what should be included in a broader horizon.

Bioethical normativity

The critique of mainstream bioethics raises familiar concerns. Justifiably focused on the liberation of the individual self in the 1970s and 1980s, the emphasis on personal autonomy and patients' rights has become sterile and one-sided. It has neglected the social and cultural context in which human beings are living. This focus on the individual person reinforces the neoliberal ideology. For some, mainstream bioethics has become a servant of the medico-industrial complex. Much of the funding for bioethical research comes from big science and technology programmes, for example connected to the Human Genome Project or nanotechnology initiatives. Independent, critical voices are exceptional. Bioethics, in the words of bioethicist Albert Jonsen, has become boring: too familiar, too domesticated.[11] It also reflects the 10/90 gap discussed in the previous chapter: the majority of bioethical discussions are concerned with issues that affect a minor percentage of the global population. Bioethics therefore needs therapy. It should no longer be concerned solely with medical and scientific problems but with institutional and global challenges. It also should liberate itself from the interests of the medico-industrial complex and from bioscience and technology. Critical perspectives demand reassessment of the conceptual and normative foundations of bioethics. One aspect is the limited conception of the individual as a rational, self-actualizing person focused on maximizing self-interest. Bioethical problems are framed as individual decision issues, interesting for healthcare providers and policy-makers. This framing disregards the social and economic context which is more the concern of politics. One implication is that for bioethics certain issues such as poverty, drug use, immigration or environmental degradation are not directly relevant. Another implication is that bioethics is more reactive than proactive: cases of assisted suicide or non-treatment decisions are drawing attention rather than long-term effects of changes in managed care and health insurance. Another aspect of mainstream bioethics is its reduced image of society. This is the procedural space within which individuals interact. It does not bring any normative requirements or commitments, unless they are voluntarily adopted by individual members. Notions such as 'common good' or 'public interest' do not have any meaning beyond the collection of individual goods and interests. A third aspect is the limited role of the government. It should create the conditions for individuals to flourish by limiting interference with individual freedom, warranting individual rights and freedoms. Health, for example, is an individual right and persons should be free to pursue it. But it is not the obligation of governments to provide it.

Neoliberal normativity

The critique of neoliberal ideology provides another opportunity to articulate the horizon of global bioethics. German philosopher Jürgen Habermas has argued that this ideology has specific normative understandings.[12] It presents an anthropological image of the human person as rational decision-maker, a social image of a post-egalitarian society that accepts marginalization, expulsion and exclusion, and an economic image of democracy with citizens as consumers and the state as service organization for clients. As discussed in the previous chapter, these understandings are driving the dominant process of globalization. The emphasis on individual choice implies that poor living circumstances are the result of poor choices. The primacy of personal responsibility provides a rationalization of inequality; equality of opportunity is important, not equality of outcome or status. The significance of social structures and social arrangements is denied. According to Ayn Rand '... there is no entity as "society," since society is only a number of individual men...'[13] Ethics has nothing to do with our relationships with others; it is primarily concerned with our own interests. Ethics is not social. Thus, there is no sense of collective goods or rights. Social justice, for Friedrich von Hayek, is an empty phrase without content.[14] Preservation of individual freedom is in fact more important than justice. Terms like 'common good' do not have any definite meaning to determine a particular course of action.

These normative understandings are increasingly criticized. Human beings are more than market actors. They are not just consumers, traders or buyers, regardless of their transactions. They have value and dignity themselves. Furthermore, they are interrelated, connected and dependent. This interrelatedness is not just a characteristic facilitating commerce or transactions but it has a fundamental significance for each human being. Individuals cannot develop into autonomous decision-makers without other people; they need sociality to flourish. Social institutions and structures are merely procedural arenas for individual action but they embody values such as solidarity, social responsibility, justice and cooperation.

Expanding the horizon

The shortcomings of the actual horizon of bioethics, as identified in the above critical analyses, support global bioethics to expand its horizon and to extend its vision and imagination. In this new, global horizon four major components are discernible.

a   *Individual person.* Bioethical discourse should proceed from a broader view of the individual human being, going beyond the insistence on the primacy of the free self-actualizing individual. Aspirations are part of a wider context in which individuals live together; they are never isolated individuals but formed in interactions within social life.

b   *Society.* A richer image of society is needed. Articulating that human beings can only flourish within relationships, the role of cooperation (rather than competition) and social responsibility (rather than individual responsibility) must be re-evaluated. Contrary to ideology, the role of society is also evident for markets; these are not autonomous, neutral forces but are created, nurtured and sustained by human efforts and through social and political policies.

c   *Common good.* Human beings share substantial resources essential for the survival of humankind. The future entails 'living together'. This will imply solidarity, and sharing of cultural and social values. It furthermore requires rethinking what kinds of public goods (for example, education and care) will be basic for interactive solidarity necessary for human survival as a species.

d. *Collective action.* In mainstream bioethics various forms of action have developed: making judgements, deliberating in ethics committees, recommending policies and developing guidelines. New forms of engagement must be employed in the global context. Influencing and changing social conditions require collective action. The interlocking patterns of global and local imply also that responses must be developed at various levels at the same time. Global developments influence national systems of bioethical governance, and vice versa. Constructing consensus on global principles on the one hand and building of national bioethics infrastructures on the other are therefore not a matter of deduction but of mutual interaction. Global action means combining local activism with horizontal, global networking.

These components provide an elementary structure to reconceive bioethics as a global endeavour. Building-blocks for a new vision and approach are available.

This global horizon can help to introduce new language, deconstructing the dominant vocabulary in health and ethics saturated with neoliberal presuppositions. The current emphasis on notions such as self-management, self-care, self-control, empowerment, individual responsibility, competition and consumer choice can be complemented and replaced with other images: citizen of the world, cooperation, solidarity, participation, inclusion, vulnerability, mutual care and social responsibility. Injecting new concepts into the bioethical debate is not just a matter of language; it also creates possibilities for new images, approaches and visions. It allows an escape from the dominant vision of the market, to go beyond the reign of competitive individualism. It opens the capacity to aspire to and change the possible future. Threats of globalization, manifested in exploitation, extraction, exclusion, expulsion and social regression must be named and analysed. Global bioethics can introduce new visions through the activity of framing, as will be explained in Chapter 11.

The task of global bioethics in this conception is to improve the global context of health and the social structures within which care is provided. Ethics is no longer the primary concern of individuals but also of communities, populations, states and transnational organizations. Since human beings share their fate on the same planet, bioethics cannot be indifferent to the problems of globalization that are jeopardizing the survival of humankind.

Global bioethics responses

The components that become visible within a wider horizon provide concepts and experiences that inspire responses to global bioethical problems. This will be elaborated in four areas in the following chapters.

Global ethical frameworks

Is it possible to identify or construct a global ethical framework for bioethics? Answering this question will demand an examination of efforts to advocate a 'world ethics'. They are inspired by the moral ideal of cosmopolitanism: all people everywhere should understand themselves as citizens of the world. This ideal is associated with an emphasis on what people share: they live in a global moral community and have a common heritage. The standard example is the international discourse of human rights, based on the idea that human beings have fundamental claims, whether or not they belong to a particular culture or are citizens of a specific state. In bioethics it is exemplified in the Universal Declaration on Bioethics and Human Rights (UDBHR).

Global governance

Cosmopolitanism is not only a moral ideal but also a political project. How can institutions of global governance in bioethics be created and reinforced? How can global arrangements be instituted that respect human beings and reduce social inequality? Can solidarity without boundaries be constructed? Of course, there are already international instruments that can be applied in cooperation between countries, organizations and individuals. But setting standards is not the same as implementing and applying them.

Global practices

Responses to global bioethical problems are not simply produced by global principles or institutional arrangements; they must be constructed and perfected in cooperation and action. Global practices will not result from imposing an ethical framework. They will occur within the dichotomy between universalism and particularism when the locality of moral views will be inspired by a global discourse that shows what common future human beings may share. Global solidarity will emerge as the result of cosmopolitanism from below.

Global discourse

Philosopher Jean-François Malherbe argues that there are various ways of doing bioethics.[15] Although a pragmatic style focused on solutions (for example in clinical ethics and research ethics) currently dominates, it is often combined with a philosophical style, attempting to retrieve traditions of conceptual analysis and rational judgement. But there also is a religious style bringing in enriching perspectives from faith, as well as a political style aiming at creating partial agreements within societies. These styles of bioethics will be continued in global bioethics. But the global perspective will imbue new visions and concepts such as social responsibility, vulnerability, solidarity and sustainability into the bioethical discourse, so that perhaps a new 'global' style will emerge. This style will refer to a broader scope of concerns, encompassing individual, social, cultural and environmental values.

This chapter has argued that global bioethics will be able to provide responses to global problems. When the major bioethical problems of today are produced by the dominance of neoliberal market ideology, bioethics should redefine itself as critical global discourse. Focusing attention on the social, political and economic context will be a first step but will not be enough. Bioethics must argue for a reversal of priorities in policy and society: economic and financial considerations should serve ethical principles such as human dignity and social justice, and no longer be ends in themselves. It should also argue that more emphasis is placed on vulnerability and social responsibility. This implies specific strategies for social inclusion but also institutional support and social arrangements. It will be necessary to demonstrate more vigorous advocacy and activism, supplementing academic enquiry. Social inequalities and conditions that produce vulnerability are not beyond social and political control. It will require that the voices of the disadvantaged, the deprived and the poor are more often heard within the bioethical discourse, involving these groups in policy development and implementation. Global inequity and vulnerability are furthermore enhancing the significance of cooperation. Forging global alliances and new networks of solidarity should be the preferred way to face global threats. An individualistic perspective makes it impossible to address the root causes of inequity, exploitation and vulnerability. Influencing and changing social conditions requires collective action. But how can this collective capacity to act be mobilized in response to global bioethical problems? This will be the subject of the next chapter.

CHAPTER SUMMARY

- Global bioethics is criticized for not being able to provide responses to global bioethical problems:
  - It is nothing new: global bioethics is in fact globalizing bioethics.
  - It is not possible; moral diversity is paramount and insurmountable.
  - It is not desirable: global bioethics means bioethical imperialism.
  - It is not necessary; problems can be addressed in a pragmatic way.
  - It is presumptuous while it is in fact too broad and impotent.
- These criticisms are one-sided since they proceed with distinctive presuppositions:
  - Binary and static thinking, separating the global and the local while the processes of globalization are marked by interaction and interdependency.
  - The focus on diversity and disagreement does not recognize shared views and common practices.
  - The idea of ethics is primarily theoretical and context-free while ethics is also characterized by practical concerns about ways of life and co-existence.
  - Bioethics is disconnected from bio-politics while in practice individual and political decision-making are interacting.
- The need for global bioethics to address global problems is argued with three claims:
  - Global issues and problems cannot be isolated but demand a global response.
  - Ethics is more than identifying and applying principles; it entails understanding the human condition.
  - Ethics, like culture, is dialogue between tradition and aspiration; they imagine possibilities to future human existence.
- Global bioethics is able to provide answers to global problems from a broader horizon that articulates what is missing in present approaches, using the criticism of mainstream bioethics as well as the neoliberal ideology of globalization.

- The expanded horizon of global bioethics includes:
  - a broader view of the individual person;
  - a positive notion of society;
  - a focus on the common good; and
  - an emphasis on collective action.
- Global bioethics responses will cover four major areas:
  - global ethical frameworks;
  - global governance;
  - global practices; and
  - global discourse.

Notes

1 H. Tristram Engelhardt (ed.) (2006) *Global bioethics: The collapse of consensus*. M&M Scrivener Press, Salem, p. 15.
2 H. Tristram Engelhardt (2006) *Global bioethics*, p. 40.
3 Callahan's critique of bioethics as 'handmaiden' is made in: Daniel Callahan (1996) Bioethics, our crowd, and ideology. *Hastings Center Report* 26(6): 3–4.
4 Renzong Qiu: The tension between biomedical technology and Confucian values. In: J. Tao (ed.) (2002) *Cross-cultural perspectives on the (im)possibility of global bioethics*. Kluwer Academic Publishers, Dordrecht/Boston/London, pp. 71–88.
5 Amartya Sen (1997) *Human rights and Asian values*. Sixteenth Morgenthau Memorial Lecture on Ethics and Foreign Policy. New York, Carnegie Council on Ethics and International Affairs, p. 30.
6 H. Tristram Engelhardt (2006) *Global bioethics: The collapse of consensus*. M&M Scrivener Press: Salem, p. 23.
7 Arjun Appadurai (2013) *The future as cultural fact: Essay on the global condition*. Verso: London/New York.
8 Pierre Hadot: *Qu'est-ce que la philosophie antique?* Gallimard: Paris 1995.
9 The notion of 'cultural aspiration' is introduced by Appadurai (2013) *The future as cultural fact*. Verso: London, New York, p. 195.
10 See, Kenan Malik (2014) *The quest for a moral compass: A global history of ethics*. Atlantic Books: London; Steven Pinker (2011) *The better angels of our nature*. Penguin Books: London; Peter Singer (2011, original 1981) *The expanding circle: Ethics, evolution, and moral progress*. Princeton University Press: Princeton and Oxford.
11 Albert Jonsen (2000) Why has bioethics become so boring? *Journal of Medicine and Philosophy* 25(6): 689–699.
12 Jürgen Habermas, *Die Zeit* 2001 (www.zeit.de/2001/27/Warum_braucht_Europa_eine_Verfassung, accessed 5 August 2015).
13 Ayn Rand (1964) *The virtue of selfishness: A new concept of egoism*. Signet/Penguin: New York, pp. 14–15.
14 Friedrich Hayek (1944) *The road to serfdom*. University of Chicago Press: Chicago, p. 57.
15 Jean-François Malherbe: Orientations and tendencies of bioethics in the French-speaking world. In: Corrado Viafora (ed.) (1996) *Bioethics: A history*. International Scholars Publications: San Francisco/London/Bethesda, pp. 119–154.

7

GLOBAL BIOETHICAL FRAMEWORKS

In the debate on the globalization of ethics, global ethics is often regarded as a two-level (or layered) phenomenon: at one level there is a self-standing international discourse defining a minimum set of standards agreeable to all.[1] At a second level, there is a multiplicity of different ethical approaches and views. These particular, 'local' moralities define what is ethically required beyond and above the minimum standards. The same distinction can be used for global bioethics. On the one hand, there is a set of global principles on which traditions and cultures agree; this is expressed in international human rights language and elaborated into specific bioethical principles. On the other hand, there are many efforts to articulate more specific bioethics standards within the context of particular religious and cultural settings. Representatives of these localized moral communities bring their views in the global debate through constructive dialogues and sometimes negotiations, so that the dialectic of global and local also helps to construct and produce global bioethics. In addition, specific cultures and traditions are important for the interpretation and application of global standards. Thus, the universal principles of global bioethics are the result of continuous and multilateral articulation, deliberation and production. As this chapter will argue, this two-level model is too simple. First, distinguishing two 'levels' suggests a hierarchy, while in fact global and local interact at the same level. Second, the universality of principles identified at the global 'level' is the outcome of interactions with and within the local 'levels', so that the global principles are in fact shaped by particular settings and approaches. Global bioethics therefore has several constitutive components (rather than two levels) while the global framework is 'post-universal'.

The adoption of the Universal Declaration on Bioethics and Human Rights (UDBHR) was a major step in the development of global bioethics.[2] The framework of ethical principles that it presents goes beyond the well-known principles of mainstream bioethics: autonomy, beneficence, non-maleficence and justice (which are in fact integrated). The UDBHR reflects Potter's encompassing notion of bioethics, covering concerns for healthcare, for the biosphere and future generations, as well as for social justice. The Declaration assumes the existence of a global moral community in which citizens of the world increasingly connect and interrelate but also share global values and responsibilities. This global community generates certain common principles, for instance the principle of protecting future generations, the principle of benefit sharing, and the principle of social responsibility. Various ethical systems in different cultural settings are converging into a single normative framework for all citizens of the world. This process is driven by the moral ideal of cosmopolitanism with concerns about common heritage, global solidarity and the future of the planet, and thus humanity. At the same time, it is energized by the practical experiences with human rights discourse. The idea that people have fundamental claims, independent of their citizenship in a country or their belonging to a specific culture, is not merely a theoretical claim. Human rights language is attractive because it is a public discourse in which everyone can participate, and because it has legal and political implications.

This chapter will examine the efforts to develop global bioethics frameworks as they are situated between the practical language of human rights and the moral ideals of cosmopolitanism. It will start with the human rights tradition and the search for common values in the 1990s, before examining efforts to develop a framework for global bioethics.

Human rights

The Nuremberg Code (1947) formulated ethical principles for medical research based on the human rights of subjects (with voluntary consent as the first requirement). Emphasizing the rights of subjects rather than the obligations of medical professionals, it demonstrated that the professional ethics of virtues and duties was no longer sufficient to assure ethics in healthcare. The Code is viewed as the beginning of the modern era of human rights. It inspired the Universal Declaration of Human Rights (UDHR) adopted by the United Nations in 1948.

The emphasis on human rights became influential in the 1990s when international criminal tribunals were established as well as numerous human rights organizations. With the growing impact of globalization but also atrocities and human rights violations in the Balkans, Rwanda and Somalia, as well as the end of apartheid in South Africa and the collapse of the Soviet Union, human rights provided an appropriate global framework for two reasons.

- *Universality*. The chief novelty of the UDHR is its universality. Everyone is entitled to human rights because they belong to the human species. This universality implies that a person is more than an individual with specific characteristics, determined by a particular culture and tradition, and exposed to injustice, discrimination and expulsion. For global problems that cannot be solved at the local level, this is a useful perspective. Moreover, it is a perspective that transcends the issue of cultural diversity. Finally, it provides a discourse that can effectively counter the impact of neoliberalism as a global ideology; it clearly states that rights and human dignity are more important than economic growth and free markets.

- *Emancipatory force*. Although human rights have been formulated by governments and international organizations, their global dissemination has been due to social movements, political struggles within particular arenas and resistance against oppression and humiliation. They have inspired poor and homeless people, disabled persons, patient organizations and indigenous populations. Claiming respect and equal treatment transforms an individual problem into a political and social one. It also turns vulnerable subjects and victims into persons with rights that need to be respected. This implies more than protecting individual rights and freedoms. It provides inspiration and empowerment, facilitating and promoting images of a better future, creating new opportunities for people, and changing the conditions of human existence. Human rights discourse is attractive to feminist bioethics; for example, the idea of equality can be used to liberate rather than oppress women. Disadvantaged groups such as indigenous populations have strengthened their positions with an appeal to human rights. The right to access available medical treatment inspired social activism in the field of HIV/AIDS. Human rights discourse therefore has a transformative power beyond its legal scope. It connects institutional processes with existing practices, civil initiatives and activism. Human rights provides an effective bridge between the moral and legal language of common humanity and practical actions in specific settings.

UNIVERSAL DECLARATION OF HUMAN RIGHTS (UDHR, 1948)

The first sentence of the Preamble states that 'recognition of the inherent dignity and of the equal and inalienable rights of all members of the human family' is the foundation of freedom, justice and peace in the world.

This leads to Article 1: 'All human beings are born free and equal in dignity and rights. They are endowed with reason and conscience and should act towards one another in a spirit of brotherhood.'[3]

Human rights discourse expanded within the field of medicine, life sciences and healthcare, more or less concomitant with the emergence of global perspectives in bioethics. International and intergovernmental organizations (WHO, WMA, CIOMS, UNESCO, and Council of Europe) have produced bioethical standards within the context of the human rights tradition.

Searching for common values

Formulating, specifying and implementing human rights will be important but is it enough for a global ethical framework? This question inspired a search for shared values, particularly during the 1990s. An example is the Commission on Global Governance, a group of prestigious personalities convened in 1992 at the occasion of the fiftieth anniversary of the UN. Its report forcefully expresses the view that all inhabitants of the world are in the same predicament; they share the same 'global neighbourhood' where the neighbourhood is the planet. Without a 'neighbourhood ethics' the planet will not survive.

OUR GLOBAL NEIGHBOURHOOD

'We call for a common commitment to core values that all humanity could uphold: respect for life, liberty, justice and equity, mutual respect, caring, and integrity. We further believe humanity as a whole will be best served by recognition of a set of common rights and responsibilities.'[4]

This search for common values was motivated by two factors. The first is the global nature of bioethical problems. They cannot be addressed in a piecemeal manner by separate actors or from a specific, 'local' perspective. Since the future is shared, humanity needs a common mission. This view motivated all UN members to translate shared values into policy goals, and to formulate specific targets to be achieved by 2015.

UNITED NATIONS MILLENNIUM DECLARATION (2000)[5]

'Thus, only through broad and sustained efforts to create a shared future, based upon our common humanity in all its diversity, can globalization be made fully inclusive and equitable.' Fundamental values essential to international relations are:

- freedom;
- equality;
- solidarity;
- tolerance;
- respect for nature;
- shared responsibility.

The second, related motivation is the inequality in capacity to deal with global problems. Bioethics is well developed in Western countries but less so in other parts of the world. This may produce a disparity between bioethical practices, often to the disadvantage of people living in countries without a strong bioethical infrastructure (as the Trovan case exemplifies). The fact that moral values differ and that moral practices vary cannot be accepted as excuses not to identify fundamental ethical principles. This was the reason to call for a global agenda for bioethics (for example in the *Declaration of Ixtapa* in 1995 by CIOMS).[6] It was an important motivation for the UNESCO initiatives. The request to develop a common framework of ethical principles was explicitly made by representatives of developing countries. They were concerned that the rapid evolution of medical science would insufficiently benefit them, disproportionally harm them, or discriminate them with double standards. This call from developing countries to create a global normative framework demonstrates that global bioethics principles are not necessarily imposed by rich and powerful countries on the rest of the world. The role of such framework is first of all to protect parties that are weaker.

The search for common values was primarily a practical effort. It is demonstrated, for example, in the activities of the Parliament of the World's Religions. In 1993, approximately 200 leaders from more than 40 religious and spiritual traditions signed the statement *Towards a Global Ethics*. This statement, drafted by German theologian Hans Küng, declares that all traditions share common values such as respect for life, solidarity, tolerance, non-violence and equal rights. The document shows what world religions have in common rather than point out how they differ. It affirms the priority of ethics over the market economy.[7]

In the same period of time, the challenge to identify common values, specifically in the area of medical science and technology, was taken up by UNESCO. The next section discusses why and how this international organization engaged with global bioethics.

Declaring global bioethics

UNESCO's Constitution (1945) declares that peace must be founded upon the intellectual and moral solidarity of humanity. Julian Huxley, the first Director-General of the organization, points out that, in order to make science contribute to peace, security and human welfare, it is necessary to relate the applications of science to a scale of values. Guiding the development of science for the benefit of humanity therefore implies 'the quest for a restatement of morality ... in harmony with modern knowledge'.[8]

Being a UN specialized organization, UNESCO's activities must accomplish goals that are relevant for all member states. Consequently, promoting science and international cooperation should serve as a channel to address the basic problems and needs of the world population. Science is not regarded as an end in itself but as a means towards the development of nations and the resolution of global problems such as poverty, environmental degradation and child mortality. Furthermore, the activities of the organization must take into account all perspectives that are relevant to all member states. In order to facilitate this, for example, six official languages are

)

used (Arabic, Chinese, English, French, Spanish and Russian), which can substantially enrich debates and enhance the inputs from diverse cultures.

Respect for cultural diversity is one of the main concerns. UNESCO has put in place programmes to preserve and protect cultural accomplishments in, for example, architecture, arts, literature, philosophy and science. Identifying and preserving accomplishments in all regions of the world shows that all civilizations and cultures have contributed to the present condition of humankind. However, in all this richness and diversity, one can also discover the expression of common values and shared interests.

Universal Ethics Project

UNESCO's interest in bioethics dates back to the 1970s when bioethical concerns emerged in many countries and the word 'bioethics' was introduced. The organization started to convene symposia and conferences on bioethics, related to the development of genetics, life sciences and reproductive technologies. The concern is particularly with the relation between scientific and technological progress and human rights. In June 1992, Federico Mayor, the Director-General at that time, decided to set up an International Bioethics Committee (IBC), chaired by French lawyer Noëlle Lenoir. The task of the Committee was to explore how an international instrument for the protection of the human genome could be drafted. Extensive consultations are focused on five themes: genome research, embryology, neurosciences, gene therapy, and genetic testing. For each theme various dimensions are studied: the current state of progress in research at the world level, the application of the results of this research, and the principal ethical concerns for the present and for the future. These preliminary studies encourage the launch of a bolder initiative: the Universal Ethics Project in 1997. Will it be possible to formulate bioethical principles that can guide not merely genetics but global bioethics?

International standard-setting

Developing international normative standards is one of the objectives of the work of UNESCO in ethics. The UN is the only existing platform for all nations to explore and discuss possibly shared values and principles, and to negotiate and agree on normative instruments. Other efforts to determine common standards have been undertaken at regional levels. The feasibility of reaching consensus in Europe in the Oviedo Convention stimulated the search for global consensus. On the one hand this Convention, but also the Declaration of Helsinki (adopted by the World Medical Association) refers to human rights, so that connecting bioethics and human rights is not a novel enterprise. On the other hand, UNESCO could build on previous normative instruments in genetics, notably the Universal Declaration on the Human Genome and Human Rights (1997) and the International Declaration on Human Genetic Data (2003).

Development and contents of the UDBHR

The 193 member states mandated UNESCO in 2003 to develop a universal declaration on bioethics. In principle, all bioethical topics were on the table. Building consensus on global principles requires subtle and critical processes of deliberation, consultation and negotiation. It is clear that given the short time frame for drafting the declaration, the development of the text and the resulting consensus has been vulnerable to criticism since not all relevant actors could be consulted while others did not feel represented by the experts involved.

One of the contentious issues in the elaboration was the scope of bioethics. At least three views were advanced: bioethics has to do with (1) medicine and health care; (2) the social context, such as access to health; and (3) the environment. In different parts of the world, different conceptions, definitions and histories of bioethics are evident. The scope of the adopted text of the Declaration is an obvious compromise between these views, linking the ethics of medicine, life sciences and associated technologies as applied to human beings with social, legal and environmental dimensions.

The core of the Declaration is presented in 15 ethical principles. They determine the different obligations and responsibilities of the moral subject (*moral agent*) in relation to different categories of moral objects (*moral patients*). The principles are arranged according to a gradual widening of the range of moral objects: the individual human being (human dignity; benefit and harm; autonomy), other human beings (consent; privacy; equality), human communities (respect for cultural diversity), humankind as a whole (solidarity; social responsibility; sharing of benefits) and all living beings and their environment (protecting future generations and protection of the environment, the biosphere and biodiversity).

UNIVERSAL DECLARATION ON BIOETHICS AND HUMAN RIGHTS (UDBHR, 2005)

The following principles are to be respected:

- human dignity and human rights;
- benefit and harm;
- autonomy and individual responsibility;
- consent;
- persons without the capacity to consent;
- respect for human vulnerability and personal integrity;
- privacy and confidentiality;
- equality, justice and equity;
- non-discrimination and non-stigmatization;
- respect for cultural diversity and pluralism;
- solidarity and cooperation;

- social responsibility and health;
- sharing of benefits;
- protecting future generations;
- protection of the environment, the biosphere and biodiversity.

Some of the principles are already widely accepted (e.g. consent). Others have been endorsed in previous Declarations (e.g. sharing of benefits). The set of principles in the new Declaration balances between individualist moral perspectives, and those orientated towards community, society, culture and environmental context. The UDBHR recognizes the principle of autonomy as well as the principle of solidarity. It emphasizes the principle of social responsibility and health which aims at reorienting bioethical decision-making towards issues urgent to many countries (such as access to quality healthcare and essential medicines especially for women and children, adequate nutrition and water, reduction of poverty and illiteracy, improvement of living conditions and the environment). Finally, the UDBHR anchors the bioethical principles firmly in the rules governing human dignity, human rights and fundamental freedoms. The section on the application of the principles provides the spirit in which the principles ought to be applied. It calls for professionalism, honesty, integrity and transparency in the decision-making process; the setting up of ethics committees; appropriate assessment and management of risk; and ethical transnational practices that help in avoiding exploitation of countries that do not have an ethical infrastructure.

The status of the Declaration

Unlike the Oviedo Convention, the UDBHR does not constitute a binding normative instrument in international law. It has weak mechanisms of implementation, and no reporting and monitoring procedures. It is equally true that the text is very general. Definitions of crucial terms are not provided and the wording of principles is not specific. Interpretation and application will probably vary widely. Nonetheless, the unanimous adoption of the text is not a merely symbolic gesture. For the first time, all states of the international community have committed themselves to respect and implement the basic principles of bioethics, set forth within a single text, and within the broader context of international human rights law. Previous international documents have been adopted by special interests groups (e.g. the WMA with the Declaration of Helsinki). Declarations adopted by UN organizations, however, are part of international human rights legislation, although as 'soft' law. The UDBHR illustrates that bioethics has developed into a global endeavour. During this process of maturation, common principles have been identified. It is important to note that the four principles of mainstream bioethics are now integrated into a broader set of 15 principles, taking into account not only individual and interpersonal perspectives but also communal, social and environmental ones.

The components of global bioethics

The process of elaborating the UDBHR shows that global bioethics seems to proceed according to a two-level model. At the global level, bioethics identifies general principles, defining a set of standards agreeable to all. Common principles are 'declared' to express the moral imagination and to guide the aspirations of the global community rather than imposed upon everyone across the world. Controversial ethical issues such as abortion, euthanasia and stem cell research, however, are addressed at the local level within the context of specific ethical traditions and particular communities. At this local, operational level, the common principles need to be interpreted and applied within a multiplicity of different ethical views and moral cultures.

The problem with this two-level model is that it presupposes a hierarchy. It assumes that global principles are basic; they provide an underlying set of values for diverse and particular ethical systems. The search for common values is inspired by the idea that global ethics (founded on basic principles) already exists and needs to be discovered within different cultural traditions. Global principles are a matter of exploration and discovery. One only needs to recognize the shared values that are already there; they are not the result of ongoing dialogue. Thus, in this two-level model, universal bioethical principles are embedded in local settings; they only must be 'excavated' in an intellectual effort of identification and determination.

The relationship between global and local 'levels', however, is more complicated. On the one hand, the global principles are not simply pre-given but the result of interactions with multiple local settings. They are not discovered but shaped by particular contexts. It is more appropriate to say that they are 'post-universal' principles; they are not a priori presupposed as basic or underlying principles but the outcome of critical dialogues with particular ethical traditions. They are located between abstract universalism and concrete multiculturalism. Universality, in this perspective, does not refer to pre-established principles that transcend all differences and that are abstracted from concrete and individual experiences. The view of the universal as a priori, prescriptive and rational necessity is typical for Western civilization, and is not shared, as the French philosopher François Jullien has pointed out, by other cultures.[9] From a global perspective, the universal is rather a regulating idea guiding the search for the common. Commonalities are not given but experienced; they create conditions in which individuals can flourish; they emerge in a process of universalizing.

On the other hand, the local bioethical contexts are not the exploration areas to discover universal principles but they need to be taken seriously as diverging ethical views. The main point is that global aspirations and local operations are not disconnected; they continuously interact. The dialectics of global and local determines global bioethics. Rather than a finished product, it is in the making.

Global bioethics is the provisional result of exchange, learning, deliberation and negotiation, articulating disagreement but also the possibility of convergence.

Such a dialectic view entails that global bioethics is constituted by three components of reflection and action. One is developing and articulating global ethical frameworks. In this domain the aspirations of global bioethics are declared and clarified, providing guidance to applications and implementations. The major challenge here is the substance and acceptability of the framework as a global one. The second component is the local context of cultural diversity. Here, specific problems in particular contexts are addressed and the question is not only how global frameworks are impacting on local approaches but also how local ethical concerns and viewpoints feed back into the global framework and modify it. The major challenge here is the governance of global problems. The third component is that of global practices; here global and local settings are interacting. The notion of 'interculturality' is useful to explain the dialectic interchange (it will be further developed in Chapter 8). Global frameworks are not simply applied but modified and adapted to local circumstances. The question here is which conditions promote fruitful interchange so that global principles are translated into practical arrangements for healthcare and medical research (see Figure 7.1).

The UDBHR is the outcome of a political process in which consensus is constructed, perhaps fabricated. It does not explicitly refer to rational explanations or foundations of the decisions that have been made during the negotiations. Nonetheless, it is a crucial document since it entails sub-texts of underlying ideals that are able to guide the further development of global bioethics. These ideals compose the ethical substance of the global framework. They also determine the acceptability of global bioethics as a discourse that can address global problems and provide a critical assessment of the sources of these problems within the ideology of neoliberalism.

Components of global bioethics

set of common standards (human rights; global principles)	specific standards within diverse ethical traditions
aspirational level of defining and declaring	operational level of interpretation and application
global community	particular communities

Global domain   ⟸⟹   Local domain

dialectic interaction: mutual exchange, inspiration, articulation, deliberation, learning, negotiation

possibility of convergence

post-universalism

FIGURE 7.1 Components of global bioethics

Two sub-texts will be important to further explore the underlying ideals: the connection with human rights, and cosmopolitanism.

Bioethics and human rights

One of the new elements of the Universal Declaration on Bioethics and Human Rights is that it connects bioethics and human rights. This is a risky stance since human rights discourse is often criticized for precisely the same reasons as global bioethics itself: there is no agreement on the foundations of human rights; they impose dominant Western views; they are weak and unfamiliar in many countries; and they are primarily focused on social change (thus undermining academic scholarship). Therefore, what makes human rights discourse attractive for global bioethics? Five advantages can be pointed out.

Global aspiration

The human rights framework satisfies the need to make transcultural and transnational normative judgements in a diverse world. It presents a framework that is transcending culture, nationality and religion. Human rights and bioethics therefore share several common characteristics: they have the same origin (the horrors of the Holocaust and the need to prevent future atrocities), the same goal (never again should individual human beings be used as a means to another end), and the same claim to universality. Human rights are applicable to everyone. Connecting bioethical principles with human rights provides a global outreach to bioethics. The underlying idea is that human well-being should not be defined by location (geographically or culturally) or determined by specific characteristics such as race, gender, nationality and ethnicity. The ideals of freedom and equality transcend any specific setting or context. Every human being has the same dignity that demands unqualified respect.

Context of interpretation

Taking human rights as the context within which bioethical principles are developed has the advantage that it refers to values and principles that are already generally (though not universally) accepted (e.g. respect for the dignity of the human person) relating to a growing body of normative instruments adopted by the international community. This context implies that human rights discourse functions as constraint and final authority for bioethical practice. The principles of bioethics cannot be restricted unless in accordance with international human rights law. The formulation of several principles in the UDBHR (for example, consent) underlines that exceptions can only be made if they are consistent with human rights. The new principle of respect for cultural diversity and pluralism is qualified with the wording that it cannot be invoked to infringe upon human rights or upon the other principles of the UDBHR. This restriction means that a specific practice can only be justified on the basis of respect for cultural diversity if it is in compliance with the other principles such as consent, non-discrimination, and benefit sharing.

Normative amplification

International human rights law adds to the normative force of bioethical discourse. Human rights promote principles and norms that are not negotiable and cannot be compromised. For example, the commitment to the integrity of the human body implies that torture, cruel punishment and organ trafficking are always wrong. There might be arguments, however, to justify these practices. Torturing one person might result in information that can save the lives of thousands of other persons. Trafficking organs might help persons with end-stage renal disease on the waiting list for organ transplantation who might otherwise die. Particularly in healthcare, utilitarian argumentation is influential since the results of medical intervention (saving lives, curing diseases, preventing illnesses) are usually predominant. In the past, result-driven activities have led to the use of new technologies and devices without informing and taking the consent of patients. This has been specifically clear in the context of medical research where it is commonly argued that the interests of many might weigh more heavily than the interests of a few persons. Human rights discourse presents a framework of principles and norms that need to be upheld regardless of the results and consequences since humanity itself is at stake.

The series of scandals and abuses in medical research has instigated mainstream bioethics in Western countries to develop a framework of basic principles and policies to introduce legislation and oversight mechanisms (see Chapter 2). Global bioethics nowadays is confronted with similar challenges. In the Trovan case it is argued that new medication is important to help people in developing countries but that the principle of informed consent is difficult to implement in populations that are illiterate or that have a tradition of community or family consent. Another argument underlines that the standard of care in Western hospitals cannot be used in developing countries. These arguments have justified medical and research practices with double standards: in developing countries lower standards are used than in developed countries because it makes those practices more feasible. Human rights discourse can counter such arguments, emphasizing that ethical principles are universal (research that is not ethical in the US is also not ethical in Nigeria) and that the ends do not justify the means (improving healthcare for a population does not justify exploitation of some citizens, taking advantage of poverty, lack of development or social misery to advance knowledge).

Practical application

Many activities in bioethics today relate to policy-making. Bioethics committees at various levels are drafting recommendations for policy. At national level, they analyse guidelines, propose legislation and assist policy-makers. At local level they advise hospital boards or research institutions regarding institutional guidelines and policies. Bioethicists are members of expert committees or participants in public forums. Human rights discourse is often helpful in these policy efforts since it has a practical edge, emphasizing rights that people have because they are human beings. One aspect is that human rights developed as a theoretical discourse as well as a practice. Although discussions continue about the universal claims of human rights, and their philosophical and theological justifications, they did not impede the discourse to become practical and public. The right to health, for example, could be applied in practice by courts and advocacy groups although there is a fundamental philosophical debate about the notion of health and what the right entails. Enjoyment of the highest attainable standard of health is already mentioned as a fundamental right in the Constitution of WHO in 1946. Numerous international documents have recognized this right but until recently it was not influential. Since 2000 this has changed. The normative content of the right as well as the obligations of states and other actors have been clarified and specified. Independent experts have been appointed by the Human Rights Council as Special Rapporteurs on the Right to Health (since 2002). They publish annual reports, examine country situations and deal with individual complaints about violations of the right. Citizens and NGOs can use this growing body of legal interpretation and evidence to put pressure on governments to improve access to treatment and care. The right to health is now included in the Constitution of a substantial number of countries.

THE RIGHT TO HEALTH

'8. The right to health is not to be understood as a right to be *healthy*. The right to health contains both freedoms and entitlements. The freedoms include the right to control one's health and body, ... and the right to be free from interference ... By contrast, the entitlements include the right to a system of health protection which provides equality of opportunity for people to enjoy the highest attainable level of health.

11. The Committee interprets the right to health ... as an inclusive right extending not only to timely and appropriate health care but also to the underlying determinants of health, such as access to safe and potable water and adequate sanitation, an adequate supply of safe food, nutrition and housing, healthy occupational and environmental conditions, and access to health-related education and information, including on sexual and reproductive health.'[10]

Another aspect of human rights language is a redefinition of the humanism that underlies both human rights and bioethics. Policy-making in healthcare is driven by concerns for individual patients and vulnerable populations in need of care and protection. But using human rights translates the moral language of compassion, concern, solidarity and needs into one of rights and dignity. For example, it is argued that severe poverty should be regarded as a human rights violation since the poor are denied access to the basic necessities of life. Rights dignify rather than victimize. People are no longer regarded as needy victims but as citizens of the world with the same claims and rights as everyone else. Human rights make people equal and more powerful. They provide a universal and objective standard to assess human behaviour without blaming individuals.

New modalities of action

The benefits of interconnecting bioethics and human rights are demonstrated in the rise of a new type of activity: advocacy. Globalization of healthcare and research makes evident how variable the infrastructures for bioethics teaching, research, consultation, policy-making and public debate actually are across the world. Bioethical principles (and legal regulations) cannot be equally applied and implemented in countries. Now that a global bioethics framework has been adopted, advocacy can help in reinforcing these infrastructures and better implement the principles. Advocacy is well known in the area of healthcare and social work. Especially for nurses, advocacy is described as a core responsibility. Patient advocacy groups play an important role in care and clinical research. Advocacy organizations can speak on behalf of homeless people or HIV/AIDS patients. Child advocacy is regarded as a core paediatrics task in response to child abuse. Advocacy work has become important in other areas, for example in international aid, recognizing that the power of global economic institutions is so strong that without activism and interventions nothing will change, even if the causes of poverty and marginalization are well understood. In the context of globalization, advocacy is proposed as a means to reinvigorate civil society and participatory democracy since it helps foster critical thinking. It not only argues for policy or legislative change. It often directly involves vulnerable, marginalized and excluded people or groups of people in order to achieve their rights. For global bioethics advocacy is a means to effectively influence daily practices and practical policies. Advocacy helps to translate agreement on paper into activities within everyday life. It is an important component of various global practices that will be elaborated on in Chapter 11.

ETHICAL WATCHDOGS

WEMOS Foundation is a non-profit organization founded in 1981 by medical students and tropical disease specialists in the Netherlands. Its mission is to create a world in which everyone has the optimal health to which they have the right. The activities are lobbying governments, building local capacity, campaigning against brain drain, and advocating affordable medication. These activities also include monitoring of the ethical context, making sure that ethical principles are applied in research and access to medication. Examples of unethical practices are publicized, together with testimonies of research subjects. The Foundation cooperates with similar organizations in Kenya, Zambia, Bolivia and Bangladesh. The Centre for Studies in Ethics and Rights in Mumbai is one of the partners. Together with Dr Amar Jesani, founder of this Centre, WEMOS produced a video about clinical drug trials in India, showing how vulnerable populations are recruited as research subjects without much protection. The number of NGOs in India is approximately 2 million (compared to 1.5 million in the US). For global health, the number of NGOs in the world is difficult to estimate but there are more than 60,000 NGOs related to AIDS alone.[11]

Cosmopolitanism

The second sub-text that inspires the development of global bioethics refers to the ideals of cosmopolitanism.[12] These ideals, often expressed in history, for example in Stoic philosophy, consider each human being as a citizen of his or her own community or state (*polis*) as well as at the same time a citizen of the world (*cosmos*). In the first, they are born; they share a common origin, language and customs with co-citizens. In the second, they participate because they belong to humanity; all human beings share the same dignity and equality. Being a citizen of the world liberates the individual from captivity in categories such as culture, tradition and community, but also gender and race. Humanism replaces communitarianism. It implies that it is possible to overcome the limitations of being born in a particular place within a specific culture. Cosmopolitanism expresses the aspiration to live beyond specific, bounded horizons. It allows a broader solidarity without boundaries. The moral ideal is that human beings belong to a universal community ('humanity'); human well-being is not defined by a particular location, community, culture or religion. Global citizens therefore have responsibilities towards other human beings, near or distant. Cosmopolitanism often uses the metaphor of expanding circles of moral concern discussed in the previous chapter.

THE IDEALS OF COSMOPOLITANISM

- Unity of humanity: human beings belong to the cosmos; world citizenship.
- The cosmos includes the whole of humanity; universal community.
- Boundaries have no moral significance.
- Openness to differences.
- Focus on what human beings have in common.
- All human beings have equal moral status.
- Global citizens have responsibility to show solidarity with others, not merely rights.

The ideals of cosmopolitanism are contested. It is argued that 'citizen of the world' is a metaphor or an abstraction, not reality. There is no world community or state to which such a citizen belongs. The nation state is the only basic political community. Cultural identity can only be constructed within the specific territory of such a nation. Social bonds with distant others are ephemeral and illusionary.

Processes of globalization over the last few decades, however, demonstrate that 'citizen of the world' has become more than a metaphor. Globalization is associated with 'cosmopolitization' of the world, not only subjectively, but also at the objective and political level.

First of all, it is argued that there is an emerging global consciousness, a growing sentiment of living in a common world. This sentiment has been facilitated by three experiences. First, the experience of the finiteness of the world. Currently, every place and space in the world is known; there no longer is terra incognita; distances have vanished. Second, the phenomenon of the 'small world'. Television and internet bring events from all parts of the world immediately close to us; we share the same planet; relationships and interconnections are unavoidable. Third, the unity of the world. There is only one world. Even if the world is not a community like the traditional *polis*, there is a common humanity; if this one planet is ruined, all will suffer and perish. Global consciousness is often constituted in a negative way: through disasters, horrors and violations of human rights, or as a reaction to crises. The suffering of distant others makes us aware that we all share the same vulnerability and similar basic needs. The point is that global interaction and interdependency expands our moral sensibility. Wherever they are, people recognize that they share the same predicament.

SMALL WORLD

In 1967 social psychologist Stanley Milgram published his small world experiment. Take two randomly selected people in the world, what is the probability that they know each other? Milgram found that only five intermediaries suffice to link the persons (or six degrees of separation). His conclusion is: 'we are all bound together in a tightly knit social fabric.' The experiment was conducted only in the USA and before the use of internet and social media. Social networks like Facebook argue that they make the world even smaller, reducing the six to four degrees of separation.[13]

Second, there is objective cosmopolitization. The autonomy of nation states is eroded by economical, political and legal global developments. States are increasingly subjected to international law with global jurisprudence (for example, the International Criminal Court established in 2002 can prosecute individuals such as leading politicians for crimes against humanity). At the same time, risks are globalized; they require collective responses. Finally, there is a rise of global organizations and actors, particularly non-governmental organizations.

Third, at the political level, cosmopolitanism questions the notion of sovereignty. Individual states are either powerless or often bypassed in responding to global challenges. Politics is nowadays increasingly the domain of civil society. Global activities are undertaken by communities of citizens, distinct from traditional political authorities. They participate in direct and horizontal communication, sharing information and using publicity to put pressure on these authorities. Instead of using existing institutions, citizens engage with particular causes, develop new collective structures, create social movements, and open up new problem areas, using the latest technologies to set up global networks and organize world forums and global summits.

Is ethical discourse changing?

Though globalization is increasingly associated with cosmopolitanism, theoretical and practical consequences of global processes are precarious. Do these processes promote growing interconnection of human beings and increasing concerns with humanity as a whole? Or do they reinforce conflict and discord? The picture is not only positive. Human rights are continuously violated. Global values are recited but without changing practices. There is also a recent backlash against human rights and international law with some states, especially the US, arguing that formerly agreed universal standards such as the prohibition of torture no longer apply in the face of national security.[14] Social movements come and go but mobilization of world citizens is temporary and fragile. Such mobilization is not necessarily positive. It can be used for global humanitarian action or terrorism and jihadism. For these reasons the question is asked whether a global identity is really emerging. Is cosmopolitanism as a moral ideal more than a future utopia?

To answer this question, it is important to consider whether the direction of ethical discourse is changeable and changing. In a globalizing context two basic changes are occurring. First, the notion of 'world' has assumed a different meaning. Initially being the location of origin or residence, the world used to be regarded as a neutral space in which interactions take place between individuals within the same territory. In a global context, 'world' acquires a broader and active meaning. Rather than space, it defines the community of human beings to which singular individuals belong. The world is not just the geographical locality in which human beings reside but the human society in which they are living. As an arena for interaction, the world is more than territory. It is a constellation of values, languages, ideas and customs. This world influences human beings just like human action constitutes and transforms the world which is not neutral but ours. We depend on our world that is the result of common efforts. This interdependence explains the role of ecological motives in global discourse. The world has become a moral concern: it is not merely given as a resource for human beings but is the condition that makes human existence possible. Philosopher Hannah Arendt has used the term *mundus* for this notion of world.[15]

The second change is the use of the term 'humanity'. Under the influence of human rights discourse and cosmopolitanism, concern for humanity as a whole has become a fundamental criterion to assess not only individual conduct but also policies and interventions of states, corporations and communities. Not obtaining informed consent from research subjects is condemned as a 'crime against humanity'. This expression refers to universal principles that should be upheld regardless of the circumstances. It also allows civil society to have a moral function; it can speak on behalf of everyone, not so much because it represents the rest of the world population but because it expresses concerns about the common good of humankind. The new meaning of 'world' as well as the notion 'humanity' inspires ethics since it focuses on commonalities rather than differences. It opens up a discourse that emphasizes time-honoured but neglected issues: global community, common heritage and global commons. These issues will be discussed in the following chapter.

CHAPTER SUMMARY

- Development of global bioethical frameworks has been inspired by human rights discourse and the moral ideals of cosmopolitanism.
- Human rights are attractive as global discourse because of:
  - universality
  - emancipatory force.
- The search for common values in the 1990s prepared the way for the UNESCO Universal Declaration on Bioethics and Human Rights, adopted in 2005.
- This Declaration is the first global ethical framework in bioethics, adopted as soft law by the international community.
- It incorporates 15 ethical principles, covering a widening range of moral objects: from individuals to communities to humankind to the environment.
- Global bioethics in this approach is not a two-level phenomenon but has three continuously interacting components: a global framework of principles, local diverse contexts of interpretation and application, and global practices of exchange, inspiration and negotiation.
- Two ideals are underlying the global framework of principles: human rights discourse and cosmopolitanism.
- Human rights discourse is attractive for global bioethics because:
  - it has similar global aspirations
  - it provides an accepted context of interpretation
  - it amplifies the normative force of bioethics
  - it has practical applications
  - it facilitates new modalities of action such as advocacy.

- Cosmopolitanism provides global ideals that inspire global bioethics. Individuals redefine themselves as 'citizens of the world'. Cosmopolitanism is growing at three levels:
  - subjective: increasing global consciousness
  - objective: expanding global jurisprudence; multiplication of global organizations
  - political: limited sovereignty of nations; growing importance of civil society.

Notes

1 The two-level model of global ethics is presented by William M. Sullivan and Will Kymlicka (eds) (2007) *The globalization of ethics*. Cambridge University Press: New York, pp. 4, 207 ff; see also: David Held (2010) *Cosmopolitanism: Ideals and realities*. Polity Press: Cambridge (UK) and Malden (MA), p. 80 ff.

2 *Universal Declaration on Bioethics and Human Rights*, UNESCO, Paris, 2005; http://unesdoc.unesco.org/images/0014/001461/146180e.pdf (accessed 4 August 2015).

3 *Universal Declaration of Human Rights*, UN General Assembly, December 1948. www.ohchr.org/EN/UDHR/Documents/UDHR_Translations/eng.pdf (accessed 4 August 2015).

4 Commission on Global Governance (1995) *Our global neighbourhood*. Oxford University Press: Oxford/New York, p. 336.

5 Nations Millennium Declaration (adopted in September 2000); www.un.org/millennium/declaration/ares552e.htm (accessed 4 August 2015).

6 CIOMS (1995) A global agenda for bioethics: Declaration of Ixtapa. *Canadian Journal of Medical Technology* 57: 79–80.

7 Parliament of the World's Religions (1993) *Toward a global ethics*. Chicago: Council for a Parliament of the World's Religions.

8 Julian Huxley (1946) *UNESCO. Its purpose and its philosophy*. Preparatory Commission of the United Nations Educational, Scientific and Cultural Organization. Paris, p. 41; http://unesdoc.unesco.org/images/0006/000681/068197eo.pdf (accessed 4 August 2015). See also: Henk ten Have and Michèle S. Jean (eds) (2009) *The UNESCO Universal Declaration on Bioethics and Ruman Right: Background, principles and application*. UNESCO Publishing, Paris.

9 For a philosophical analysis of the relations and distinctions between the notion of 'universal', 'uniform', and 'common', see François Jullien (2014) *On the universal, the uniform, the common and dialogue between cultures*. Polity Press: Cambridge (UK) and Malden (MA).

10 UN Economic and Social Council: *General Comment 14*, August 2000.

11 The WEMOS video is accessible via: www.youtube.com/watch?v=aoMnvUyCPuE

12 See: Kwame Anthony Appiah (2006) *Cosmopolitanism: Ethics in a world of strangers*. Allen Lane (Penguin Books): London; Robert Fine (2007) *Cosmopolitanism*. Routledge: London and New York.

13 Stanley Milgram (1967) The small world problem. *Psychology Today* 1(1): 61–67. See also: Lars Backstrom, Paolo Boldi, Marco Rosa, Johan Ugander and Sebastiano Vigna (2012) *Four degrees of separation.* Proceedings of the 4th ACM International Conference on Web Science (see: http://arxiv.org/abs/1111.4570).
14 Jens David Ohlin (2015) *The assault on international law.* Oxford University Press: Oxford and New York.
15 Philosopher Hannah Arendt has used the term 'mundus' in her book *The human condition.* University of Chicago Press: Chicago, 1958. The human world in her view is 'not identical with the earth or with nature, as the limited space for the movement of men and the general condition of organic life. It is related, rather, to the human artefact, the fabrication of human hands, as well as to affairs which go on among those who inhabit the man-made world together.' (*The human condition,* p. 52). See also: 'Mundalization' used by In-Suk Cha (2008) Toward a transcultural ethics in a multicultural world. *Diogenes* 219: 3–11.

8

SHARING THE WORLD
Common perspectives

International human rights law and cosmopolitan ideals inspired the development of global ethical frameworks. At the same time, global bioethics cannot simply be the application of universal human rights to moral issues and queries. One problem is that views about the content of human rights differ. Some argue that they are primarily negative rights (emphasizing non-interference so that individuals are protected against the state). Civil and political rights are therefore more important than social and economic rights. Others, particularly from the global South, argue that human rights are also positive rights (as entitlements to certain basic goods that need to be provided by the state). This controversy is connected to a minimalistic interpretation of human rights as rights of individuals.[1] In this view human rights discourse is the language of individual empowerment; at its core is moral individualism. Its main purpose is to guarantee that individuals are free to choose how to conduct their life. Human rights discourse does not impose one vision of a good human life. On the other hand, minimalism is criticized since separating negative and positive rights seems artificial. If basic conditions for human existence are not provided, civil and political rights cannot be exercised. All human rights are interdependent. The right against torture is as important as the right to subsistence. The recent growing importance of the right to health demonstrates that human rights do not only have an individual dimension but also a dimension of solidarity and collective good. It is therefore important to stress the commonalities of the human condition. Human rights discourse is global because human beings share common needs and vulnerabilities.

The ideals of cosmopolitanism provide a broader context for the interpretation and application of human rights within global bioethics. Importantly, they connect what pertains to the individual as well as the community. Human beings are embedded in particular communities but are part of a universal community. Individualistic approaches are therefore inadequate. The individual person can only be empowered within a relational context with others. This broader view is especially articulated in non-Western perspectives such as the African worldview of Ubuntu.

UBUNTU ETHICS

In Bantu languages, *Ubuntu* describes a particular African worldview. It expresses that a person becomes a person through other people: 'I am because we are.' It is the community which makes and defines the individual. Being a person is not given but the result of a process, of integration into a community through rituals and learning social rules. Because the individual is always a node in a tissue, the good of the community has priority. Emphasis is on the commonality and interdependence of the members of the community. Individuals therefore have duties and responsibilities towards each other, rather than merely rights.[2]

Another aspect of cosmopolitanism is that rights cannot be separated from duties and responsibilities. In a world that comprises one community without boundaries, citizens have responsibilities towards each other. This aspect is usually expressed in non-Western approaches.

Cosmopolitanism therefore provides global bioethics with a richer vocabulary to address global problems. It illustrates that ethics is expressed in different languages: the language of rights but also of responsibilities; the language of principles, but also of values and virtues. Cosmopolitan ideals furthermore can help a rethink of how to implement moral principles in practices and settings around the world. Human rights discourse is often criticized because implementation is left to states that are either not interested or themselves violators of rights so that implementation is not effective or politically influenced. In an era of globalization there is a range of non-state actors such as transnational companies that can be involved in human rights violations. In the area of bioethics, enforcement and implementation of principles is even more difficult since there is no body or entity that can examine and monitor their application and impose sanctions. Cosmopolitanism suggests other modalities of application (as will be discussed in the following chapters). It expands the range of actors and stakeholders involved. Another advantage of cosmopolitanism is that it can guide the application and interpretation of human rights in diverse settings. Rights can conflict. Individual liberty can clash with equality, the right to private property with justice. Cosmopolitanism focuses on what human beings have in common. In a global moral community in which all human beings have equal moral status it is important to determine common perspectives. This is not simply an empirical determination of the basic needs of human beings or the conditions for human flourishing. Human rights specify the needs and conditions shared among all human beings and necessary for individual existence. But the determination of common perspectives has most of all a normative function. If human beings have similar basic needs and share the same vulnerability, the focus of ethical discourse should not be on individuals but on the conservation, protection and amelioration of commonalities that are crucial for everyone. Such emphasis on common perspectives is particularly requested if global bioethical problems (as argued in Chapter 5) are associated with the neoliberal ideology of globalization. Human rights discourse as well as cosmopolitanism proposes a different view of globalization in which the focus is on the human person *within* the social and cultural context and the environment. Universalism is not enough to challenge neoliberal globalization. What is needed is a different orientation. It is not sufficient to protect the dignity of the individual person against possible exploitation and marginalization, although this will be a necessary first step. What is even more important is that the existential conditions are enhanced and standards of life improved. This requires a shift towards what connects human beings; in other words, an expanded ethical horizon that goes beyond individual perspectives and concentrates on commonalities and collective action. The area of healthcare amply demonstrates the connection between individual and common good. Health is a necessary and universal condition for human functioning. It is an individual good that allows each person to live his or her life. At the same time, it is only realized if certain preliminary conditions are fulfilled: sanitation, clean air and water, diet and nutrition, essential medication, not as private commodities but as common goods available for everyone.

Global moral community

Globalization of bioethics has brought the notion of 'community' into the spotlight. In many non-Western cultures, individuals are not privileged over communities. Global bioethics, therefore, should recognize that in many countries, individual rights can be less significant than responsibilities towards family, community and society. Another reason for increased attention to community is the recent policy emphasis on social determinants of health. When health is the outcome of social and economic conditions rather than individual healthcare and medical technology, promoting health implies reinforcement of justice, not only locally and nationally, but globally.

The emergence of global bioethics has not only stimulated the interest in community but at the same time expanded the idea of the moral community. An illustration is the debate on protecting future generations and on intergenerational justice. Here, the human community includes more than the present generation of human beings. Responsibility to posterity is cardinal to ensure the survival of humankind. Similar concerns about community have arisen in the debates on the principle of benefit sharing. This novel principle is important in the context of bio-prospecting, i.e. the search and collection of natural substances that might be used for the development of drugs. Natural resources are abundantly available in developing countries with rich biodiversity such as Brazil and Indonesia. In many developing countries traditional medicine is based on such natural resources. These resources and the traditional knowledge of indigenous populations are increasingly being appropriated (a practice condemned as 'biopiracy') by commercial companies to fabricate new profitable substances without any compensation to the indigenous communities. With the current emphasis on property rights (as discussed later in this chapter), traditional knowledge is regarded as the property of nobody, and thus free for the taking. Against this background the principle of benefit sharing has been advanced in order to counteract injustices.

BIOPIRACY

Basmati rice has been cultivated for centuries in South Asia. Local farmers have improved the quality of the rice by seed selection and breeding practices. In September 1997 the Texan company RiceTec Inc was granted a broad patent on Basmati rice lines and grains. This caused a public outcry. NGOs in India started an international campaign that led to the withdrawal of some patent claims in 2002. Another example is the Japanese cosmetics firm Shiseido. It has patented several formulas of herbs and spices to make anti-ageing agents and hair tonic. These patents are based on the knowledge and practices of traditional healers and farmers of Central Java in Indonesia. Due to protests and media campaigns calling for a boycott of its products, Shiseido retracted some of the patents in 2002.

These new debates in fact refer to a fundamental discourse which regards humanity itself as a moral community. Two interrelated arguments are used. One argument is that the global community includes not only human beings but all nature. The concept of community is broadened to include more than humans; non-human species need to be considered members of our community since we all share dependency and vulnerability. The second argument is that Earth is not the possession of one particular generation. Each generation inherits it and should transfer it to future generations. Because of the interdependence of human life and the fragility of our planet, a new vision of community should encompass past, present and future generations. The continued existence of the human species can only be guaranteed if humanity itself is regarded as a 'global community' that takes care of the global commons that are under the custody of humanity as a whole and that need to be preserved to safeguard the survival of humanity.

Both arguments expand the notion of global community in two directions: synchronically, by including not only human beings but all forms of life, and diachronically, by including various generations. The implication is that 'global community' becomes a morally relevant notion because it refers to extent (a worldwide scope involving 'citizens of the world') as well as content (the identification of specific global values and responsibilities as well as the establishment of global traditions and institutions). The values defining the global community refer to commonalities shared by humankind. Especially two concepts are connected with the notion of global community: common heritage and commons. They emphasize that all human beings have common needs and common vulnerabilities; that they can only survive and flourish under certain shared conditions; and that life on the planet is only sustainable if humans cooperate. The next two sections will elaborate on these concepts.

Common heritage

The notion of 'common heritage of humankind' was introduced in international law in the late 1960s to regulate common resources such as the ocean bed and outer space. A milestone was the speech of Maltese ambassador Arvid Pardo to the UN General Assembly (November 1967).[3] He argued that the sea-bed and the ocean floor are a common heritage, and should be used and exploited for peaceful purposes and to the benefit of humankind as a whole. The new concept in fact went back to the older tradition of Roman Law that distinguished the separate category of *res extra commercium* (things outside of commerce; property that cannot be exchanged), for example common property (such as seas) and public property (such as rivers). This category defines objects of law that cannot be economically exchanged, thus not sold or owned by anybody. The distinction between private and common property was famously used in 1609 by Hugo Grotius in his book *Mare Liberum* where he argued that the sea is *res omnium communes* (belonging to everybody; common property) like the air and the sun: these are objects that are used and enjoyed by everyone but they cannot be owned by anyone.

Initially applied to common areas with material resources outside the borders of nation states, such as the ocean floor, the moon, outer space and the Antarctic, the use of the notion expanded to vital resources within the territory of individual nations, such as tropical rainforests. Labelling areas as common heritage means that they are vital for the survival of humankind. It also means defining global responsibilities. Common areas cannot be appropriated. They demand international cooperation in order to create common management. Possible benefits should be equitably shared among states, irrespective of their geography. They should only be used for peaceful purposes. And finally, it is necessary to preserve them for future generations. In the 1970s, the concept came to be used to include culture. When cultural accomplishments (e.g. Machu Picchu or the Great Wall of China) have outstanding universal value (being exemplary, unique and irreplaceable) and when they are exceptionally important for the sustainability and quality of life on Earth, they can be regarded as common heritage. The HUGO Ethics Committee was the first to apply the notion of common heritage on the human genome. It was followed by UNESCO in its Universal Declaration on the Human Genome and Human Rights (1997), declaring that the human genome is the heritage of humanity.

UNIVERSAL DECLARATION ON THE HUMAN GENOME AND HUMAN RIGHTS (UDHGHR, 1997)

Article 1: 'The human genome underlies the fundamental unity of all members of the human family, as well as the recognition of their inherent dignity and diversity. In a symbolic sense, it is the heritage of humanity.' This basic statement has several practical implications: the genome cannot be appropriated as someone's property and financially exploited (Art 4); benefits from scientific advances should be available to all (Art 12); research results should be used for peaceful purposes (Art 15); scientific knowledge and information should be freely exchanged and publicly accessible (Art 19).

A further step is to apply the notion in bioethics itself. When the Council of Europe was founded in 1949 its Statute affirmed that spiritual and moral values were the common heritage of the peoples uniting in the Council. Values are transmitted from one generation to another, they form the basis of cooperation, and are necessary for the preservation of human society and civilization. The ethical framework laid out in the UDBHR is developed within the same mindset. Ethical principles are identified and declared that must be considered as heritage of humanity. These principles represent a coherent register of moral values that enable global citizens to act and live together in a global moral community.

Common heritage as a bridge between universal and particular

Extending the notion of common heritage may contribute to developing the idea of 'global moral community'. Like specific communities can only thrive through commonly shared ideas and symbols, a global community is supported through identifying particular moral values and cultural objects as world heritage. It is heritage, precisely because it is essential for community-building. When the idea of heritage is applied at the global level, and considered heritage of humanity, it aspires and creates a global community of common values as well as cultural symbols. These values and symbols are always specific. They are expressions of particular identities. They reflect diverging characteristics of human beings in history and across the world. But to regard them as common heritage means that they have significance for humanity. Their particularity can be universalized, showing that they are no longer representative of one particular culture but of human culture in general. This does not mean that they lose their specific characteristics and become homogenized or assimilated in a broader framework. The interaction equally affects this framework. Specific materials, objects and values are recognized as heritage of humanity when they combine universality with uniqueness. They should be different from other heritage, showing diversity as a defining feature of human beings. Here, the universal (what is typical for being human) is particularized. Diversity itself becomes common heritage.

The notion of common heritage brings together the universal and the local. It highlights what humanity is sharing in all diversity. But, using the notion has normative implications. First, heritage should be safeguarded for the benefit of present and future generations. Second, it is not a burden but a benefit to humanity; it should be used as a shared source of exchange, innovation and creativity; it is as necessary for the future of humankind as biodiversity for nature. Third, it is more than an economic resource. Heritage does not call for exploitation but for inclusion and participation of all human beings for the benefit of everyone. 'Declaring' ethical principles such as respect for human vulnerability, social responsibility, and protecting future generations as principles of global bioethics, and recovering them as common heritage of humankind, is not simply projecting them into the world as one single space for human activity and creativity. Heritage is not static; it helps to construct humankind as an imagined moral community, it provides a general structure for organizing and expressing divergence. The notion of common heritage is thus an instrument of a cosmopolitan project employed to create a global moral community that is growing into existence, expanding, and premised upon a shared symbolic universe, common interests and global solidarity. Global bioethics therefore is not simply a project to advocate universal values or to acknowledge moral diversity. It is a dialectical effort to bridge universalism and particularism. The challenge is to combine convergence and divergence.

Interculturality

How can recognition of divergence in moral views and approaches be reconciled with the convergence towards commonly shared values? As argued in Chapter 6, answers emerge if simplistic views of globalization are overcome. Globalization does not produce either uniformity or multiplicity; it does both. People nowadays participate in multiple cultures. All cultural traditions are hybrid and dynamic, not frozen but changeable. Similar arguments can be made for bioethics. Of course, different ethical perspectives exist, but differences do not exclude that there is a common core. The term *interculturality* is therefore more appropriate than 'multiculturalism'.[4] The idea of multiculturalism has become problematic: while acknowledging the existence of multiple cultures and value systems, it does not really examine how people can live together and can construct new syntheses and social relationships. In practice, multiculturalism is often associated with policies of acculturation (the 'other' is integrated or assimilated into the dominant culture), indifference (the 'other' is tolerated in peaceful co-existence of cultures, producing parallel and separated communities that do not interact) or articulating and even retreating into traditional identities (reinforcing the differences between 'us' and 'them' since the other produces fear of losing one's self). A global world, however, is not merely characterized by the existence of multiple value systems, but first of all by the continuous interaction and reciprocal learning of these systems. The term 'interculturality' emphasizes interaction. 'Inter' refers to separation and also to linkages and communication. While multiculturalism emphasizes respect for diversity, individual freedom, justice and equal treatment, interculturality introduces a moral vocabulary of interaction, dialogue, participation, trust, cooperation and solidarity. Interculturality is more interested with what unites people than what divides them. It has a more positive thrust than multiculturalism; it is not enough to have co-existence but one should strive to produce practices that can create community. If there is common ground it needs to be cultivated through interchange and communication. Intercultural dialogue is driven by the quest for unity or rather commonality, not uniformity. Convergence will result from a continuous process of 'translation'. Since there is not one moral language that is pre-given, underlying or more fundamental than other languages, there is no possibility to step outside of the communication process. A global, 'trans-cultural' reference point that is universally acceptable does not exist. There are only 'interstitial' spaces where cultures interact and overlap, and where people communicate. The first step in reaching common understanding is to recognize that there are radically different 'languages'. Consensus only becomes a possibility after differences are expressed and acknowledged. We have no choice other than to interact in our various languages and search for common heritage. Convergence is not given but the result of an ongoing activity of deliberation, consultation and negotiation.

INTERCULTURALITY

- focus on interaction, dialogue, reciprocity, and communication;
- concern with synthesis, sharing, similarities, and commonalities across differences;
- recognition of dynamic identities and evolution of cultures;
- promotion of unity and (social) cohesion;
- ways of learning how to live together.

Commons

While common heritage refers to the past, the notion of 'commons' is orientated towards the future. Both notions go beyond the perspective of the individual; they emphasize what human beings share and what they need to respect and preserve. They emphasize the central role of transmission; human beings need to safeguard what they have received from previous generations and transfer it to future generations. Both notions evoke the context of loss, finitude and concerns about survival. The emphasis on commons, however, shifts the attention more clearly from shared past to future. Commons raise the question of how we can be good ancestors. Commons inspire concerns for planetary resources, future generations and social transformation.

In the history of humankind, commons were the rule.[5] A classic example is land available for public use, and managed by the surrounding community. The land as 'commons' is not owned by anybody. Sustaining it is a shared interest and requires cooperation and collective action. Genetic diversity is another example.

PLANT GENETIC DIVERSITY

Genetic diversity is essential for the survival of humanity. It is regarded as common heritage as well as agricultural commons. Traditionally, in local commons, farmers exchanged seeds to improve existing plant varieties so that yields would increase and crops become less vulnerable to drought, diseases and pests. These local commons increasingly disappeared with the rise of industrialized agriculture. Breeders started to collect and store seeds in seed banks, and thus created a breeders' commons. In the 1980s public breeding programmes were privatized. This led to the emergence of agro-businesses that control seeds and protect genetic varieties with intellectual property rights. The commons to which breeders had free access ended. Five companies (e.g. Monsanto and Du Pont) control 30 per cent of global seed sales and 38 per cent of agricultural patents. Concerns with diminishing genetic variety, however, reactivated the idea of commons. In 2008, the Svalbard Global Seed Vault was opened deep inside the permafrost on the island of Spitsbergen, funded by the Norwegian government, with a storing capacity of 4.5 million seed samples, creating a non-commercial global pool of crop genetic diversity.

Different types of commons are distinguished: natural commons (such as fishing grounds, forests and water supplies), social commons (for example, caring arrangements, public spaces, waste removal and irrigation systems), intellectual and cultural commons (knowledge as well as cultural products), digital commons (notably the internet and the world wide web), and global commons (e.g. oceans and outer space). These types have different qualities. They can be depletable (natural commons) or renewable (social and cultural commons). They can refer to rivalrous goods (use by one person diminishes the amount of goods left for others as is the case in many natural commons) or non-rivalrous goods (using knowledge, ideas and information does not engage in competition that decreases opportunities for other people but is in fact increasing opportunities). For rival goods it is therefore important to restrict access, while for non-rival goods open access will be required. Global commons are non-excludable (they are open to everybody since access cannot be restricted) and non-rivalrous (use by one individual does not have an impact on the use by others).

Despite heterogeneity, all commons share basic features. First, they do not fit into the usual distinction between private and public ownership; they refer to collective property, jointly owned by a group of people (as in local commons) or belonging to all persons on Earth (as in global commons). Second, they are essential for human subsistence and long-term survival (since they provide water, food, shelter but also health and knowledge). Third, commons need to be protected for future generations so sustainability is important. This is the reason that they are often connected with mechanisms of inclusion and exclusion, regulating and monitoring access and preventing overexploitation. Commons, finally, are not simply resources; they are social practices (some advocate the use of the verb 'commoning'). They express a discourse of social cooperation, reciprocity, sharing and social harmony. Commons refer to togetherness ('commonwealth'), not only with people but with nature, environment and land. Human beings use commons but they are also part of them. Commons are social arrangements based on shared interests and ideals.

New interest in the commons

For a long time, commons have been regarded as archaic social practices that have disappeared in developed countries and are nowadays only maintained in isolated indigenous communities. On the one hand, they were considered tragic since they promoted free-rider behaviour. The problem with collective property is that nobody feels responsible. Individuals will maximize their benefits without sharing the costs so that individual self-interest will ruin everybody's long-term interest. On the other hand, they are the best examples of neoliberal projects, transforming common goods into private property. Globalization reactivated the interest in commons. For example, the Commission on Global Governance (1995) discussed the global commons as an opportunity.[6] They are resources for the survival of humanity; they are the global neighbourhood that is the home of future generations. The negative effects of turning commons into private property, and restricting access to commons, started to receive increasing attention. Privatizing a commons blocks people from using it. The area of drug research and innovation is an example. Patenting of discoveries may lead to multiple owners of, for example, gene fragments. Too many property rights covering the same thing means that nobody can use it. Ownership is fragmented and the use of the underlying resource is impeded. This is called 'anticommons', because it reverts the idea of sharing.

ANTICOMMONS IN BIOMEDICAL RESEARCH

'In the past 30 years, drug R&D has been going steadily up, but discoveries of major new classes of drugs have been declining. Instead, drug companies focus on minor spin-offs of existing drugs for which they already have assembled the necessary property rights. How did this new drug discovery gap happen? Patent anticommons. Paradoxically, more biotech patent owners can mean fewer life-saving innovations. Drugs that should exist, could exist, are not being created.'[7]

The notion of commons is interesting because it emphasizes social sharing rather than private property, common rather than individual interests, and collaboration rather than competition. It is an important component in a discourse that provides: a) general criticism of neoliberalism; b) a specific critique of property rights; and c) connects to the environment and biosphere.

a   The idea that there are commons that are collective property, belonging to all persons on Earth, or to local and transnational communities implies that people are always involved. Commons are not simply resources that can be appropriated, harvested and used; instead, they are developed, sustained and managed by social practices of communities who depend on them for daily subsistence, survival and flourishing. Commons are produced in human efforts of cooperation. Examples are new forms of common property that have emerged, such as the world wide web, free software and initiatives such as Creative Commons, Public Library of Science, and General Public Licensing that promote sharing of knowledge and information. People engage in collective enterprises because they are concerned about the common good. Commercialization and commodification threaten the flourishing of present and future generations since they make the commons no longer accessible. This is the point of the commons argument in the area of healthcare. Health is determined, for example, by clean air, healthy water and safe food; these should be accessible to all members of a population since they are part of the public health commons that have been created over time (as systems of providing hygiene, sanitation, water, sewage disposal and vaccination), not as a privilege or commodity but as a right. For example, groundwater and aquifers have long been regarded as commons, as shared resources, but are now increasingly privatized. Almost 900 million people lack access to safe drinking water; 40 per cent of the world's population has no access to reliable sanitation. Approximately 10,000 people are killed every day by preventable diseases caused by unsafe water and poor sanitation. This data is used to argue that water should be a commons since it is the only way to make it accessible to all people.[8]

WATER WARS

Cochabamba, the third largest city of Bolivia, privatized the municipal water supply in 1999 at the request of the World Bank. The private company drastically raised water prices. A community coalition organized a series of protests. In 2000 the government had to reverse the privatization. The President of the World Bank repeated his view that free or subsidized provision of water will lead to abuse. In 2010, at the initiative of the Bolivian government, the UN General Assembly declared that access to clean drinking water and sanitation is a human right. As a commons, it is essential as a basic human necessity. However, the chairman of Nestlé, the leading water bottling company in the world, insists that water is 'a foodstuff like any other', and therefore should have a market value.

The language of commons activates a third option in-between the neoliberal dichotomy of private and public goods, of market and state. It argues that there are common areas, domains and resources that should be publicly accessible because they play a special role for all human beings.

b   Commons discourse is critical of the intellectual property rights (IPR) regime that is associated with globalization (particularly, copyrights, trademarks and patents). Property rights have existed for centuries and have been connected to innovation and creation of new knowledge and technology. Nowadays, they are strongly connected to trade. Since the 1980s, patent claims have proliferated, not only for new medications but for genetic resources, traditional knowledge, biological organisms, and all forms of life as well. A patent is a temporary grant of monopoly on the rights to make, use, offer for sale, or import an invention. It is usually granted for 20 years. The global expansion of IPR over many domains of contemporary life is recent, especially in life sciences and medicine. It has become a major component in globalization.

PATENTING AND BIOMEDICINE

1980   US Bayh-Dole Act: university patents are allowed on results from publicly funded biomedical research; this led to a boom of new biotech companies. In 2014, US bioscience firms employed 1.6 million people.

1980   US Supreme Court in Diamond vs Chakrabarty: a bioengineered microbe is patentable.

1984   US Moore case: patent granted on human cell line.

1988   US patent on Harvard Oncomouse: first patent for genetically modified animal.

1994   Agreement on Trade-related Aspects of Intellectual Property Rights (TRIPS)

1995   Establishment of World Trade Organization (WTO)

2001   Doha Declaration on the TRIPS Agreement and Public Health

2011   European Court of Justice: human embryonic stem cells are not patentable.

2013   Supreme Court of India: dismissal of Novartis' patent on cancer drug Glivec.

2013   US Supreme Court: 'genes and the information they encode are not patent eligible ... simply because they have been isolated from the surrounding genetic material.' However, synthetic DNA is patentable.

The major critique of the global IPR regime is that it reinforces global inequality. Patent activity is concentrated in a relatively small number of companies in the global North. This is especially clear in biotechnology: 90 per cent of all patents on life forms are held by Northern companies. But also within developed countries property rights are usually concentrated by a few rights holders. Patents create a monopoly, allowing a single owner to block access to a resource. Studies have shown that monopolies increase the prices of drugs. Monopolies prevent less expensive generic drugs from entering the market.

The focus on intellectual property rights is, moreover, associated with the phenomenon of biopiracy.[9] From a commercial point of view, collecting biological or genetic materials is interesting because it might result in commercial products that can be patented. There are many examples of drugs derived from plants: quinine from the cinchona tree, or vincristine from the rosy periwinkle. These substances have been extracted, patented and marketed by Western companies for treatment of malaria and as chemotherapy, respectively. The point is that they have been used for centuries by indigenous populations as part of traditional knowledge. Quechua people in Peru have used the bark of cinchona trees to reduce fevers while the periwinkle was known for centuries as a folk medicine in Madagascar. Derivation of drugs from plants in this context is expropriation. What has been common knowledge for ages is transformed into private property. The significance of indigenous communities in generating this knowledge is disregarded. These communities could not prove that they have discovered the medicinal uses of these substances (there are no written claims); their knowledge was communal and open; it was not an individual accomplishment but represented an ancient practice of benefit sharing.

The global IPR regime is not only reinforcing inequalities but itself is the result of an unfair global institutional order (as argued by Pogge, Chapter 4). This order has deliberately been established by the World Trade Organization (WTO) and the Agreement on Trade-related Aspects of Intellectual Property Rights (TRIPS). It was the outcome of coordinated pressures by Western countries and international businesses as the owners of property rights on developing countries. There was no fair representation of countries involved, no sharing of full information, no democratic bargaining but a mixture of political and economic threats and coercion. Public involvement was also absent; all negotiations were behind closed doors. Countries were pressured to comply through bilateral trade agreements. The WTO has a dispute settlement system that can apply punitive measures if countries violate the rules. But it is not only the process that is unfair. The globalization of intellectual property has primarily benefited Western countries. The international legal context has been created by owners of intellectual property, and is in their primary interest. The intellectual property rights regime is an illustration that the global context of health and healthcare itself can be unfair.

Due to growing criticism, particularly the lack of access to affordable medication, the strict implementation of property rights has been mitigated. The Doha Declaration is regarded as a success for developing countries arguing that public health and the right to health is more important than protecting patent rights.

DOHA DECLARATION (2001): PATENT RIGHTS VERSUS RIGHT TO HEALTH

The TRIPS agreement aims at the global protection of intellectual property rights. It includes 'flexibilities' in order to protect public health. Because many developing countries have not been able to use these flexibilities, the Doha Declaration created more opportunities to promote access to essential medicines. Countries can use compulsory licences for generic drugs to produce or import patented drugs without permission of the patent holder. They can also use parallel importation of patented drugs from one country to another at the lowest price.

However, in practice developing countries cannot use the flexibilities to promote access to medicines. A major reason for this is that regional and bilateral free trade agreements are signed with the European Union and the United States including intellectual property rights provisions that are more stringent than the requirements of the TRIPS agreement. For example, they extend the duration of patents and they introduce exclusive protection of test data for drugs. In the last case, data obtained in clinical trials and submitted to get approval of a new drug cannot be used to get approval for a generic drug. The result is that countries cannot develop or buy less expensive generic medication for their population.

REDUCING ACCESS TO MEDICINES

The World Health Assembly in 2008 stated that intellectual property rights 'do not and should not prevent Member States from taking measures to protect public health'.[10] Nonetheless, reality is different. For example, the Central America Trade Agreement signed in 2004 provides strong property protection including data exclusivity. This allows foreign pharmaceutical companies to market drugs without competition of generic drug companies. In Guatemala, where 75 per cent of the population lives below the poverty line, the effect was that prices of medication increased. Several generic drugs were removed from the market and others could not enter. The trade agreement therefore reduced access to medication.

The dominance of the IPR regime raises questions about the status of the public domain. What exactly is available to all; what is the common space in which we can collaborate? Is knowledge a private or communal good? Are there any limits to what can be privatized and commodified? The more strictly the property regime is applied, the more it restricts access to knowledge and information. This has consequences for healthcare but equally for science. Traditionally, scientific information is openly accessible; one does not need permission to use and elaborate a specific scientific theory or discovery. New ideas not only emerge from competition but also from cooperation: sharing ideas in networks, personal communication, open publications, and settings in which critical ideas can flourish. Creative activity requires free exchange and discussion; it builds upon and transforms the ideas of others.[11] However, the current tendency is to move from a free culture to a permission culture where property law is used to control information and protect existing commercial interests. Intellectual property rights may therefore infringe upon human rights such as freedom of expression and the right to health. In the current context, protection of property rights seems more important than providing for the basic needs of human beings. These rights are no longer considered as instrumental rights that should help to implement human rights so that the flourishing of all human beings is promoted. They have become the tools of the powerful while human rights protect, or at least should protect, the powerless. This basic criticism evokes the need for a new global discourse in which the ethical value of property rights is balanced against that of health, education, culture and science. It furthermore demands a critique of the technocratic conception of the prevailing intellectual property law which does not take into account the rising ethical conflicts. Property rights are now the specialty of a limited community of experts.

c   Third, the notion of commons connects human beings, the environment and the biosphere. Commons as social practices link communities with specific areas, domains or resources shared as common property. Managing this requires social cooperation and individual participation so that social norms are developed, boundaries set, systems monitored and sanctions applied. Collective governance aims at sustainability. Care is taken not to exhaust the commons. Traditionally, forest commons were regarded as reservoirs of biological diversity, containing a community of species which need to be preserved for humanity; forests were not collections of trees, or economic assets for paper and wood that could be replaced by more profitable assets such as eucalyptus or palm plantations. This traditional feature of commons as harmonious relationship with nature, as a bond between inhabitant and habitat, has become more interesting nowadays because of global environmental degradation. The environment, in the view of the World Commission on Environment and Development is common property; ecosystems are shared. Human life should be integrated in a wider context; it is only sustainable in harmony with all life and the environment. Therefore, commons are often associated not with growth but with sustainability. It is interesting that currently, especially in Latin America, new worldviews are promoted that re-actualize traditional connections between living beings and nature. The concept of 'living well' promotes a vision of life that differs from the neoliberal ideology. A basic element is respect for the integrity of nature as a source of life. This vision has been incorporated in the constitutions of Ecuador (2008) and Bolivia (2009), countries with large indigenous populations. At the initiative of Bolivia, the United Nations proclaimed 22 April as International Mother Earth Day, acknowledging that Earth and its ecosystems are our home.

BUEN VIVIR (SUMAK KAWSAY): LIVING WELL

Ecuador used to have a flourishing economy in the 1970s. Between 1995 and 2000 it became one of the poorest countries in Latin America (the number of poor people rose from 34 per cent in 1995 to 71 per cent in 2000). Public services such as healthcare and education collapsed due to political instability, corruption and neoliberal economic policies. This background created the need for new social and political approaches. The worldviews of indigenous peoples in the Amazon and Andean regions provided inspiration. In Ecuador it is expressed as Sumak Kawsay (from the Kichwa language), in Bolivia as Suma Qamaña (from the Aymara language) but in fact a plurality of views exists among various populations. For example, aboriginal societies in Canada have a worldview that connects individual, land, family, values, spirituality and everyday life. This view is symbolized as a tree: individual behaviour is like the leaves; community customs are like small branches; ethics are like large branches; values are like the trunk; but the whole tree is rooted in the earth.[12]

These alternative approaches use the idea of commons in two senses. The first sense is global: the planet is our home. Mother Earth (or Pachamama) is the basis for existence. It cannot be owned. We, as human beings, belong to it and we all share it. The second sense is local: since human beings are part of communities and these communities are intimately connected with nature, they are responsible for respecting all living creatures within their communal scope.

Bioethics and the commons

The new interest in the commons has several impacts on the global bioethical debate.

- The first is that the notion of patenting itself is critically reviewed.[13] The implementation of the IPR regime in developing countries since the 1990s has negatively changed the accessibility and affordability of medicines. Even with flexibilities allowed, developing countries are pressured by developed countries and industries to apply even more stringent property protection than required by TRIPS and the Doha Declaration. There is no evidence for the argument that patent protection is necessary to promote research and development in developing countries. This has led to pleas to abolish patents, or at least to develop other approaches. Patents do not encourage innovation, and damage public health and social welfare. Moreover, the IPR regime conflicts with human rights. Protecting intellectual property should not be an end in itself but should contribute to human flourishing. Health should be more important than trade.

- Another impact comes from the argument that the set of 'objects' that could be patented should be reduced.[14] In 2002 biotech activists proposed a treaty to share the genetic commons. They argued that plant, animal and human life should not be patented. This proposal reiterates the idea that the genome is the common heritage of humankind. However, since 1980 patents on living organisms and genetic materials have increasingly been granted. This practice of patenting human genes is now reconsidered.

THE MYRIAD CASE: HUMAN GENES ARE NOT PATENTABLE

In 1990 it was discovered that two genes, BRCA1 and BRCA2, were associated with a higher risk of breast and ovarian cancer. Some years later, biotech company Myriad Genetics was awarded patents on these genes. Genetic testing for breast cancer was now the monopoly of the company that charged $4,000 for a diagnostic test. The impact on public health and the practices of Myriad to prevent cheaper tests led to legal action in the US to contest the patents. In June 2013, the US Supreme Court ruled that naturally occurring human genes are not patentable. A distinction must be made between products of nature and human inventions. Modified DNA can be patented. The decision endorses the idea that the human genome is the heritage of humanity. Access to knowledge should not be restricted and scientific ideas freely exchanged. The public domain is redefined and opened up. Not only will diagnostic tests be more affordable but also scientific research will benefit from the decision.[15]

In 2013, the Supreme Court of India rejected the patent application of pharmaceutical company Novartis for the cancer drug Glivec.[16] The Court was not convinced that the drug was an 'invention', i.e. sufficiently different from an earlier version. Generic drug makers can continue to provide the drug at significantly lower costs.

- The third impact is on the debate on access to medication. Lack of access to essential medicines in developing countries may be the result of various factors. The 10/90 gap in medical research (Chapter 5) is one. Poor infrastructure for healthcare is another. But patenting of pharmaceutical products, restricting generic competition and raising prices is certainly an important factor. There are several approaches to limit the negative impact of patents on the accessibility and affordability of care and treatment. Ethically, the global moral order can be criticized as inherently unjust. Human rights approaches can strengthen the implementation of the right to health. Politically, flexibilities can be provided in the legal framework of property rights. Economically, the production and use of generic medication can be encouraged. But there are also more targeted ethical approaches such as appealing to the special responsibilities of academic researchers and universities.

EXPANDING ACCESS TO HEALTHCARE: THE RESPONSIBILITY OF UNIVERSITIES

Nearly 20 per cent of the most innovative drugs are patented by universities (for HIV drugs this is 25 per cent). Universities can agree to humanitarian licensing for generic production of drugs in developing countries. This modality was first used in 2001 to provide less expensive medication to AIDS patients in South Africa. Yale University had in 1986 filed a patent for stavudine, an antiretroviral drug. The patent was licensed to a pharmaceutical company that developed a medicine (Zerit) that was approved for the market in 1994 and included in the WHO Essential Medicines list. For a time, stavudine was the most prescribed antiretroviral in the world. It earned Yale $261 million in royalties. In South Africa, it was not affordable by many because the daily dose cost $2.23. The NGO Medicine without Borders wrote to Yale authorities to ask permission for importing the generic version of stavidune produced by a company in India that was 34 times less expensive. The university rejected the request. The researcher who had discovered stavudine with largely public funding wrote to the *New York Times* to support the request. Yale students joined the action. Ultimately, the university agreed to not enforce the patent. As a consequence, the price of the medication dropped by 96 per cent. In 2001, the students established Universities Allied for Essential Medicines (UAEM), a worldwide organization of students from research universities with the goal to emphasize the responsibility of universities and researchers to enhance global access to public health goods.

- Data sharing is another area where the notion of the commons is used to redefine the public domain.[17] Results of clinical trials are used to apply for marketing approval of new drugs with regulatory agencies; often, but not always, results are published in scientific journals. But the patient-level data is not itself publicly accessible. They are considered the property of sponsoring companies. It is now argued that these practices should change. Sharing data will improve medicine and will benefit patients. Clinical trials data is complex; they need to be analysed and evaluated by different stakeholders, including critical and independent researchers, so that evidence is corroborated. Claims of interested parties about safety, efficacy and effectiveness can then be scrutinized. Too many recent cases have shown that published clinical evidence is selective, biased or incomplete. The public benefit of having more reliable information is ethically more important than data protection or trade secrets. Data sharing also demonstrates that scientific activity is a cooperative enterprise.

TAMIFLU

In June 2009, the WHO declared the global outbreak of swine flu (H1N1 influenza) a pandemic. Two months later WHO recommended treatment of symptomatic patients with Tamiflu (oseltamivir), an antiviral medicine, as soon as possible. In response, governments started to stockpile Tamiflu. The Department of Health in the UK bought 40 million doses, the US 65 million. The WHO recommendation was based on one meta-analysis of ten clinical trials published in 2003. The Cochrane Collaboration, an independent not-for-profit organization of researchers, wanted to review the evidence. They requested the clinical study reports with the raw data from clinical trials from the manufacturer (rather than the published trials). The request was rejected with the argument that the data is a trade secret. Years later, the Cochrane team finally got access to the complete data from all clinical trials. In April 2014 it concluded that there is insufficient evidence that the drug is an effective treatment of pandemic flu. Over $20 billion of public money has been wasted.[18]

The European Medicines Agency announced that from January 2015 it will publish the clinical reports that are supporting applications for authorization of medicines as soon as a decision has been taken. From 2016 a new clinical trials law in the European Union will require that all trials are registered and clinical study reports are publicly available. Some major drug companies have changed their policies and now provide access to data. The campaign for data sharing brought together scientists, media (for example the *British Medical Journal*) and NGOs. Data sharing is also gaining momentum in emerging research fields such as synthetic biology.

- The fifth impact is visible in efforts to redefine science as an open and shared activity. Due to commercialization of biotechnology and privatization of biomedical research, over the past few decades science has shifted from an academic into a corporate endeavour. This has affected the traditional norms of the scientific community. With a growing number of cases of scientific misconduct and conflicts of interest, concerns increased that scientific integrity and objectivity are compromised.

SCIENCE COMPROMISED

In February 2000, the editor of the *New England Journal of Medicine* made a public apology for failures to apply its conflicts of interest policy. Almost half of the articles on drug therapy published in the journal over the previous three years have been by authors with financial support of the companies that manufacture the drugs discussed in the articles.[19]

These concerns have led to more attention on the ethics of science and research. Policies and regulations should guarantee that science will be an independent and collaborative endeavour for the sake of basic values such as knowledge and health, rather than for profit. These efforts argue that science is based on commons: ideas and knowledge that are widely available and shared. Open communication and free exchange of ideas is indispensable for scientific growth. This is illustrated by the two major technological developments of our time. Publicly available genomic data facilitated access to genomic information and was essential for the success of the Human Genome Project. Similarly, without publicly shared codes and open source software the internet could not have developed so rapidly. A science commons is a necessary condition for health research for another reason. Health is not only promoted by medical products and services but also by reliable information that motivates individuals to modify behaviour. Changing diet, exercising more often, and abstaining from tobacco resulted from scientific information and reduced the incidence of cardiovascular diseases. But the precondition is that such information is publicly available and reliable. The idea of a science commons has furthermore inspired the movement for open access publications. Unrestricted access to publications is essential for the progress of science and dissemination of knowledge.

PUBLIC LIBRARY OF SCIENCE

Starting in 2003 as a non-profit project of scientists to publish open access scientific journals, the company now publishes seven peer-reviewed journals (for example, in biology, clinical trials, genetics and medicine). For readers, all publications are freely available after acceptance. Authors are charged a publication fee; researchers from specific low-income countries will not be charged a publication fee. In response, other journals have also changed to open access online publishing. Universities, societies and funding bodies are increasingly requiring that results of research they have funded are open access.

Common perspectives

The argument so far has been that global bioethical frameworks are inspired by human rights discourse and the ideals of cosmopolitanism. Both sources of inspiration emphasize the rights and responsibilities of individuals as citizens of the world. But they also assume that individuals are interdependent and that they share a common predicament: they are all vulnerable, have similar basic needs, and are dependent for their survival on the cooperation of others and the sustainability of the biosphere. The focus on commonalities was elaborated in this chapter. How to think about what is common in a contemporary context that is dominated by economic and financial powers in the service of private interests? Notions such as global community, common heritage and commons are often regarded as either archaic or utopian, as a romantic return to traditional ways of life or as a parochial kind of thinking that can never change the universal impact of globalization. This chapter argues that these notions are pertinent to global bioethics. While having a global reach they are nonetheless firmly embedded in local practices. Bridging the distinction between global and local, and highlighting cooperation and collective agency, they face the nature of global challenges. They also connect different dimensions of ethical concern: individual, common, social and planetary. Furthermore, these notions can be used to show that a different kind of globalization is possible – one that is not dominated by the neoliberal discourse of privatization and commodification. They can help to strike a balance between trade, health and justice, between freedom and control, between individual and public interests, and between individual flourishing and the survival of humankind.

What makes the notions of common heritage and commons useful for global bioethics are their normative implications. These implications are restrictive as well as prescriptive.

Restrictive implications

Since common heritage is outside the sphere of commerce and requires the sharing of benefits, there are limitations to human activities. Commons are vital for the continuation of human life. They refer to 'interests beyond borders' since humanity is at stake. It is therefore necessary to protect them against exploitation by individuals, states and companies. There are also limits to scientific and technological interventions (contrary to the maxim of Benjamin Franklin that the only limitation to exploitation will be that of technology; what can be done, will be done). These limitations pose constraints on the neoliberal ideology. Commons should not be owned by anybody, but even if they do, they should be used and enjoyed by everyone. What is regarded as common heritage and commons should not be transformed into commodities that are tradable and have exchange value. Its value is different. What makes the commons valuable is that it is necessary for the survival of the human species (e.g. water), that it safeguards the free and harmonious development of human beings (e.g. knowledge and information), that it is essential for active life and human flourishing (e.g. health and education), and that it determines the context for creativity and innovation (e.g. digital commons).

Prescriptive implications

The notions of common heritage and commons furthermore focus attention on what should be done. They provide an underlying rationale for *global* bioethics principles and can therefore re-orientate the bioethical debate. They expand, complement and encompass the individualistic orientation of mainstream bioethics. Human beings are not isolated individuals. Commons as well as common heritage imply connectedness; they are not merely material objects or immaterial resources but societal institutions in which communities cooperate because they share concerns for human flourishing and survival. Principles focused on individual flourishing should therefore be complemented with principles concerned with the well-being of the community, society and the biosphere. Global bioethics is not only concerned with the individual good but, more importantly, with the common good. Notions of commons and common heritage introduce and articulate ethical principles such as benefit sharing, protecting future generations and the environment, solidarity and cooperation that facilitate this re-orientation.

In conclusion, the common perspectives discussed in this chapter provide a rationale for the principles that are proposed in the global bioethical framework reviewed in the previous chapter. These principles are justified if the moral significance of the notions of common heritage and commons is recognized for global discourse. These notions provide a moral perspective that differs from the mainstream one. They expand the horizon of bioethics so that it can develop into a global endeavour. This different moral vision articulates common rather than individual interests; cooperation rather than competition; sharing in a community rather than exchanging in a market; citizens caring for the commonwealth rather than consumers and producers; preservation and conservation rather than usage and exploitation; future rather than current needs; inclusion rather than exclusion; belonging, collaboration and networking rather than individual autonomy and self-sufficiency.

Common perspectives are particularly relevant for bioethics since they foster a different view of science and research, as well as healthcare practice. Considering these areas of human activity as commons demarcates them from the dominant reign of neoliberalism. Commons, however, are always at risk of being privatized and turned into private goods. They require continuous scrutiny of all parties who come together in their concern for what they share. Commons therefore require governance, the subject of the next chapter.

The question also is whether a 'bioethical commons' is emerging that will allow bioethics to be more critical of the dominant discourse. The challenge is how global ethical frameworks are practically elaborated and applied. Ethical considerations may be fine and satisfying but will they have any effect in the real world? Given the pervasiveness of neoliberal globalization and the ferocity with which the system (e.g. the IPR regime) is defended by powerful stakeholders, bioethics discourse seems impotent and futile. However, historic examples show that ethical discourse is not powerless. The best example is the elimination of slavery.[20] This was a very profitable practice. Its economic importance only grew in the nineteenth century after it was officially prohibited in countries such as the US and the United Kingdom. However, people continued to voice moral arguments against this practice. The abolition of slavery was the result of a moral movement. Not just ethical arguments have been used but various strategies and tools for social change, transforming moral ideals into practical activities. The next few chapters will discuss how global bioethics may effectuate practical changes.

CHAPTER SUMMARY

- Human rights discourse and cosmopolitanism inspire global ethical discourse. They do so because they share common notions: global community, common heritage and commons.
- Global bioethics has increased interest in the notion of community and has expanded the idea of moral community (including all forms of life as well as future generations).
- Common heritage of humankind:
    - This notion refers to what is outside of the framework of private and public property, transmitted from generation to generation.
    - It has specific characteristics: non-appropriation; common management; benefit sharing; peaceful use; preservation for future generations.
    - Its application evolved from common areas to culture, to human genome, to ethical principles.
    - It provides a bridge between the local and the global; it creates a global moral community with its own values and symbols.
    - It refers to interculturality.
- Commons:
    - There are different types: natural, social, intellectual and cultural, digital, and global commons.
    - Their characteristics are: collective property; essential for survival; collective action and cooperation; sociality and sharing.
- Global bioethics can use the notion of commons:
    - As general criticism of neoliberalism.
    - As specific critique of the international property rights regime that reinforces global inequalities.
    - As an argument to connect human beings with the environment and the biosphere.
- The current bioethical debate shows a rethinking of the notion of commons:
    - Pleas to abolish or curtail patenting practices.
    - Restricting the objects that are patentable.
    - Increase access to medication.
    - Data sharing.
    - Open science and publishing.
- Normative impact of 'common heritage' and 'commons':
    - Restrictive: limiting commercial and technological interventions.
    - Prescriptive: promoting specific ethical principles related to benefit sharing, vulnerability, future generations, justice, solidarity, social responsibility, environment and biosphere.

Notes

1 For the minimalistic interpretation of human rights: Michael Ignatieff (2001) *Human rights as politics and idolatry*. Princeton University Press: Princeton and Oxford (especially pages 57 and 66).
2 Ubuntu ethics is explained in: Leonard Tumaini Chuwa (2014) *African indigenous ethics in global bioethics: Interpreting Ubuntu*. Springer: Dordrecht. See also: Thaddeus Metz (2010) African and Western moral theories in a bioethical context. *Developing World Bioethics* 10(1): 49–58.
3 For the speech of Arvid Pardo in the United Nations General Assembly, 22nd session, 1 November 1967: www.un.org/depts/los/convention_agreements/texts/pardo_ga1967.pdf (accessed 4 August 2015).
4 Michele Lobo, Vince Marotta and Nicole Oke (eds) (2011) *Intercultural relations in a global world*. Common Ground Publishing: Champaign (Ill); Ted Cantle (2012) *Interculturalism: The new era of cohesion and diversity*. Palgrave Macmillan: New York.
5 Derek Wall (2014) *The commons in history: Culture, conflict, and ecology*. MIT Press: Cambridge (MA) and London (UK).
6 UN Commission on Global Governance (1995), see https://humanbeingsfirst.files. wordpress.com/2009/10/cacheof-pdf-our-global-neighborhood-from-sovereignty-net.pdf, especially pp. 251–3 and p. 357 (accessed 4 August 2015).
7 Michael Heller (2013) The tragedy of the anticommons: A concise introduction and lexicon. *The Modern Law Review* 76(1): 6–25 (quotation on page 21).
8 COMEST (World Commission on the Ethics of Scientific Knowledge and Technology) (2004) *Best ethical practice in water use*. UNESCO, Paris. (http://unesdoc.unesco.org/images/0013/001344/134430e.pdf) (accessed 4 August 2015).
9 Daniel F. Robinson (2010) *Confronting biopiracy. Challenges, cases and international debates*. Earthscan: London/New York.
10 World Health Assembly: Global strategy and plan of action on public health, innovation, and intellectual property, 24 May 2008: http://apps.who.int/gb/ebwha/pdf_files/A61/A61_R21-en.pdf (quotation on page 6, item 8) (accessed 4 August 2015).
11 Lawrence Lessig (2004) *Free culture: The nature and future of creativity*. Penguin Books: New York.
12 Alberto Acosta (2014) *Le Bien Vivir: Pour imaginer d'autres mondes*. Les Éditions Utopia: Paris.
13 Michele Boldrin and David K. Levine (2012) *The case against patents*. Working paper. Research Division, Federal Reserve Bank of St. Louis: St. Louis (http://research.stlouisfed.org/wp/2012/2012-035.pdf). Alternative approaches are elaborated in: Dan L. Burk and Mark A. Lemley (2009) *The patent crisis and how the courts can solve it*. The University of Chicago Press: Chicago and London.
14 Donna Dickinson (2013) *Me medicine vs. We medicine: Reclaiming biotechnology for the common good*. New York: Columbia University Press.
15 For the US Supreme Court ruling (2013) www.supremecourt.gov/opinions/12pdf/12-398_1b7d.pdf (accessed 4 August 2015).
16 The ruling of the Supreme Court of India (2011) is given in: http://indiankanoon.org/doc/1692607/ (accessed 4 August 2015).
17 Marc A. Rodwin (2012) Clinical trial data as a public good. *JAMA* 308(9): 871–872.
18 Tom Jefferson, Mark Jones, Peter Doshi, Elizabeth A. Spencer, Igho Onakpoya and Carl J. Hennighan (2014) Oseltamivir for influenza in adults and children: Systematic

review of clinical study reports and summary of regulatory comments. *British Medical Journal* 348: g2545.

19 David Weatherall (2000) Academia and industry: Increasingly uneasy bedfellows. *The Lancet* 355: 1574; Robert Cook-Deegan (2007) The science commons in health research: Structure, function, and value. *Journal of Technology Transfer,* 32(3): 133–156.

20 Seymour Drescher (2009) *Abolition: A history of slavery and antislavery.* Cambridge University Press: New York.

9

GLOBAL HEALTH GOVERNANCE

Determining principles of global bioethics is one thing. Another is the application of principles. At the local and national levels, bioethical problems are addressed with the usual mechanisms of government: legislation, political decision-making, professional self-regulation, public debate, expert recommendations and practice guidelines. Globalization has created challenges to these approaches to government. At the global level, there is no authority that is responsible for the application of principles. The global nature of the problems will make national approaches inadequate. Practices that are ethically rejected in one country, and are sometimes legally prohibited, are permitted in another country. The case of surrogate motherhood mentioned in Chapter 1 is a good example. Countries such as France have prohibited all forms of surrogacy. Commercial surrogacy is illegal in countries like the United Kingdom while it is legal in, for example, India and some states in the US. These differences illustrate that the ethical assessment of surrogate motherhood varies, but also that the application of this assessment is limited in practice. It is not possible to enforce an ethical position within one country at global level. Even when all countries agree about the significance of moral values and principles it is still challenging to implement these values in healthcare practices around the world, as recurrent cases of gender discrimination, organ trafficking and lack of informed consent demonstrate. The problem here is what today is called 'governance'. If there are global ethical frameworks, how can they be applied at a global level to address global problems? Ethical principles, whether or not they are universal from a theoretical perspective, only become meaningful in practical conditions where they are incorporated in local laws, values, customs, institutions and practices, and where people can appeal to them so that they are really applied in daily healthcare settings. The question is how this can be done at a global level when there is no world government or global political authority.

This chapter will elaborate on the notion of 'governance' in the field of healthcare, medicine and medical research, and especially examine the role of governance in global bioethics. It will first explain the notion of 'global governance'. Next, it will elaborate on mechanisms and activities of global governance focused on health. Problems of governance are visible in the management of the current Ebola epidemic. These problems are explored in the third section of this chapter and related to different approaches of globalization. The chapter will then argue that new forms of governance are needed, particularly because of the global nature of problems. Not only is there a variety of ways to deal with global challenges but most approaches are tentative, disorganized and not very effective. Bioethics is implicated in global governance in two ways. This chapter discusses one way; it will argue that the notion of global governance implies normative motives and choices. Global health governance demands critical analysis of goals and methods. Rather than being a technocratic instrument, it raises ethical questions: What is the value of health compared to trade, economic growth and security? Should interventions focus on specific diseases or on healthcare system infrastructure? What does global solidarity require when faced with global threats such as Ebola virus disease? These questions open up a first avenue for bioethics: critical reflection on the mechanisms, directions and outcomes of global governance. The next chapter will address a second way of involvement when bioethics itself becomes a privileged mechanism of governance.

Global governance

The concept of global governance became known after its use in the report of the Commission on Global Governance (1995). It is not the same as 'government', which is linked to the power and authority of states. The new term 'governance' is introduced because the role of states in addressing global problems is diminished due to globalization. However, the concept is contested as vague and not effective. For some scholars it will only work when there is a world government, which is a utopian idea. Other scholars doubt whether globalization can be controlled, regulated or managed at all. Nonetheless, it has become increasingly clear that global problems such as climate change, pandemics, migration, disaster relief and poverty cannot be adequately addressed by states and interstate cooperation alone.

GLOBAL GOVERNANCE

'Governance is the sum of the many ways individuals and institutions, public and private, manage their common affairs. It is a continuing process through which conflicting or diverse interests may be accommodated and co-operative action may be taken.'[1]

'Global governance' is a broad concept. It has at least five facets.

1   Focus on global problems. Contemporary threats are no longer local or directed at individual countries but global and interconnected. They are too complex for one state or actor. The nature of current risks and problems therefore requires a new approach.

2   Necessity of collective action. Cooperative policies and measures are required to create new principles, norms, institutions and procedures of decision-making. Partnerships and collective approaches are essential, based on consultation, transparency and accountability.

3   Variety of actors. Addressing global problems involves not only governments but a range of actors: intergovernmental organizations (e.g. WHO and UNESCO); multilateral economic institutions (WTO, World Bank and IMF); international law; NGOs (such as Amnesty International, Human Rights Watch and Transparency International); social movements; multinational corporations (e.g. pharmaceutical companies); professional organizations (WMA); philanthropic agencies; media; religious institutions and universities (with epistemic communities of scientists).

4   Various levels of activity. Collective action needs to take place at global, regional, national and sub-national levels.

5.   Diverging objectives. While global governance is focused on common concerns, there is no agreement on what governance aims to accomplish. Objectives can differ from promotion of order, stability, human rights, peace, democracy, equality, and justice in international life. This divergence depends on different understandings of global governance. Is it primarily a technocratic approach concerned with managing problems? Or is it a normative and political approach that aims to eliminate the causes of problems and to criticize the global system that produces them? In the first view, knowledge, technology and expertise are required. In the second view there is a need for global norms, ideas and actions.

One of the oldest objects of global governance is health. Today, health is a central topic of international cooperation, as demonstrated in the Millennium Development Goals (see Chapter 7). While individual states are responsible for the health of their citizens the global nature of problems requires common action. At the same time, in the absence of a supreme political authority, the global health problems need to be addressed, managed and coordinated in a different, non-hierarchical manner, making global cooperation a necessity.

Global governance of health

International cooperation in the field of healthcare started in the last part of the nineteenth century. A series of cholera epidemics beginning in the late 1820s in India and spreading across Europe in the 1830s initiated the convening of international sanitary conferences since 1851 and resulted in conventions that were generally not effectively implemented. The main motive for collaboration was to keep diseases out of Western countries, emphasizing health measures in the source countries outside of the West. At the same time, countries were primarily concerned that such measures (mainly quarantine) would not disrupt international trade. Only in the beginning of the twentieth century, did international cooperation for health purposes become more consolidated with the first international health agreement (1903: International Sanitary Regulations) and the first formal global health institutions (1902: International Sanitary Bureau of the Americas; 1907: Office International d'Hygiène Publique). The World Health Organization was established in 1948. Since the 1990s, global governance entered a new phase with an enormous growth of interest in global health, with a rise of partnerships, aid and funding.[2]

Global health

The new interest in global health over the last two decades is attributed to several developments.[3] First is the emergence of new diseases, especially novel infections. Over the past 30 years one new infectious disease has emerged every year (Ebola, West Nile virus, or SARS). Known diseases such as tuberculosis are re-emerging because of drug resistance. These infections pose global threats to human health even in countries where they do not originate. It is estimated that 30 infectious diseases exist just in developing countries, while there is only one disease that exists only in the developed world (Legionnaire's disease).[4]

The second development is the connection between trade and disease. Though this connection is old and explains the disagreements about quarantine in the early stage of global governance, globalization has multiplied the effects. Pathogens can travel in hours to another part of the globe. Internet and media can instantaneously disseminate information of outbreaks. For example, environmental disasters have multinational dimensions, involving governments, NGOs, companies and international organizations. The same is true for food contamination. Industrially produced food is exported to many countries. If safety standards are not applied it will not only produce domestic victims; it will have also a negative impact on trade. An example is the Chinese baby milk scandal in 2008. Melamine, a toxic chemical was mixed with milk and baby formula to increase protein content. Tens of thousands of babies were hospitalized. The reputation of Chinese food collapsed, and several countries banned Chinese dairy products.

TOXIC WASTE POLLUTION IN CÔTE D'IVOIRE

Late August 2006 about 3,000 people experienced intestinal and respiratory problems in Abidjan, the capital of Côte d'Ivoire with 4 million inhabitants. The complaints were caused by fumes of toxic substances dumped by the vessel *Probo Koala* during the night at various sites around the lagoon of

Abidjan. The Ministry of Health had authorized the dumping believing it was sewage. Analysis showed that at least two toxic substances were involved: hydrogen sulphate (which is volatile) and organochlorines (that persist in the environment and accumulate in the food chain). The government only took action one week later. It reported to the UN that it does not have the capacity to deal with the problem; international assistance was requested in September. French experts urged the removal of the toxic sludge. Health problems increased with more than 10,000 medical consultations a day; 23 people were hospitalized and 17 died.

The third development is the growing impact of neoliberal policies. During the 1980s and 1990s these policies had caused public health to deteriorate, especially in developing countries. Institutions such as the World Bank began to emphasize the relation between health and development. Since 2000 the Bank has been the largest external funder of healthcare globally. The policies of the WTO have complicated access to medication in many countries and became the focus of international struggle since the TRIPS agreement of 1994.

The interest for global health is finally reflected in the exponential growth of partnerships. While in the 1990s total spending on global health stagnated, and healthcare was significantly reduced in a number of developing countries, expenditures have exponentially grown since then. More resources for health assistance are available now than ever before. Remarkable is the growth of civil society groups (particularly NGOs) and global health partnerships. Many new actors have entered the field of global health: intergovernmental and humanitarian organizations, NGOs, private businesses and philanthropic foundations. Broad-based partnerships have been created such as the Global Fund to Fight AIDS, Tuberculosis and Malaria (in 2002).

World Health Organization

As the major institution in international health policy, WHO has as its objective: 'the attainment by all peoples of the highest possible level of health.'[5] The basic idea is that health is a fundamental right of every human being, while health at the same time is broadly defined ('not merely the absence of disease or infirmity'). WHO has been successful in specific areas. Smallpox was eradicated in 1980. Guinea worm disease, leprosy and polio have been significantly reduced due to long-term campaigns. The management of the SARS epidemic (2002–2003) is regarded as one of the success stories of effective management. On the other hand, WHO has been criticized for responding too quickly to the swine flu epidemic in 2009 (H1N1 influenza), thus creating global panic.

Collective management of global health affairs is problematic for WHO for at least two reasons. First, as a UN agency specializing in health it is centred on states.

The programme, as well as budget, is determined by member states. WHO's regular budget, based on member contributions, has been declining since 2011. Two-thirds of the resources are extra-budgetary donations, earmarked for specific purposes. The organization therefore hardly controls its own finances, reducing its flexibility and capacity to set priorities. The second reason is that more and more financial aid for global health is independent from WHO. Not only are other institutions such as the World Bank providing resources but also wealthy private foundations with larger funds than WHO. States have deliberately created new institutions and partnerships separated from WHO with their own budgets and mandates (for example, the Global Fund as a separate entity), undermining the credibility and leadership of the organization.

ACTORS IN GLOBAL HEALTH GOVERNANCE

- World Health Organization.
- Other UN organizations: UNICEF (children's immunization, breastfeeding, and oral rehydration); UN Population Fund (reproductive health); UNDP (child health, maternal health and HIV/AIDS; caretaker for the MDGs).
- Other intergovernmental organizations: WorldBank, IMF and WTO.
- NGOs. For example: International Committee of the Red Cross (established in 1958); MSF (1971); Physicians for Human Rights (1986); Partners in Health (1987); People's Health Movement (2000); Global Health Watch (2005); Food and Water Watch (2005).
- Philanthropic foundations: Institut Pasteur (1887); Rockefeller Foundation (1913); Aga Khan Foundation (1967); Carter Center (1982); Bill and Melinda Gates Foundation (2000).
- Policy forums as G8 and G20; they established the Global Fund to Fight AIDS, Tuberculosis and Malaria in 2002.
- Public–private partnerships, combining state and non-state actors. Examples: GAVI (Global Alliance for Vaccines and Immunization, 2000); IAVI (International AIDS Vaccine Initiative, 2001); UNITAID (2006).
- Civil society organizations, national and international; for instance, the Treatment Action Campaign (1998, South Africa); Health Gap (Global Access Project, 1999); the Treatment Advocacy and Literacy Campaign (2005, Zambia).
- Health celebrities and goodwill ambassadors for the UN and NGOs; musicians such as Bono and Elton John; Chinese actress Peng Liyuan as WHO ambassador for tuberculosis and HIV/AIDS.

Many actors, no director

Due to the above developments, the concept of global health governance has become elusive. Initially associated with institutions such as WHO, responsible for collective responses, it is now connected to many stakeholders in global health and with institutions outside of the health sector. These organizations have different objectives and interests, making health one of the values to consider among others. The World Bank is focused on economic growth and development, balancing healthcare against the economy. The WTO usually prioritizes promotion of trade over regulation of health. Multinational corporations aim to maximize profit for shareholders rather than to provide for basic health needs. NGOs demonstrate a wide variety of activities such as monitoring and reporting, disseminating information, advocating specific causes, and providing relief and assistance, but their range and mission is often limited and concentrated on specific issues.

Governance is not government. The field of global health demonstrates that there is no centralized authority that can impose its will. There is no coherent framework of action but only series of sometimes overlapping, sometimes conflicting rules, norms and principles. There are many actors with different interests and agendas. Many scholars argue that there is an urgent need for new governance arrangements.[6] Not only should there be more coherence and coordination, but also a better focus on priorities and specific goals such as access to medication, protection of the vulnerable, marginalized populations, poverty and global justice.

Problems of governance

During the 1960s policy-makers were convinced that infectious diseases were no longer a serious threat (the US Surgeon General in 1967 declared that it is 'time to close the book on infectious disease'). Nowadays, these diseases are regarded as major challenges; they are the 'dark side of globalization'. Now that human communication and transportation is faster and more intensive, known and unknown diseases are spreading across the globe. Efforts to contain them should necessarily be global. Although global health governance has traditionally been focused on infectious diseases, and the fight against contagion can bring together a broad coalition of actors, an effective system of governance has difficulties in manifesting itself, as the recent example of Ebola illustrates.

Ebola threat

First identified in 1976 in Central Africa, Ebola (haemorrhagic fever) is not an unknown disease. There have been 24 outbreaks in various countries such as Congo, Gabon, Sudan and Uganda. These have been limited, with a maximum of a few hundred cases, often in poor, rural villages. Although the disease kills half of those affected, it is not very contagious. It cannot be transmitted through air like influenza. Countermeasures are known: isolate symptomatic patients; trace contacts; and observe those contacts for symptoms (for 21 days). As long as contact with the body fluids of infected patients can be avoided, the spread of the disease can be contained. This was a successful strategy in countries like Senegal and Nigeria. Unfortunately there is no treatment or vaccine.

EBOLA VIRUS DISEASE

On 23 March 2014 the Ministry of Health of the Republic of Guinea notified the WHO of an outbreak of Ebola virus disease in a remote area of the rainforest close to Sierra Leone and Liberia. A total of 49 cases were reported, including 29 deaths. The outbreak, however, had already started in December 2013. Doctors without Borders (MSF) had sent teams to the area in February. First cases were reported in Liberia in March and in Sierra Leone in April. Then in May the disease exploded in Monrovia, the capital of Liberia. A month later MSF warned WHO that this was an unusual outbreak of Ebola; again in June that the epidemic was totally out of control.

In early August 2014, two American aid workers became infected; they were brought to the US and treated with ZMapp, an experimental drug. Now the world seemed to wake up to the problem. On 8 August, WHO declared Ebola a 'global emergency'. By then, 2,240 cases were confirmed, with 1,229 deaths. A special UN coordinator was appointed but a coordinated response was still missing. In October 2014, the first Ebola patients died in Spain and the US. In the summer of 2015, the total case count was close to 25,000 with over 11,000 deaths.

The management of the Ebola epidemic is an example of failed global governance.[7] Though MSF tried to raise awareness, responses were very slow or absent. Ministries of Health were unprepared. Policies were disorganized. Only since August 2014, when the personal tragedies of Western missionaries overshadowed the anonymous statistics of casualties, were global responses formulated. The US government, labelling Ebola a 'security threat', decided to send thousands of troops to help build treatment centres. But even in September 2014, a major UN response was absent.

In this case, in the words of critical authors, what have been missing are large-scale, coordinated humanitarian, social, public health and medical responses. The relevant actors, knowledge, expertise, preventive strategies were all there. Criticism was particularly focused on the lack of leadership by the WHO. The organization was late in recognizing the extent and impact of the epidemic. It did not take initiatives in the early stages. It did not coordinate relief efforts. WHO later admitted to having mismanaged the emergency. It could have taken a robust coordinating role. But others also pointed out that the blame is not only with the WHO. In recent years, member states have severely reduced the organization's budget. Recently, the budget for health crises has been halved, shifting efforts away from infectious diseases, and hundreds of staff members have been laid off. The tardy global response is thus also the result of the austerity politics of member states.

A second explanation for the failure of governance refers to the technocratic approach mentioned earlier. In principle, it is known how to contain the epidemic: isolate, canvass and observe. Measures should be taken, and biohazards suits flown in. But this approach underestimates the social, political and economic context of the epidemic. Guinea, Liberia and Sierra Leone are among the poorest countries in the world (with respectively 55, 64 and 53 per cent of the population below the national poverty line). Guinea has a history of military dictatorships until 2010, while Sierra Leone and Liberia were devastated by civil wars in the 1990s that ended in 2002 and 2003. Given this history, people simply don't trust their governments. The health facilities and infrastructures in these countries were destroyed. Many health professionals left. Most of the healthcare is delivered with support from donors (60–70 per cent in Sierra Leone; 80 per cent in Liberia). Life expectancy is low (48 years in Sierra Leone; 59 years in Guinea). Against this backdrop, countries were not merely unprepared but unable to take the necessary measures. A major problem was the lack of health professionals (Guinea has 940 physicians for a population of 10 million; Sierra Leone 136 for 2 million; and Liberia 51 for 4 million). Experts estimated that Ebola treatment requires four highly trained staff members per patient so that thousands of additional health workers will be needed. Moreover, more than 300 health professionals have died from the disease.[8]

A third explanation has to do with lack of moral engagement, or rather the absence of global solidarity. Poor global governance is primarily the result of moral failure. Lack of international assistance and solidarity demonstrate indifference.[9] The concerned countries could not cope with the epidemic, but international assistance was, at least initially, limited and uncoordinated. No initiatives were taken by larger countries while NGOs (for example, MSF) sent volunteers, and small countries like Cuba, hundreds of health workers. Most Western countries were more concerned with protecting their own vulnerability, attempting to halt the threat at their borders rather than eliminating it at the source. Ebola was first of all considered as a security threat for the developed world. Perhaps this was reinforced by the already existing perception that this virus was extremely dangerous. During the Cold War Ebola was part of the bio-weapons programme of the former Soviet Union. In response, the US had invested in research to develop drugs and vaccines in special biosafety labs of the army. The funding for this research stopped in 2012 as a result of budget cuts. The limited amount of experimental medication that was available in August 2014 for the expatriated missionaries was not developed for African patients.

In the summer of 2014, WHO convened a teleconference on the ethical issues of Ebola infection. The focus was on whether unproven drugs could be used on patients. No ethical questions were raised concerning the deficient coordination at the global level, the dilemmas at the local level due to deteriorating conditions in the affected countries, and the indifference and lack of solidarity of the global community. The ethics concentrated on the promise of individual treatment rather than the actual public health disaster that was unfolding, as if the catastrophe can be eradicated with a drug, even if not much is known about its efficacy and risk.

Five types of gaps in governance

International scholars Thomas Weiss and David Held explain the difficulties of global governance as a discrepancy between the nature of the problems and the means that exist to address them.[10] Many intergovernmental and international institutions have been established (in the twentieth century, on average more than one international organization has been founded per day) but they are not capable of solving transnational issues. Originally these institutions were based and initiated by states and resulted from cooperation between states but there have been difficulties in moving from the international (inter-state) to the global level. WHO, for example, is an organization of member states; it can coordinate international cooperation but under the direction of states. International responses are usually short term and local, rather than long term, global and sustained. This is a reminder of the problem of politics that Potter identified earlier. Weiss distinguishes five types of gaps in global governance.

GAPS IN GLOBAL HEALTH GOVERNANCE

- *Knowledge*: no agreement on the nature of the problem.
- *Norms*: no agreement on international norms and how to address the problem.
- *Policies*: disagreement on the formulation, adoption and implementation of norms.
- *Institutions*: absence of robust global institutions with sufficient resources and authority.
- *Compliance*: limited monitoring and enforcement; no clarity about responsibility, authority and capacity to monitor commitments.[11]

Diverging normative perspectives

The Ebola case illustrates that lack of knowledge is not the decisive problem: the virus has been identified, diagnostic tests are available, the mechanisms of contagion as well as preventive measures are known. However, knowledge can be ignored. The international sanitary conferences in the nineteenth century were concerned with delays of trade and ignored growing scientific evidence that infections were spread from human to human so that strict quarantines were justified. The lack of agreement on the best policies is more often influenced by different normative views.

The functioning of global institutions, especially WHO over the past six decades, shows two sources of tension, both related to the interpretation of the notion of health: should health be considered in a broad or restricted sense, and how is health related to other relevant global concerns such as security, trade and rights?

Health: broad or narrow?

In its Constitution, WHO presents a broad definition of health, giving the organization an encompassing mandate. In practical reality, however, member states have favoured a disease-focused approach with WHO providing 'technical assistance'. Many programmes are addressing specific diseases while assistance is often focused on providing medication and vaccination without ameliorating the healthcare systems. Research is also concerned with developing new technologies to control diseases and test new vaccines for eradication, rather than examining the social and economic conditions of vulnerable populations. This tension between a broad and narrow conception of health is reflected in the Ebola case.

Health and other global values

Another source of tension exists between health as global common good and other global values. As discussed earlier, health can be regarded as a human right. In a globalized world, health is often in competition with trade and commerce. Health is also connected to development. Without a healthy population, countries will not sufficiently develop. Finally, health is increasingly related to security. Epidemics are threatening health but also the stability of countries; they impede global exchange, travel and trade; they create uncertainty, fear and sometimes panic. At the same time, there are concerns about bio-security; micro-organisms can be used as bio-weapons.

Diverging policies

Different normative frameworks of health translate in diverging policies. Interventions can be vertical or horizontal. Vertical interventions are directed against specific diseases or health issues. Examples are the WHO campaigns against malaria and poliomyelitis, or the Carter Center's efforts to eradicate guinea worm disease. These approaches focus on biomedical concerns, individual subjects, and the expected progress of science and technology. Horizontal interventions are directed at strengthening the healthcare system so that an infrastructure is created that in the long run can cope with the structural determinants of health. These approaches articulate the interconnections between health and global inequalities; they are targeting populations and the socio-economic context. The two approaches not only lead to different programmes and activities, but they imply different discourses. Horizontal interventions are often critical of neoliberal policies. Public health infrastructures in many countries have been damaged by decades of privatization of health services, introduction of user fees, and reduced budgets for public health, producing increased health inequities. Neoliberalism has emphasized individual responsibility rather than state responsibility; global health has not been treated as a common good. Strengthening and rebuilding health infrastructure therefore is a first priority. Governance can only be effective if the underlying structures are addressed. The problem is who actually leads and takes responsibility for such long-term efforts. Vertical approaches, on the other hand, are attractive since they have specific and measurable targets; results are clear and can be used to attract more funding. At the same time, prioritization of certain diseases (HIV/ AIDS, malaria, tuberculosis) leads to neglect of other health concerns, such as tropical diseases (e.g. Chagas disease, endemic in Central and South America) and non-communicable diseases. Since little attention is paid to the structural setting of health, issues such as brain drain, poverty and women's health are too extended for vertical policies.

Another effect of normative divergence is that policies are primarily driven by the interests of developed countries since they have the expertise and resources to determine the governance agenda. The global South is considered as a reservoir of dangerous diseases. Fears abound that contagion will spread across borders. The main concerns of policies are to prevent threats from moving in the direction of developed countries. These countries emphasize their vulnerability rather than the vulnerability of affected countries. There is less concern that Northern lifestyles and health hazards (unhealthy food, chronic and non-communicable diseases) create problems in the global South.

Inadequate institutions

The paradox of our times is that we are increasingly confronted with global challenges while the means to address them are weak. Global governance institutions in particular are ill-equipped and deficient for two reasons.

- *Capacity problems.* The scope and character of institutions are insufficient to deal with global risk. Governance is informal, diffuse and not hierarchical like government; there is a range of actors with problems of cooperation and coordination but no one is in charge. There is no authority and a lack of enforcement capability. A clear division of labour among agencies and organizations concerned with health does not exist. WHO itself has a complex structure with headquarters in Geneva, six relatively independent regional offices, and 150 country offices. The organization is dependent on member states; its resources are insufficient to meet all needs. Furthermore, its leadership role is contested by its own member states. The institution is simply not made up to direct global governance.
- *Responsibility problems.* Since global health governance through existing institutions is primarily based on states, there is a lack of ownership of global problems. Collective problem-solving solutions emerge if domestic interests

concur. Until that time no state will feel responsible for health threats in other states. Power differences among states play a major role; they exclude many countries from decision-making processes. Also, the agenda of international organizations is often driven by the interests of a limited group of countries. Finally, there is lack of accountability.

Lessons from Ebola

The failure of global governance for the Ebola virus disease in 2014 has produced criticism as well as new proposals. One main lesson is that health services that are underfunded, understaffed and fragmented will never be able to cope with epidemics such as Ebola. The focus of global governance should therefore be on improving health systems. In fact, this is cost-saving since building health systems will cost three times less than the current costs of responding to Ebola. Another lesson is that the inadequate health systems in countries are often the results of years of neoliberal policies. The third lesson is that the only way to prevent future health catastrophes is universal health coverage, making essential healthcare available to everyone, particularly poor and vulnerable populations.

The governance failure of Ebola is now used as the starting point for a new global health agenda. Global bioethics can have a major input in formulating and implementing this agenda. It can provide ethical arguments to give priority to health. These arguments should be used to instigate political debate. For example, the majority of African countries are spending less than 10 per cent of total government expenditures on health, while African heads of state have promised in the Declaration of Abuja in 2001 to spend at least 15 per cent on health.[12] Bioethics should articulate ethical arguments for prioritizing health systems rather than specific diseases and issues. This will imply criticism of current policies of NGOs and philanthropic agencies. The policies of global actors such as the IMF should be critically analysed from bioethical perspectives since they in fact restrict access to healthcare, and prioritize short-term economic growth over long-term health improvement. Finally, bioethics should make a strong stance in favour of the commitment to universal health coverage, arguing that it is a moral imperative to achieve that every person has access to essential quality healthcare. It would be an effective way to implement the human right to health.

Governance from above and below

Problems of governance are not new. Scholars agree that health governance was weak until the mid-1990s, especially in regard to the HIV/AIDS epidemic.[13] First, economic interests often prevailed over health considerations (see the example of IPR discussed in the previous chapter). Second, views differed about the response. Should it be biomedical, i.e. developing new technologies and drugs to control the disease and vaccines for eradication; or should it be human rights-based, emphasizing the political and social issues such as discrimination and marginalization? Third, there was lack of commitment by states resulting in denial of the problem and inactiveness. Essentially, these are the same causes of governance weakness as today. In the early 2000s, many initiatives were taken to improve governance and to broaden its scope. Actions pressed governments to provide better access to medication. The Doha Declaration gave countries, in principle, more opportunities to protect public health. The UN General Assembly in 2001 declared the HIV/AIDS epidemic as a 'global emergency' that is not merely a medical problem but that is undermining social and economic development. Furthermore, new funding mechanisms were established such as the Global Fund, expressing a stronger commitment of states but also circumventing the existing UN mechanisms.

The difficulties and weaknesses of global health governance are associated with differing views of globalization. The dialectical perspective explained in Chapter 4, implies that there is no antithesis between the global and the local. Many local events are shaped by developments far away, while global events are often influenced by specific contexts and conditions. Globalization, therefore, is not simply a process in which one global culture gets to dominate particular cultures. It is not an irresistible phenomenon that subjects local contexts to external forces, that are hard to control and that homogenize specific identities and values. Nonetheless, such 'globalization from above' seems the dominant perspective in governance policies. These policies rely on the power of states since they are the only ones that can enforce laws in the absence of powerful international organizations. When there are strong global institutions (such as the World Bank and IMF) they impose neoliberal policies that are in the interest of hegemonic economic forces, while global information is controlled by Western media corporations. An example of globalization from above, discussed by Indian anthropologist Veena Das, is the immunization campaigns carried out by the state in India, at the initiative of WHO and UNICEF.[14] Continuous progress was reported but in practice information on children born was not reliable. Records were kept by officials who wanted to advance a success story. Only numbers of doses of antigens distributed were counted, not the number of children immunized. Health workers were not encouraged to report adverse reactions to vaccines. Local epidemics soon re-emerged.

In contrast, if one takes the dialectics of global and local levels seriously, much of globalization is 'from below'. In this view everybody takes part in globalization. The 'global' is often constituted within the local. Globalization is therefore not only experienced passively but in many cases actively produced by groups of citizens, agencies and institutions at the local level. In this view, global bioethics does not merely refer to ethical values and principles that are transcending various cultures or are interacting with them from the outside, but global values are co-produced in interactions with local value systems. The global ethical framework is, so to speak, also emanating from the fast growing manifold interconnections between people worldwide. Global values are 'post-universal'; they are articulated in the sphere of 'interculturality' (as argued in Chapters 7 and 8).

Globalization from below implies a different approach to governance; it is rooted in local traditions, allows for the participation of many stakeholders (including vulnerable and excluded populations) and grassroots movements and networks, involves global civil society, and seeks global solidarity in horizontal activities of cooperation.[15] Given the importance of contextual knowledge, governance needs to go beyond the focus on individuals, and attend to structures and relationships. Like the shared management of commons (Chapter 8), global governance must involve local people, shifting power and resources from state agencies and global institutions to local communities. This approach emphasizes global practices that create reciprocity and solidarity across borders through public discourse, social action and political struggle. Cosmopolitan aspirations therefore inspire a theoretical framework but they are realized through slow, everyday efforts.

TREATMENT ACTION CAMPAIGN (TAC)

Post-apartheid South Africa adopted a new Constitution in 1996. The right to health was enshrined in this Constitution. In the same year, 3 per cent of the population was infected with HIV, rising to 10 per cent in 1999. New effective therapy became available in 1996 but was too expensive. In 1998, a group of AIDS activists launched the Treatment Action Campaign to advocate for the right to treatment. Combining protest, social mobilization and legal action, TAC campaigned to improve access to essential medicines. One focus was the excessive price of drugs. TAC supported the government in 2001 when a conglomerate of multinational pharmaceutical companies wanted to block the new Medicines Act that allowed production or importation of less expensive medication. Another focus was the South African government itself. Based on the right to health in the Constitution the government has positive duties to provide treatment. Arguing that the government is neglecting public health (thus against its own Constitution) TAC brought the case to the courts. In 2001, the Constitutional Court ruled in favour of TAC and ordered the government to implement a national anti-retroviral treatment programme. The programme was launched in early 2004. South Africa now has the largest programme in the world.[16]

New forms of governance

In developing new systems of global governance, as alternatives to governance by states, global bioethics can play a major role.[17] What is needed, first of all, according to many scholars, is a new vision of globalization and governance. Next, there should be a broader approach to governance, involving more actors and stakeholders. Finally, new practices should evolve, encouraged by different forms of leadership.

a. Broader vision of governance

The perspective of globalization from below not only implies a different view of global processes (as dialectics between global and local) but also inspires local activities to connect with global developments. In this interconnectedness, new ways of living together are developing based on a sense of a shared world and commonalities; transnational connectivity will foster global values and a sense of global citizenship while at the same time articulating specific values. These intercultural and dialectic processes should be incorporated in governance so that agreement will emerge over how global problems can best be addressed. What is required, therefore, is what the philosopher Karl Otto Apel has called a 'second-order globalization', as a novel order of human interaction, necessitating not simply management but change.[18] This approach to governance will call for reinforcement of at least some international organizations such as WHO, although they should operate in a different manner. It will also call for more intensive articulation of a common framework of shared values and objectives. This type of more explicitly directed globalization requires normative reflection and activity: articulation of values important for humanity as a whole; delineation of goals that preserve the planet for future generations; and promotion of global justice so that all can share in the progress of science. At this point, bioethics could actively contribute, recognizing that health governance always takes place within a politicized context, underlining the need to identify, clarify and criticize values, ideals and goals. The emphasis on a new vision primarily refers to the need for what can be called a 'normative web', a network of principles, values and norms that can provide structure to social activities. Within such a web, specific actors can operate, interrelate and cooperate.

b. Involvement of more actors

Current global health governance is still dominated by states. Globalization from below requires a broader, more inclusive and participatory coalition of actors and stakeholders. Global institutions such as WHO should reach out to non-state actors such as NGOs. At the moment there is little cooperation, let alone coordination with civil society. The scientific community should also be more involved in global governance. Strengthening the role of science in governance is related to the present-day significance of technology, facilitating horizontal linkages between various actors. Contemporary information technology creates more possibilities for governance, setting up networks of expert groups and individuals, research centres, ministries, NGOs and UN bodies, and increasing global surveillance capabilities. Information concerning potential outbreaks, disasters or other significant global health events is no longer dependent on reporting of states (that sometimes have an interest in delaying or concealing such information). Especially for emerging diseases, new electronic networks have been established (for example, the Global Outbreak Alert and Response Network in 2000). It shows what can be done when a broader group of actors cooperate. The same potential exists in the area of aid and assistance. Although 70 per cent of health aid is bilateral (from one state to another), the growth of global partnerships, funding and private donations makes non-state actors such as the Red Cross and MSF increasingly important.

c. Different practices and leadership

Leadership is essential to direct global health governance. WHO has been criticized for lack of leadership. However, in 1987 it took the lead with creating the Global Programme on AIDS, but this leadership role was undermined in 1996 with the establishment of a separate programme, UNAIDS. The organization also criticized China for initial denial of the outbreak of SARS; it issued travel warnings against the wishes of member states such as Canada. At the same time, efforts to articulate the social context of disease and the importance of health infrastructure, thus going beyond the targeting of individual diseases, were often half-hearted. Despite its mandate to associate health and human rights, WHO did not criticize neoliberal policies of other global organizations that have been devastating to global health. Strengthening the role of WHO will therefore not come from its member states. Processes of globalization, however, are producing new practices of cooperation that offer opportunities for global governance. The example of TAC illustrates how global ideas can be localized. A global principle such as the right to health is specified and applied within a specific context, using the advantages of the domestic law, educational campaigns, community engagement, political activities and international networking. New types of local and global activism give rise to networked governance. These practices (see Chapter 11) contribute to the core values of good governance: transparency, accountability, representation and participation. They also put emphasis on the fifth type of gap in global governance: lack of compliance. Setting standards is one thing, enacting them another.

Conclusion

Governance of global health is a major challenge in today's world. Addressing health issues requires cross-border cooperation, not only between states but between a range of different agencies and actors. It also requires sharing of knowledge and expertise, recognizing that threats to health are no longer individual or domestic but globalized; they represent common concerns. Moreover, health depends on social and economic conditions. Health has been called 'the barometer of extreme poverty and inequality in the world'.[19] This chapter has argued that bioethics can play a special role in global health governance. Bioethics can help to reduce the gaps in global governance. First, it provides knowledge that clarifies the nature of global problems. Second, it examines normative perspectives, scrutinizing divergence and identifying possibilities for convergence. Third, it assists in the formulation and adoption of policies. Fourth, it may strengthen global institutions by articulating the importance of global responsibilities, justice and solidarity.

Bioethics plays a role because governance is not merely a technical or managerial approach based on facts, scientific expertise and technology. Governance also involves values, norms and ideas. With its reflective resources bioethics can make intellectual and critical contributions to the clarification of normative perspectives that guide policies and institutions in specific directions rather than others. Of course, these contributions are potential and indirect since in everyday practice pragmatic policy concerns may be more powerful. Today, however, bioethics is more and more directly involved in global governance. As the next chapter will show, bioethics is increasingly becoming itself a mechanism of governance.

CHAPTER SUMMARY

- Global governance refers to the collective efforts of state and non-state actors to manage global problems.
- Global health governance is focused on global health, especially infectious diseases. Its major institution is the World Health Organization (WHO). Nowadays there are many agencies and organizations in global health governance, without a central authority to coordinate.
- The Ebola virus disease of 2014–15 illustrates the current problem of governance.
- Global health governance has five gaps:
  - Insufficient knowledge.
  - Diverging normative perspectives (e.g. broad or narrow concept of health).
  - Diverging policies (e.g. focus on specific diseases or health systems).
  - Weak institutions (with capacity and responsibility problems).
  - Lack of compliance.
- The dominant perspective in global health governance is 'globalization from above'. However, since the impact of states is limited, 'governance from below' will be more influential.
- New forms of governance are needed to which global bioethics contributes:
  - Broader vision of governance and globalization based on a common framework of shared values and objectives.
  - Inclusion and participation of more actors and stakeholders.
  - Evolvement of new practices inspired by different forms of leadership.
- Bioethics can contribute to global health governance through critical reflection on the mechanisms, directions and outcomes of governance.

Notes

1 Commission on Global Governance (1995) *Our global neighbourhood*. Oxford University Press: Oxford, p. 2.
2 Mark W. Zacher and Tania J. Keefe (2008) *The politics of global health governance: United by contagion*. Palgrave Macmillan: New York.
3 Sophie Harman (2012) *Global health governance*. Routledge: London and New York; Jeremy Youde (2012) *Global health governance*. Polity Press: Cambridge (UK).
4 B. Cockerham and William E. Cockerham (2010) *Health and globalization*. Polity Press: Cambridge (UK) and Malden (USA).
5 See: Kelley Lee (2009) *The World Health Organization (WHO)*. Routledge: London and New York.
6 For example, Thomas G. Weiss (2013) *Global governance. Why? What? Whither?* Polity Press: Cambridge (UK) and Malden (USA).
7 Lessons from Ebola are provided in: *Save the Children: A wake-up call. Lessons from Ebola for the world's health systems*. London, March 2015 (www.savethechildren.org/atf/cf/%7B9def2ebe-10ae-432c-9bd0-df91d2eba74a%7D/WAKE%20UP%20CALL%20REPORT%20PDF.PDF) (accessed 4 August 2015).
8 For the data on poverty, see: https://data.un.org/Data.aspx?d=MDG&f=seriesRowID%3A581 Data on the number of physicians per country: see Global Health Observatory Data Repository (http://apps.who.int/gho/data/view.main.92000). Data for Guinea are for 2005, Sierra Leone for 2010, and Liberia for 2008.
9 Critique of Ebola governance as a normative failure is made by Anthony S. Fauci (2014) Ebola – Underscoring the global disparities in health care resources. *New England Journal of Medicine* 371(12): 1084–1086. He argues that indifference and lack of coordination prevailed. What was lacking was 'international assistance and global solidarity' (Fauci, 2014, p. 1086).
10 Thomas G. Weiss (2013) *Global governance. Why? What? Whither?* Polity Press: Cambridge (UK) and Malden (USA); David Held (2010) *Cosmopolitanism: Ideals and realities*. Polity Press: Cambridge (UK) and Malden (MA).
11 Thomas Weiss (2013) *Global governance*, pp. 45–61.
12 The Abuja Declaration, 24–27 April 2001: www.un.org/ga/aids/pdf/abuja_declaration.pdf (accessed 4 August 2015).
13 Geoffrey B. Cockerham and William E. Cockerham (2010) *Health and globalization*. Polity Press: Cambridge (UK) and Malden (USA).
14 Veena Das (1999) Public good, ethics, and everyday life: Beyond the boundaries of bioethics. *Daedalus* 128(4): 99–133.
15 Jeremy Brecher, Tim Costello and Brendan Smith (2000) *Globalization from below: The power of solidarity*. South End Press: Cambridge (MA).
16 Mark Heywood (2009) South Africa's Treatment Action Campaign: Combining law and social mobilization to realize the right to health. *Journal of Human Rights Practice* 1(1): 14–36.
17 Proposals for improving global governance for health are made by the Commission on Global Governance for Health (2014) The political origins of health inequity: Prospects for change. *The Lancet* 383: 630–667.
18 Karl Otto Apel (2000) Globalization and the need for universal ethics. *European Journal of Social Theory* 3(20): 137–155.
19 Sophie Harman (2012) *Global health governance*. Routledge: London and New York, p. 1.

10

BIOETHICS GOVERNANCE

The previous chapter showed how 'governance' has developed in connection to globalization. The traditional mechanisms and procedures of government were adequate as long as they could be applied within states. However, in interstate cooperation and at the global level they were no longer sufficient. The challenge for governance is that it requires an approach that differs from government; nonetheless at the global level many approaches are still based on the premises of national and international government. The same challenge is visible in global bioethics.

Traditionally, healthcare practice was regulated by the medical profession itself (see Chapter 2). The emphasis was on the person of the individual practitioner. Ethical discourse articulated the virtues, conduct and duties that were necessary to be a responsible and reliable professional. Standards and codes were developed and implemented by professional associations. This 'government by profession' became increasingly problematic when the progress of science and technology generated moral concerns. The rise of bioethics in the 1970s can be considered as an effort to create a new platform to debate and analyse these concerns. A new system of 'governance' emerged, first in the United States, and later replicated in other countries (Chapter 3). Although in this system medical experts no longer play a dominant role, and a wide variety of actors are involved, the main driving force is the national government. It is the state that makes legislation, issues guidelines, establishes committees, sponsors research and promotes ethics teaching. At the same time, the efforts of states can only be successful if they are advanced by other actors, especially bioethicists, and accepted by the general public. This model of national governance has been extended to the international level especially since the 1990s (Chapter 4). International activities and institutions generally reproduced the basic elements of bioethics at the national level, emphasizing international cooperation and coordination. However, a global approach to bioethics governance is still in the making. This chapter will begin by examining the movement from national to international to global governance, in order to identify the elements necessary for global bioethics governance. Subsequently, a distinction will be made between two types of bioethics governance: governance *through* bioethics and governance *of* bioethics. The first emphasizes the contributions of global bioethics to various efforts to develop and manage policies and practices in research, healthcare and medicine. The second focuses on efforts to develop and manage bioethics itself so that it can more effectively address global bioethical problems.

Bioethics governance at the national level

The ethics infrastructure that has developed within many countries has the same components of governance discussed in the previous chapter. The only difference is that the problems are not immediately global. The need for bioethics governance emerged because policy-makers were confronted with a new type of problem. Scientific and technological advances are producing social debate and controversy, for example concerning transgenic animals, organ transplantation or medical research. Professional self-regulation is no longer able to prevent and reassure the social and moral concerns of citizens. As discussed in Chapter 2, scandals of medical research and ethical queries connected to new technologies triggered the transition from medical ethics to a new and broader ethical discourse. On the one hand, the advancement of science and technology demonstrates that the perspectives and interests of science, industry and civil society are different. On the other hand, traditional forms of governance are no longer adequate. These forms are technocratic, emphasizing scientific authority and expertise, and are usually non-transparent and closed; they could even further decrease public trust in science. In this context, bioethics provided policy-makers with new possibilities for governance. It could connect innovative technologies with the concerns of citizens, reconcile various perspectives and interests, and therefore pacify controversies and debates. The characteristics of the broader concept of ethics embodied in the new discipline of bioethics (elaborated in Chapter 2) made it an ideal mechanism for a more democratic approach to governance. Inclusiveness demanded the involvement of a range of disciplines and actors; reflection emphasized the need for deliberation, dialogue and argumentation; a holistic approach implied a broad vision of health and the human person; human values affirmed that facts are not the only relevant considerations. Bioethics therefore was useful to shape new forms of governance that were more inclusive, transparent and accountable, and that were based on consultation of a variety of actors and involved activities at various levels. First established as an academic discipline, bioethics quickly became a policy instrument. The creation of the first national bioethics commission in 1974 in the US, high-profile court cases, and specific legislation set a pattern that was rapidly reproduced in other countries.

HERMAN THE BULL

The birth of Herman, the first transgenic bull in the world, in December 1990 initiated an intense public debate in the Netherlands about animal biotechnology. The animal was genetically engineered so that its female offspring would produce the human breast milk protein lactoferrin. Animal protection organizations argued that animals were reduced to instruments for scientific knowledge and commercial production. A few years earlier, an outbreak of Bovine Spongiform Encephalopathy ('mad cow disease') in the United Kingdom had alerted the public to the unhealthy conditions of the bio-industry. It also showed how governments can mismanage the risks to humans, repeatedly assuring that the risks were minimal and that it was safe to eat beef; but in fact crucial evidence was withheld. Public confidence in government policy declined as the number of infections increased. In this context, the Dutch government could not continue with the usual governance, relying primarily on scientific expertise. A special national ethics committee (Committee on Animal Biotechnology, CAB) was created in 1997 with experts in ethics and biotechnology advising the Minister about ethical acceptability and licenses.[1]

Bioethics governance at the international level

Bioethics governance at the international level faces a different type of problem. Though similar social and moral concerns can arise in various countries, these problems cannot be contained within borders but are impacting relations between states. Life sciences and biotechnology are international endeavours. They require extensive collaboration. Bioproducts have economic effects in the competition for markets. Public support is necessary for their introduction and application. The problem at the international level therefore is the need for harmonization of policies, especially if countries cooperate in some common structures. How can the interests of science and industry be balanced with public opinion if there are diverse national policies?

An illustrative case is European governance. It clearly developed from technocratic to more open forms of governance. Policy problems used to be framed in terms of economic potential and scientific progress. Policies primarily relied on scientific risk assessment by panels of experts. However, the introduction of genetically modified (GM) foods in the 1990s led to increasing protests in many European countries. Consumer groups and NGOs campaigning against these biotechnology products pointed out that there are moral concerns beyond the risk perspective, for example in relation to human rights, human dignity and respect for nature. Moreover, the public perception of risk differs from the scientific one, emphasizing environmental impact and potential harms to biodiversity and organic agriculture. Furthermore, economic competitiveness was put in a global context, arguing that the interests of powerful industries, with the US as the world's biggest exporter of GM crops, is only one consideration among others but should not necessarily drive decision-making.

GENETICALLY MODIFIED FOODS

Genetically modified foods such as soybeans and potatoes started to arrive on the market in the mid-1990s. In Europe and Asia many groups and organizations emerged that oppose the technology. In many countries public opinion is strongly against GM foods ('Frankenfoods'). Protesters, even today, destroy GM crop trials. Public resistance created regulatory conflicts, especially in the European Union. Under pressure from scientific and commercial groups, initial regulation aimed at the release of GM foods. Protests and boycotts followed in countries like Austria, Germany and France. Several countries declared a moratorium on the introduction of GM crops. In this context, the European Commission had to change its policies. In 1997 it introduced mandatory labelling of all GM foods in order to enhance consumer choice.[2]

Within this controversial climate, European governance has been redesigned. The objective is to better connect to citizens and be more transparent and accountable. Basic features of the new governance practice therefore are public debate and involvement of civil society as well as participation and consultation of a wide variety of actors. However, the application of principles of good governance in the international arena is modelled on the experiences of national level governance. The focus continues to be on expert advice, though more multidisciplinary and open. Within this framework, bioethics plays a key role. Policy-makers regard bioethics as a mechanism to transcend diverging cultural and moral perspectives and to debate issues in a common language so that tensions can be mediated and opposing ethical positions overcome. The positioning of bioethics in European governance has followed two steps. First is the determination of a common ethical framework. This was accomplished in 1997 with the Oviedo Convention. Agreeing on certain values as fundamental for Europe, the Convention provided legitimacy to bioethics as a policy instrument. The second step is the establishment of specific ethics committees. The European Group on Ethics in Science and New Technologies (EGE) created in 1991 is an advisory body to EU decision-makers. Its role has gradually been expanded from providing information and policy recommendations to representing civil society and engaging the public. The Council of Europe set up the Committee of Experts on Bioethics in 1985, first as an ad hoc, later as a permanent body. The Committee prepared the Convention, and later its additional protocols.

Bioethics governance at the global level

The Universal Declaration on the Human Genome and Human Rights (UDHGHR) is credited as the first impetus to global bioethics governance.[3] This Declaration was adopted by UNESCO but also in 1998 by the UN General Assembly. It initiated a global debate on moral issues concerning the human body and human life confronted with economic considerations. The debate highlighted two relevant dimensions typical for bioethics governance at the global level. The first dimension is the focus on science as a global commons that requires shared principles. The Human Genome Project, launched in 1990, will generate knowledge that should be in the public domain, although specific applications can be privatized. The new knowledge should benefit humanity. It should be widely disseminated and available to countries that are not involved in the research endeavour themselves. There is therefore a need to go beyond a strict economic perspective since the genome is the heritage of humanity. The second dimension is the emphasis on human rights. Genetic technologies can be used to limit reproductive freedom and to promote sex selection, thus introducing new forms of discrimination and stigmatization. Access to genetic services and potential new treatments can also be limited for various reasons in different countries. The new knowledge will only benefit humanity as a whole if special attention is paid to ethical concerns, in particular the human rights implications.

These two dimensions illustrate that the nature of the problem in global bioethics governance is first of all inequity. At the global level the major concern is how global justice can be done, rather than how controversies can be pacified (at the national level) or how diverse approaches can be harmonized (at the international level). The other components of governance are similar at the various levels: a need for cooperation, variety of actors, various levels of activity, and diverging objectives, although addressing them is a much broader task at the global level. Not only are there more diverging ethical views, but there is also no implementation mechanism or supervisory process if there is agreement on basic principles (as will be elaborated on later).

The methodology of bioethics governance apparently is the same at all levels. First is the creation of a global ethics committee, the International Bioethics Committee in 1993. Second is the development of an ethical framework, initially in the area of genetics, later in bioethics in general. In this way, a separate space has been created for the exploration, examination, specification and negotiation of ethical values in connection to scientific advances. The objective of global bioethics governance is modest. The UDHGHR was intended as an incentive for national legislation. Since substantial national legislation is lacking, and international human rights law is too vague and unspecific in this area, there is opportunity for a global initiative, not to impose a framework on all countries but to start a global dialogue on how human genetics can develop for the benefit of everyone. But even this modest objective requires subtle processes and practices of deliberation and interaction in order to defuse controversies that will otherwise result in ineffective statements. The global governance of cloning is an example.

DECLARATION ON HUMAN CLONING

In February 1997 Scottish researchers impressed the world with Dolly the sheep. She was cloned from an adult somatic cell taken from a mammary gland. In the press it was immediately suggested that the same technique of somatic cell nuclear transfer could be used to clone human beings. Following a French–German initiative to draft a convention against the reproductive cloning of human beings, the UN General Assembly started discussions in 2001. There was agreement that cloning embryos to make a baby should be banned; countries disagreed about the use of somatic cell nuclear transfer for creating embryos to derive embryonic stem cells, so-called research cloning (also called 'therapeutic' cloning although therapeutic purposes are in the future). The same technique used for both purposes leads to the destruction of the embryo. For this reason, a majority of countries wanted to prohibit all forms of human cloning. No consensus could be reached. From the start negotiations have been political, conducted by representatives of states in New York, without involvement of a bioethics committee, scientists or the general public. The General Assembly adopted the Declaration on Human Cloning in March 2005 with 84 countries in favour and 34 against, with 37 abstentions. Although there was initial agreement on a legally binding treaty, the coupling of reproductive and research cloning produced a weak agreement. After the vote, many countries declared that they will not honour the Declaration.[4]

The development of bioethics governance at the national, international and global level shows that bioethics is becoming an inescapable component of global health governance. It is replacing traditional forms of governance that are no longer adequate to manage social and moral problems. Global bioethics is increasingly challenged to make contributions to address global problems. Nowadays, governance is therefore more often done *through* bioethics. But this new role of bioethics raises questions about the governance *of* bioethics. What discipline or form of expertise is required to perform this role? In what sense can it still be ethics, i.e. a normative assessment of developments in life sciences and healthcare? What kind of bioethics is needed to deal with global problems? And what does 'dealing' mean here? These questions can only be answered after a critical examination of the new role of bioethics in present-day governance.

Governance *through* bioethics

The recent incorporation of bioethics in governance transforms cultural and social concerns about scientific and technological advances into moral concerns. Bioethics provides a new language to facilitate exchange of views and to reframe problems in such a way that compromises can be reached to make a recommendation or decision. Earlier, this was the advantage of principlism for national and international bioethical debates. The conviction that bioethics basically is the application of a limited number of principles implies that bioethics has clear tasks that are useful to research and healthcare practices as well as policy-making. For a global framework other notions such as solidarity, cooperation, social responsibility and global justice will be required to expand the debate. Because of these characteristics, bioethics is helpful to global policy-makers in managing potential conflicts between scientific and economic interests and public concerns.

Four functions

The new approach to governance through bioethics is based on four functions of global bioethics.[5]

1   *Regulation.* Bioethics is involved in developing different normative instruments: guidelines, recommendations, declarations and conventions. Many countries are witnessing a proliferation of regulatory activities related to healthcare and medical science. China is an example. If it wants to be a global player in life sciences research, it needs to develop a regulatory framework that is in harmony with global standards; and it certainly has done so recently.
2   *Oversight.* A network of ethics committees has developed in many countries, providing oversight mechanisms particularly in the area of health research. These review systems are increasingly globally coordinated. Networks of research ethics committees are created to harmonize and standardize approaches. Global summits of national ethics committees are convened to exchange experiences and best practices.
3   *Deliberation.* Governance requires that developments in science, technology and healthcare are publicly discussed. The national space for debate, however, can be very different. Ethical issues raised by these scientific developments are not the prerogative of scientists or policy-makers, but in fact concern every citizen. Dialogue and exchange of views is necessary but the involvement of civil society actors is more outspoken in some cultures than in others.
4   *Interaction.* Global bioethics requires interaction about values and ethical principles. Policies and guidelines will be applied in practices by individuals towards other individuals. Researchers will interact with research subjects, physicians with patients, nurses with persons in need of care. Informed consent protocols are approved by ethics committees but there is generally little follow-up and quality control about how they are applied in practice.

Problems for global bioethics governance

With these four functions an ethical infrastructure has been built in many countries. The same functions are used to set up similar infrastructure at the international and global levels. In a global perspective these efforts are confronted with serious problems.

- *Diversity and variety*. The variety in how the four functions are effectuated is enormous. Take the function of oversight. Many countries nowadays use ethics review committees in the domain of research. But there is not one preferred model. Even when there is a national ethical review committee, review style at the local level can be different, depending on the institutional context (academic, commercial or care context). Although the regulatory context is the same, review practices can differ. Similar diversity exists in bioethics committees for policy. The first national bioethics committee was established by presidential decree in 1983 in France. It can propose recommendations for legislation that have been adopted in 1994 as 'bioethics laws'. The United Kingdom has no officially recognized national bioethics committee but several specialist committees for controversial areas such as human genetics, gene therapy, research with human embryos and human tissues. There are possibly national bioethics committees across the globe in more than 90 countries. Their goals differ: providing policy advice, improving patient care, protecting human research participants, and establishing sound professional practices. Some committees have only one task, others combine several tasks. Mandates, missions, working practices and composition vary. This diversity implies that bioethics governance is not uniform. For example, in Israel there is no national bioethics regulatory agency. There is piecemeal regulation with a multitude of relevant statutes, a web of ad hoc advisory committees dominated by experts, and no significant public engagement. The system has been characterized as a technocracy of official expert ethics committees. In Singapore, on the other hand, the government established the Bioethics Advisory Committee when it became clear that decentralized review committees could not provide a governance framework to safeguard public trust and research integrity.

  The existing diversity promotes a continuous call for streamlining and harmonization, especially in the field of health research. The argument is that international collaboration needs comparable standards and procedures. The response to international controversies usually is to tighten oversight, putting more emphasis on implementation of universal principles. The challenge is that they always need to be applied within a context. The characteristics of this context should be taken into account, particularly in an ethical assessment. Research proposals, for example, will therefore be reviewed not merely in a technical manner (e.g. focusing on individual rights) but that they are embedded in a value structure (with emphasis on the community and society). The consequence is a tension between common standards and local practices. Bioethics governance is not a matter of imposing ethical frameworks or more stringent application of principles, guidelines and regulations. Because of the dialectics between the global and the local, governance at the national level will interact with global governance in order to generate international cooperation on the basis of common concerns. This will not only influence global governance, and necessitate it to pay attention to ethical assessment of the social conditions for science and healthcare (avoiding inequity, exploitation and corruption). It will also influence national governance since this has to adapt to the global context. Regulation of science can be driven by different motivations: because scientific advances are morally problematic within the country but also because of the need to conform to global moral expectations. China is a good example. The country has recently established a regulatory framework for bioethics governance that follows international guidelines. Authorities as well as researchers considered that ethical review was necessary in order to maintain the reputation of Chinese science, to assure the legitimacy of research, and to earn the trust of the international scientific community. Although governmental governance initially was authoritarian and pragmatic, scientists themselves became more actively involved, and an energetic bioethics community emerged. In the area of stem cell research for example, ethical issues were first identified outside of the country, transforming non-ethical issues into ethical ones within China. Global standards in fact served as a mirror to reflect on local norms, leading to what is called 'internal globalization'.

RESEARCH ETHICS IN CHINA

After an examination of research integrity in China, the journal *Science* concluded that a flourishing black market in publications exists. For fees ranging from $1,600 to $26,300 authorship in Science Citation Index (SCI) journals is for sale. Shady companies are trading in SCI papers. Chinese regulatory agencies are concerned about global influence and the reputation of Chinese science. They have taken initiatives to improve research ethics through education and codes of conduct. But SCI papers are the basis of promotion in many universities; they also lead to privileges and financial rewards. The emphasis is on individual research rather than institutional research teams, encouraging competition and rivalry.[6]

• *Representation and expertise.* A second problem for global bioethics governance is related to the nature of bioethics itself. What kind of knowledge or expertise does it provide? Who may legitimately present him or herself as a bioethicist? The interdisciplinary character of bioethics that for Potter was the strength of the new discipline is at the same time a weakness in governance. For example, membership of the International Bioethics Committee (IBC) is based on cultural, geographical and disciplinary diversity. They need to be specialists in the life sciences and in the social and human sciences. Areas such as law, human rights, philosophy, education and communication are mentioned but no reference is made to ethics or bioethics. No special education, training or expertise seems to be required to qualify as a member of a bioethics committee. Most committee members are therefore scientists with bioethicists being a small minority. This composition has consequences. One is a preference for particular working methods (see the next section). But it also raises questions about the role of bioethics experts and the involvement of the public in bioethical debates. Bioethics expertise is ambiguous. In governance mechanisms the supposition is that there is specific expertise in moral issues. The purpose of these mechanisms is to offer a platform for consideration and deliberation that goes beyond merely scientific and empirical matters, thus leaving the usual technocratic approach behind. Bioethical debate should furthermore attend to public concerns. Bioethics expertise is assumed to represent 'lay' moral perspectives. In this view of governance mechanisms a distinction is made between the field (bioethics) and the actors. Some actors are specialists (bioethicists) but all operate in a dual role: as technical experts (in a variety of disciplines) and as representatives of civil society interests.

• *Public participation.* Bioethics governance generally emphasizes the need to involve the public. Often, public concerns have been the reason to establish ethics committees. For example, the EGE is mandated to organize public round tables in the EU and may invite representatives of NGOs to exchange views. Public engagement arguably has several advantages: it leads to increased trust, diminished controversy and more acceptable decisions since they include a range of perspectives. But in practice, public participation is limited. Working sessions of committees are usually private. There are different ways to organize public debate: consensus conferences, internet dialogues, focus groups, consultative panels, citizen juries and public hearings. It is not clear what the most effective approach is. Committees often make a limited contribution to public debate. The Dutch CAB organized public hearings but the debates were monopolized by small groups of 'animal experts'. A two-way dialogue did not emerge. The debate was also focused on the specific case of a license request; exchanges on broader ethical issues such as the moral status of the animal were not permitted. Critics therefore regard such ethics committees as a vehicle to facilitate the public input into a controversial debate but at the same time as a governance tool to transform, filter and limit public voices in ethical debates.[7] When committees engage in public participation they can also decide who to invite. Who will be regarded as a legitimate representative of the public? It is often known in advance which range of diverging views exists. Radical opinions can be easily marginalized or neglected. Moreover, the impact of public debate on policies and political decision-making is not clear. In 2003, public debate on GM food was organized in the United Kingdom, with more than 600 meetings involving 20,000 participants. The government did not want this debate; it restricted its terms and imposed a short timetable. The outcome was clear: the British public was not in favour of GM crops. This was not a welcome conclusion and the government simply ignored it. In March 2004 it conditionally approved the commercial growing of GM maize.

Finally, the emphasis on public participation is problematic in a global perspective. Involvement of civil society in policy-making is not uniform across the world. For example, in Japan there was little public concern about human embryonic stem cell research, compared to Western countries. The Japanese government organized national debates but social organizations were not substantially engaged. In China there was no involvement of citizens in the debate on embryo research. Scientists themselves were very active in shaping governance. Most of them were opposed to public engagement.

Objectives and forms of governance

The problems of global bioethics governance in translating its four functions into practical arrangements relate to a more basic lack of clarity about objectives: should bioethics governance primarily focus on solutions or on problems?

The objective of providing solutions is visible in the work of ethics committees. As platforms to deal with social uncertainty and conflict they want to demonstrate their usefulness as problem-solvers. For example, the Dutch CAB focused primarily on the concrete issue of licensing, although the committee was established out of public concerns with the moral status of animals. The committee took a step-by-step approach to individual cases. In this pragmatic approach it is impossible to question the status of animals in genetic modification; concepts like the intrinsic value of animals do not apply. By demarcating and restricting the domain of debate, general criticism could be defused and practical decisions reached. The same operational pragmatism is at work in national debates. In China, the main concern regarding human stem cell research was about acceptability of this research, especially to Western countries. Since ethical problems did not so much emerge within the country itself, there was no need for intensive public debate. Ethical responses, however, were needed because of foreign concerns.

The objective of clarifying problems is different. Public concerns about the commercial introduction of GM foods, for example, need to be taken seriously. What do they imply? What values are driving these concerns? Only by exploring the problem, can the different interests at stake be properly balanced. Ethics committees concentrate on problems that have a symbolic rather than pragmatic function. They show that political decision-makers take ethics seriously. They are a public manifestation of ethical concerns. Their contribution to governance is not providing solutions but creating a channel for public debate.

These two different objectives (solutions versus problems) give rise to two different forms of bioethics governance: administrative and political.[8] Each form has specific operational methods.

1   *Administrative governance.* Providing solutions requires a specific methodology. First, as indicated earlier, is pragmatism. There is a specific problem that needs to be solved. General debate, invoking abstract moral concepts should be avoided. Proceedings should concentrate on specific issues, cases or a defined

target. Second, such a demarcated approach demands a specific rationality. Fact finding and scientific evidence must be the first stage of work. If the subject of debate is clear, procedures for decision-making can be applied: detailed analysis, argumentation, justification and explanation will follow, resulting in recommendations. Third, resolving the problem requires consensus. Bioethics governance often uses the language of consensus building. The specific expertise of bioethics is to provide this language so that it is possible to deliberate about controversial issues. It also provides the conceptual framework for analysing and justifying particular problems and practices.

This form of governance is not too different from the earlier technocratic governance. It involves other notions and other discourse but it continues to focus on regulation and solution. Only, another type of expertise is now engaged. Because scientific and commercial interests are opposed to public concerns, bioethical experts are assigned the role of balancing the various moral views at stake.

2. *Political governance.* The focus on problems requires another form of governance. New policies are necessary because of public concerns about science, technology and commercialization. These concerns need to be explored and articulated. Rather than a regulatory approach, it is first advisable to engage in moral discourse, not only with policy-makers and scientists but with the general public. This engagement demands another methodology. First, an open and democratic approach will clarify the problem or problems. Ethical concerns can only be pacified if they are taken seriously. Deliberation therefore must include the concerns of civil society and should take into account various interests. Second, facts and values cannot be nicely separated. Controversies about scientific and technological advances already imply moral disputes and diverging ethical views. Scientific evidence does not present neutral facts but is value-laden. Instead of an instrumental, rational approach focused on how to solve the problem, political rationality is required that interprets and explores the problem in connection to responsibilities, obligations, relationships and human rights. The role of scientists in open deliberation is therefore limited. Science is not the only source of information and knowledge. Furthermore, public input should be different. Rather than regarding citizens as in need of information so that public consultation means informing and educating the public (assuming information deficit), citizens should be engaged in dialogue, articulating different visions on what the problem is. Consultation means participation. Third, the emphasis on consensus often silences the moral debate. It sets a particular frame for discussions and leaves no place for critical reflection. Priority is given to technical and practical matters. Political governance, on the other hand, emphasizes that the process of searching for common values is more important than consensus. The public process of deliberation taking into account all relevant views is what counts. This implies that voice is given to dissent, that controversies are not avoided and that pluralistic viewpoints are appreciated.

Both forms of bioethics governance fulfil the four functions of global bioethics (regulation, oversight, deliberation and interaction) but in different ways. Administrative governance is attractive because of its focus on output and efficiency. It helps to develop political decisions that address the interests of policy-makers and to solve societal problems. Political governance is attractive since it focuses on human rights, public participation and democratization. Its focus is more on input. It assists political decision-making on the basis of preferences of citizens and the engagement of civil society. For these reasons, bioethics has become more and more involved in governance practices.

Criticism of bioethics governance

At the same time, this involvement has led to increasing criticism. Most critique is aimed at administrative governance. The technical approach of this form of governance may help to define ethical questions but it hardly produces normative statements about their acceptability. Rather than demonstrating a normative role, bioethics is concerned with neutralizing contestation and facilitating policy decisions. Bioethics governance therefore is a new form of 'pastoral power'.[9] The consensus culture that it is fostering is devastating for the aspirations and ideals of global bioethics since broader issues connected to rights and values cannot be discussed. Emphasis on consensus also highlights an important difference between bioethics governance at the national and global levels. While at the first level, problems can be solved by narrowing the debate on specific controversies, at the global level consensus can only be accomplished by focusing on general issues and broad principles. Consensus will promote global dialogue and cooperation but at the price of avoiding controversial topics. The UDBHR could only be adopted by not attending to specific moral issues (informed consent was the exception). The debate on human cloning started with a focus on one specific issue but was immediately complicated by introducing broader ethical frameworks that could not be reconciled. Another criticism of administrative governance is that in reality it presents another type of experto-cracy. The only change with the past is that now a new type of expert is influential. Bioethicists work in the same closed and non-transparent way as scientific authorities in earlier days. They regard themselves as representing the concerns of civil society so that there is no need for a real dialogue with outsiders. Public participation is only important as an instrument for public relations to increase support for decisions; it is not important for normative reasons, for example because citizens have the right to participate in decisions, or because the quality of final policy decisions will improve.

Political governance is subjected less frequently to criticism. It is often simply dismissed as impractical. If mechanisms of governance will not contribute to solving policy questions but make them more complicated, the usefulness of bioethics for policy-makers will rapidly diminish. The emphasis on pluralism means that ethics committees have members with different views but radical perspectives are often excluded. Minority views tend to be marginalized but because they have been included in the deliberations they are simultaneously neutralized.

Both forms of governance are fundamentally criticized with the argument that bioethics has become biopolitics. This critique will be addressed in Chapter 12. Its core is that bioethics governance is effective because it balances scientific and economic interests with social and moral concerns. But doing so, it facilitates scientific and technological advances as well as commercial trade. The CAB in the Netherlands, for example, has almost never rejected an application for licensing; it is accused of primarily promoting the interests of research and industry, rather than the interests of animals. The concerns about GM foods in Europe were only taken seriously when the political context changed with the rise of 'green' political parties, and when the European Parliament became a platform for civil society. A solution was found with the emphasis on labelling of food, transforming the social concerns of ethical acceptability into a private choice of citizens/consumers. The examples illustrate the usefulness of bioethics discourse: it translates social concerns into a specific moral language of individual agency that is no longer obstructing scientific progress and commercial exchange. Bioethics helps to frame the debate in a particular manner so that the domain is demarcated and immunized against fundamental critique.

The criticism of biopolitics is more outspoken at international and global levels. Attention is focused on the role of the EGE as an ethical mediator in biopolitical disputes in the EU.[10] The committee's mandate is criticized as unclear, its membership as elitist, its working methods as opaque, and its repertoire of ethical arguments as narrow and as excluding alternative views. Nonetheless, the EGE had significant influence on EU legislation, policy-making processes and policy implementation. Also, it has expanded the territory of bioethics governance. Debates about patenting embryonic human stem cells, for example, have demonstrated that an economic and legal approach is no longer sufficient. Patenting is not a technological enterprise but requires ethical considerations. At the same time, in mediating between the values of science and commerce on the one hand, and the moral concerns of citizens on the other, preference is usually given to the first ones. The EGE is then portrayed as a mechanism to facilitate the acceptance of new technologies. It provides ethical endorsements to further development of the bio-industry. This role of bioethics is sometimes explicitly stated. The Bioethics Advisory Committee of Singapore, for example, was established in 2000 in order to promote the economic policies of the country through 'setting the ethical groundwork for a knowledge economy'.[11] Against this background, questions arise about the proper role of bioethics. If many of today's bioethical challenges emerge because of the dominancy of neoliberal market ideology, and bioethics itself has been incorporated into new governance mechanisms that facilitate this ideology, then bioethics has become part of the basic problem. Rather than scrutinizing the context in which bioethical problems are produced, bioethics has become what some observers have called, 'the political means for the creation of a global moral economy where the trading and exchange of values is normalized and legitimated'.[12] It is evident that this critique seriously questions the nature of bioethics. Can bioethics itself, when it is implicated in the governance of global problems, be 'governed' so that it will be able to develop critical and independent positions in regard to global governance?

Governance *of* bioethics

Bioethics, as illustrated in this chapter, has a growing role in global governance. It is in a unique position to contribute to the evolution of new forms of government described in Chapter 9. First, bioethics can articulate values, ideals and goals that imagine a broader vision of governance aimed at humanity and its future survival. Second, since bioethics is first developed at local and national levels and involves a broad range of actors it can engage civil societies in global approaches from below. Third, bioethics can inspire new practices of cooperation and activism. Despite these opportunities, bioethics governance is relatively new. It is facing serious challenges and criticism. Governance also raises fundamental questions about bioethics itself.

It seems difficult to apply the notion of governance to bioethics. It is not a uniform enterprise or field. It covers a variety of activities, involves many different actors, and performs heterogeneous roles. At the same time, there are many efforts nowadays to clarify the identity of bioethics, to coordinate bioethical research, to harmonize bioethical contributions and products such as guidelines and statutes, to specify bioethical expertise, and to professionalize bioethics. An example is the proposal for a code of ethics for bioethicists.

CODE OF ETHICS FOR BIOETHICISTS

Robert Baker has proposed a draft code of ethics. The basic virtues for bioethicists are competence, independence, integrity and professionalism. The code defines the responsibilities of bioethics. 'Bioethicists have a responsibility to advise professionally, honestly, competently and with integrity. They should listen to disparate voices, identify the nature of value uncertainty or underlying conflicts, gather relevant data, clarify relevant concepts and normative issues, help to identify morally acceptable options, educate, mediate and facilitate consensus building. Bioethicists may also analyze, critique and/or defend and ultimately recommend various positions, policies and practices.'[13]

Three concerns about the identity of bioethics will be examined here.

Bioethics as a field, discipline, or profession

Governance of bioethics assumes that there is a distinct field for governance. Minimally, bioethics is considered as a special field that addresses a specific set of moral problems related to health, healthcare and associated technologies. The field has several sub-areas such as research ethics, clinical ethics, public health ethics, organizational ethics and professional ethics. New specialized sub-areas are arising such as nano-ethics and neuro-ethics. At the global level, not all sub-areas are equally developed. Core activities globally are education, research, policy and healthcare. A somewhat broader consideration is that bioethics is a discipline. It has its specific concepts, theories and methodologies. Conceiving itself as applied ethics, 'principlism' is its paradigm. A maximum view regards bioethics as a profession, or at least as undergoing professionalization. Since its emergence in the 1970s (see Chapter 3) it has acquired professional paraphernalia such as specialized institutes and centres, journals and textbooks, degree-granting programmes, professional associations and standing committees. An ethics code is needed to provide guidance to bioethics professionals working in different settings, and to demonstrate to society that bioethicists are following certain standards and have specified virtues. A code is not a finished product but will need revision and reconsideration; it will help to build a community of professionals and will therefore promote professionalization.

The idea of professionalization of bioethics is contested. Although many agree that there should be some standards (in terms of knowledge, competence and experience) so that the quality of bioethics can be warranted, there is disagreement about how to proceed. Clinical ethics consultation is most often highlighted as an area for standardization. In 2006, the American Society for Bioethics and Humanities (ASBH) proposed core competencies for healthcare ethics consultation.[14] On the basis of these competencies credentialing mechanisms can be established. It is no longer acceptable that ethics consultations are done by people without appropriate training (only 5 per cent had completed a fellowship or graduate degree programme in bioethics). The current emphasis is on certification of individual practitioners (with portfolios and examinations). This will not solve the divergence of educational background as long as degree programmes in bioethics are not accredited. The ASBH has also launched a code for ethics consultants.[15] All these efforts are considered necessary to guarantee the quality of ethics consultation, and to improve accountability and transparency. It assumes that clinical ethics is sufficiently different from bioethics, and in need of professionalization.

CODE OF ETHICS FOR HEALTHCARE ETHICS CONSULTANTS

In January 2014, the Board of the American Society for Bioethics and Humanities approved the first edition of the Code of Ethics and Professional Responsibilities for Healthcare Ethics Consultants. It includes the following core ethical responsibilities of individuals performing healthcare ethics consultation (HCEC):

1   be competent (practicing in a manner consistent with professional HCEC standards);
2   preserve integrity;
3   manage conflicts of interest and obligation;
4   respect privacy and maintain confidentiality;
5   contribute to the field;
6   communicate responsibly;
7   promote just health care within HCEC.

Bioethics as an epistemic community

Another concern particularly for global governance is whether bioethics can be regarded as an epistemic community.[16] Members of such an expertise-based community may have very different backgrounds but they share similar knowledge that can help policy-makers to address global problems. What is the specific expertise that bioethics can offer? Bioethical expertise has two components: knowledge and skills. Knowledge concerns moral arguments and moral concepts. Skills relate to moral reasoning. Bioethics experts can therefore provide reliable moral advice but also reasons that justify the advice. This view is not generally accepted for two reasons. The first is that bioethics experts do many things but they do not often provide normative direction. For example, ethics consultants may have particular knowledge and skills that may be useful in healthcare but these are not particularly associated with *moral* expertise. They act as mediators, consensus-builders, value interpreters and educators. The ASBH Code of Ethics describes what ethics consultants are able to do: 'facilitating communication among key stakeholders, fostering understanding, clarifying and analyzing ethical issues, and including justifications when recommendations are provided.'[17] Ethics consultants can clarify and recommend but not advocate a particular normative view. They facilitate decision-making; they are not the ultimate decision-makers. This is an important role but the question is whether it is ethics as a normative endeavour. The second reason for contesting specific bioethics expertise is related to the interdisciplinary nature of the field. Bioethics requires collaboration with a wide variety of disciplines. Many bioethical practitioners are trained in different professions: healthcare, law, philosophy, theology, anthropology or science. Clinical ethics consultations are most often done by physicians and nurses. The majority of ethics committee members usually are not professional ethicists. Bioethics experts may therefore have heterogeneous knowledge and skills, besides quite different ethical views. For this reason, it is not uncommon to reject the label 'bioethicist'. Bioethics expertise is not an individual capacity but is located at the level of the epistemic community. On the other hand, it does not exclude that there are specialists. In healthcare, paediatrics and geriatrics developed into medical specialties while other physicians should have sufficient expertise to deal with children and the elderly.

Reinforcement of mainstream bioethics

The process of professionalization implies the marginalization of alternative approaches. In the past, scientific and academic medicine has prevailed over a variety of alternative and traditional healing systems. The fear is that the same will happen in bioethics: professionalization will articulate mainstream bioethics and exclude other approaches. The core competencies promoted by ASBH and the role of the bioethics consultant as facilitator presuppose that respect for individual autonomy is the basic ethical principle. Critics argue that instead of scrutinizing the context in which moral problems are produced, bioethics itself, with its emphasis on individual autonomy, becomes a symptom of bureaucratization, managerialism and proceduralism, and is therefore subservient to neoliberal ideology.[18] In order to be recognized as a profession, bioethics accepts that it is operating in a context that is rational, calculable and competitive. It will gather facts and evidence, and clarify values, but will not challenge and critique them. Particularly from a global perspective, this reinforcement of mainstream bioethics will be problematic. Respect for autonomy is one of the moral principles to address bioethical problems but as argued in earlier chapters, global bioethics should attend to the social, cultural and economic conditions that produce these problems.

Governance *of* global bioethics

At the global level efforts to strengthen bioethics so that it can play a stronger role in global governance are less focused on professionalizing its practitioners and more on creating institutions and reinforcing the infrastructures that are necessary for the flourishing of bioethics. On this basis, global bioethics can better scrutinize the social conditions that determine global health. This section will discuss the bioethics institutions as well as the infrastructures that operate at global level. Both are relatively new and growing; all need support and reinforcement in order to enhance the impact of global bioethics around the world. The role of international organizations in this regard is finally examined.

Global bioethics institutions

Following national and regional models, various bioethics institutions at global level have been established.

Global bioethics committees

Shortly after the first standing national bioethics committee was set up in France (1983), international committees were established. The Council of Europe created a committee on bioethics in 1985; the EU did the same in 1991. The first global body was the IBC formed by UNESCO in 1993. Global committees may also have a more limited scope. HUGO established an ethics committee in 1992 tasked to explore the social, legal and ethical issues in relation to human genome research. At the same time, another approach is to set up ad hoc committees, such as the Warnock Committee in the United Kingdom, focused on in vitro fertilization (1982–1984). An example at global level is the ethical committee convened by WHO about the ethical issues of the Ebola epidemic. These committees share two features. Their composition follows three conditions: independency, multidisciplinarity, and pluralism. Second, their task is to advise governments (or Boards), not so much to stimulate public debate. They produce reports, statements or opinions in order to influence policy-making and public discussion.

Educational programmes

A growing number of educational activities have a global outreach. Teaching programmes at national level offer scholarships for foreign students, or set up global courses. Examples are the International Bioethics Summer School in New York, organized by the Global Bioethics Initiative, and the Erasmus Mundus Master in Bioethics taught at three universities in Belgium, the Netherlands and Italy with scholarships of the European Commission.[19] A substantial effort in ethics education is sponsored by the Fogarty International Center, itself funded by the National Institutes of Health (NIH) in the US.[20] Its primary focus is on research bioethics in developing countries. It awards grants for educational initiatives, for example setting up training programmes with researchers in Tanzania, Thailand, China and Guatemala. Responsible conduct of research is the aim of online training programmes provided by the Collaborative Institutional Training Initiative (CITI) and used by thousands of institutions in more than 40 countries.[21] UNESCO has produced a basic bioethics curriculum that can be used in different settings and cultures, based on the principles of the UDBHR.[22] The organization also provides training courses for ethics teachers as well as educational resources. WHO has published educational materials such as a casebook on ethical issues in international health research.[23] Global bioethics education will certainly further expand. In many countries basic education in bioethics is not available. If it is available, there is a wide variety of educational activities primarily in research ethics.

Professional associations[24]

The International Association of Law, Ethics and Science established in France (1989) has set up a francophone network with connections to Latin America, China and Japan, with annual conferences and meetings across the world. In 1990, it started the *International Journal of Bioethics* (in English, French and Spanish). The International Association of Bioethics was formed in 1992. Besides organizing conferences every two years, it has created thematic networks of scholars, for example in clinical ethics, environmental bioethics, genetics and public health ethics. It is affiliated with two scholarly journals, *Bioethics* and *Developing World Bioethics*. The International Society for Bioethics was founded in 1996 in Spain. It has organized eight world conferences on bioethics and published its own journal (Spanish and English). The Society awards a biennial prize on bioethics. In 2000, the first prize was awarded to Van Rensselaer Potter. Recently, more specialized global associations have been launched: the International Society for Clinical Bioethics, founded in 2003, and the International Association for Education in Ethics in 2011.

Global networks

There are numerous NGOs and international networks in global health but less so in global bioethics. Specific NGOs such as 'Global Bioethics Initiative' and

'Bioethics International' are not-for-profit organizations based in the US that provide educational services as well as exchange of information and newsletters. Other networks are focused on local needs. An example is the network 'Law, Ethics and Health' established in 2003 in Senegal.[25] It brings together all stakeholders interested in promoting the right to health in the country. Other examples are provided by national bioethics societies that aim to improve the domestic bioethics infrastructure in cooperation with foreign bodies. The internet facilitates global networking and mechanisms of support. The Bangladesh Bioethics Society, for instance, organizes human rights training workshops for students with the help of national and international members.[26]

In many cases, bioethical concerns are promoted by organizations and networks that have a broader scope. An example discussed in Chapter 8 is 'Universities Allied for Essential Medicines'.[27] Established by Yale law students, UAEM developed into a global NGO of university students advocating for better access to medicines, and public health goods in general, in poor countries. In 2013, the organization launched a Report Card evaluating and ranking top research universities in North America on their contribution to global health research and access to treatment. Other examples of NGOs with a similar mission are the WEMOS Foundation mentioned in Chapter 7, and the TAC in South Africa discussed in the previous chapter. Physician for Human Rights, founded by medical doctors in 1986, is another example of an active, global NGO that works in areas that are closely connected to the concerns of global bioethics. It is using medical science to document and denounce human rights violations and take action to stop them. Other NGOs collect and publish data that are useful for bioethics initiatives. The Access to Medicine Foundation ranks the 20 largest pharmaceutical companies for their efforts to improve access to medicine in developing countries.[28] Every two years since 2008 an Index has been published showing what companies do to enhance access to their products. The Global Health Impact Project is a collaboration of researchers across the world with a similar aim: how to advance global access to essential medicines? In 2014, they launched the Global Health Impact Index. This ranks drugs by their impact on tuberculosis, malaria and HIV/AIDS as well as pharmaceutical companies by the impact of their drugs on alleviating the global burden of these diseases.[29]

The various global bioethics institutions presented are connected in different ways to the development of global bioethics. Some are set up as clear bioethics organizations from the start. For others, bioethics is only one concern among others. Other organizations present information, advocate for causes, or undertake actions that offer opportunities for global bioethics activities, theoretical or practical. All institutions demonstrate the five facets of global governance mentioned at the beginning of Chapter 9. First, they are focused on global problems, and are important for setting the agenda for global bioethics. Second, they are the result of cooperation across borders and flourish because they embody collective action. Third, they include a variety of actors. Fourth, they operate on various levels of activity. It is no longer relevant where they are established or based since due to modern communication technology their outreach is global. Fifth, they have diverging objectives. Some institutions aim to promote justice, others human rights; some provide knowledge and information, others engage in action and normative assessment.

Global bioethics infrastructures

Global governance of bioethical problems assumes that at least some basic bioethics infrastructures exist at national levels. From the perspective of governance from below, ethical concerns will best be addressed within the social and cultural context in which they emerge. Global bioethics can contribute to the strengthening of these national infrastructures. Precisely because of its global outreach and international networking it can mobilize support. In countries where, for example, specific legislation is lacking, examples and model laws can be provided to help policy-makers to take initiatives. The role of global bioethics will then be to close the gaps in global governance so that the means to address global bioethical problems will be improved. These gaps relate to knowledge, norms, policies, institutions and compliance (see Chapter 9).

Sharing of information, experiences and best practices

Disseminating, testing and advancing knowledge is an essential contribution of global bioethics to health governance. There is a range of current initiatives. Two types can be distinguished: data collection and interactive exchange.

The first type aims to collect and provide relevant bioethics information. These initiatives facilitate knowledge about bioethics developments elsewhere, and they allow access to journals, books, official publications and news items. An example is NIH Bioethics Resources on the Web, a compilation of web links to bioethics information.[30] Another is the Ethics CORE Library that has more than 5,000 training items for responsible conduct of research.[31] A third example is the Bioethics and Law Observatory at the University of Barcelona in Spain.[32] Although these initiatives provide information, the coverage is usually limited to activities in specific countries and to specific language materials.

The second type of initiative aims at interactive exchange. An example is the Global Ethics Observatory launched by UNESCO.[33] It comprises six databases: on individual experts, ethics institutions, ethics teaching programmes, ethics related legislation and guidelines, codes of conduct, and resources in ethics. The advantage is its global outreach and the presentation of information in six major languages. All information stored is obtained, vetted and updated in close interaction with national experts and bodies. The main purpose is to facilitate international cooperation. For example, one can look at the available information for Morocco, learn about the Moroccan Association for Bioethics, and the continuous ethics education programme at the University Hassan II in Casablanca. Since contact data are provided, one can get in touch with colleagues to learn more.

Capacity-building

Addressing gaps in norms, policies and institutions requires the availability and functionality of bioethics institutions such as ethics committees, ethics teaching programmes, legislation and public engagement. If these institutions are lacking or weak, the capacity to deal with bioethical challenges will be limited. Efforts to build bioethics capacity can be focused on specific countries and on the global level. Examples for specific countries have been discussed in the previous section. What are the best approaches to accomplish capacity-building at the global level is an open question. Governance from above is not possible since there is no global lead agency in charge of bioethics, at least not with sufficient funding and authority to initiate activities across the world. The only option is to stimulate and promote cooperation from below so that horizontal networks and collaborative patterns will be created. This is the purpose of the International Dialogue on Bioethics, organized by the European Commission since 2009.[34] It brings together approximately 50 European and non-European national ethics committees. A similar objective but with global coverage is envisioned by the Global Summit of National Bioethics Advisory Bodies, organized by WHO, and meeting since 1996.[35] The development of bioethics in low and middle income countries is also enhanced by the creation of a network of collaborating academic centres for bioethics. A more hands-on approach to capacity-building is undertaken by UNESCO.[36] It has practical programmes that aim to expand expertise primarily in developing countries. One is focused on setting up national ethics committees, and providing bioethics education to their membership. Another is to train ethics teachers in specific courses. A third aims at training journalists and judges in bioethics. It is clear that this kind of capacity-building requires a long-term effort. Global initiatives cannot establish national infrastructures but they can initiate and support them through inclusion within a broader network of activities.

The role of international organizations

Finally, governance of global bioethics raises questions about the role of international organizations. Nowadays, many of these organizations are active in bioethics, have set up programmes, committees and activities. The UN Inter-Agency Committee on Bioethics (since 2003) promotes coordination and collaboration among various UN organizations and agencies (e.g. UNESCO and WHO) and other international organizations (e.g. Council of Europe and EU). The two driving forces in global bioethics are UNESCO and WHO. The bioethics programme of UNESCO has been established since 1992. WHO created the Global Health Ethics unit in 2002. As intergovernmental organizations they play an important role. First, they provide a global forum. Because they represent all countries and work with different languages they are able to convene a wide range of stakeholders. This platform function is an opportunity for dialogue but also for fostering consensus and standard-setting. Second, the organizations engage in practical activities. They mobilize resources and experts to provide training. They bring together centres and bioethics scholars in new global networks of mutual support.

However, as intergovernmental organizations they face challenges. Their budgets are more and more restrained so that they are less able to programme and execute activities. Participation of developing countries in bioethics activities is often relatively low. The level of expertise and input into deliberations is unequal. The legitimacy of their activities for the bioethics community is contested, while many bioethics experts do not even know their activities. The interdisciplinary nature of bioethics can also hamper the translation of bioethics principles within a domestic context (with competing ministries of health, science and technology, education and culture). The major problem, however, is that the organizations are often subservient to the interests of member states. It is states that determine the priorities, activities and budgets. This context also determines the success of bioethics activities, as illustrated by the failed attempt to regulate human cloning. France and Germany submitted the proposal to make a convention against reproductive cloning of human beings to the UN, not to UNESCO or WHO. While there initially was agreement on the need for a convention, after four years of negotiations there was only increased dissent. Negotiations were not among bioethics experts but politicized among state representatives. The debate expanded into general ethical views regarding human life and abortion. The result was a non-binding declaration that not even explicitly prohibits cloning.

In the previous chapter the need for new forms of governance has been highlighted. UNESCO and WHO, as leading intergovernmental organizations in bioethics, can broaden global bioethics governance in two ways. The first is to involve more actors. They should produce 'normative webs' that are wide and inclusive. At the moment, their bioethics activities have limited participation of other international organizations and non-state actors. They should involve actors such as professional associations, academic centres and NGOs. Activities should be transparent and accountable so that their legitimacy will increase. What WHO has been doing in the field of surveillance of infectious diseases, and health aid and assistance, increasingly relying on networks of non-state actors, can provide a model for global bioethics. The second way to broaden bioethics governance is to take the lead in establishing new practices. The organizations can identify where actions are needed. For example, it is well known that bioethics activities are weak or absent in the Arab region; national bioethics committees do not exist or are inactive, regulations are lacking, bioethics teaching in universities is deficient or inexistent. Rather than waiting for demands of states, the organizations can proactively undertake initiatives in cooperation with non-state actors. In the past UNESCO profiled itself as teacher of norms. Between the 1950s and 1970s its mission was to set up science policy organizations in member states. There was no demand of states but the mission was driven by the organization itself, collaborating with professional experts and science organizations, and based on the norm that states are responsible for science. Such a proactive approach should be undertaken in the area of global bioethics. Rather than waiting for demands of assistance, the

organizations should start promoting and implementing the principles of global bioethics, redefining bioethics as a concern of the global community.

Conclusion

The challenge to global governance, as illustrated by the Ebola epidemic, is how global problems can be addressed when there is no global governing agency or central authority. At the same time, global governance is unavoidable since global problems transcend the domestic level and are beyond the reach of individual states. This chapter has argued that global bioethics is increasingly incorporated in the emerging mechanisms and procedures of global governance. Healthcare practices at domestic level require various forms of bioethics governance. Similar approaches can be observed at global level. Governance of global problems in connection to health is currently most often done through bioethics. In this manner, bioethics provides regulation, oversight, deliberation and interaction. Bioethics mediates between social and moral concerns, and the interests of science and commerce. It therefore has become a useful and indispensable component of governance for present-day policy-makers.

However, at a global level bioethics governance faces significant challenges. The variety and diversity of approaches is enormous; there is not a preferred approach that can be imposed from above. Bioethics expertise is heterogeneous and unequally distributed among countries. Public participation in societal debate and policy-making differs across the world. These challenges and the different forms of governance to which they give rise, raise questions about bioethics itself. Is it possible to apply the notion of governance to bioethics? The chapter answers this question affirmatively. Global bioethics can better address global bioethical problems if governance efforts are directed to strengthening global bioethics institutions and infrastructures that are also preconditional for the flourishing of bioethics at local levels.

Gradual improvement of global bioethics governance does not necessarily guarantee that bioethical practices will emerge that implement the global ethical frameworks. Setting standards is not the same as respecting them in practical contexts, even if formal and informal governance mechanisms exist. From the perspective of individual patients and citizens, healthcare professionals and scientists, policies may be important but what affects them most are the daily intricacies of concrete practices. This brings us to one of the five gaps in governance that have not been discussed in this chapter and that will be the focus of the next chapter: compliance. How are global ethical principles introduced and embodied in scientific and healthcare practices? How do practices emerge that are inspired by global principles of cooperation, solidarity and social responsibility, rather than the mainstream principles of individual autonomy and individual rights?

CHAPTER SUMMARY

- Bioethics governance has first developed at national levels. The same approaches and methods have been applied at international and global levels.
- The nature of problems and major concerns are different at various levels:
  - National:
    - ☐ Problem: controversies
    - ☐ Concern: pacification.
  - International:
    - ☐ Problem: diversity of approaches
    - ☐ Concern: harmonization.
  - Global:
    - ☐ Problem: inequity
    - ☐ Concern: global justice.
- A distinction is made between governance through bioethics and governance of bioethics.
- Governance *through* bioethics refers to the use of bioethics in governance efforts to develop and manage policies and practices in research, healthcare and medicine.
  - Functions: regulation, oversight, deliberation, and interaction.
  - Problems: diversity, representation and expertise, public participation.
  - Two forms: administrative and political governance.
  - Criticism: bioethics is biopolitics, facilitating neoliberal ideology.
- Governance *of* bioethics refers to efforts to develop and manage bioethics itself so that it can better address ethical problems. The incorporation of bioethics in global governance invites basic questions about bioethics itself:
  - Is it a field, discipline or profession?
  - Is there an epistemic community of bioethics?
  - Does professionalization of bioethics reinforce mainstream bioethics at the expense of alternative views?
- Governance of global bioethics should create and reinforce institutions and infrastructures necessary for the flourishing of bioethics.
  - Global institutions: ethics committees, educational programmes, professional associations, and global networks.
  - Global infrastructures: sharing of information, capacity-building.
- The role of international organizations in global bioethics (notably UNESCO and WHO) needs to be reinforced and redefined:
  - Broader involvement of non-state actors.
  - Proactive initiatives for new practices and agenda-setting.

Notes

1 The example of the Committee on Animal Biotechnology in the Netherlands is studied by L.E. Paula (2008) *Ethics committees, public debate and regulation: An evaluation of policy instruments in bioethics governance.* Thesis Vrije Universiteit Amsterdam.

2 Les Levidow, Susan Carr and David Wield (2000) Genetically modified crops in the European Union: regulatory conflicts as precautionary opportunities. *Journal of Risk Research* 3(3): 189–208; Nuria Vazuez-Salat, Brian Salter, Greet Smets and Louis-Marie Houdebine (2012) The current state of GMO governance: Are we ready for GM animals? *Biotechnology Advances* 30: 1336–1342.

3 For the global impact of the Genome Declaration, see: Brian Salter and Charlotte Salter (2013) Bioethical ambition, political opportunity and the European governance of patenting: The case of human embryonic stem cell science. *Social Science & Medicine* 98: 286–292.

4 United Nations Declaration on Human Cloning, www.nrlc.org/uploads/international/UN-GADeclarationHumanCloning.pdf. Also: UNU-AIS report: *Is human reproductive cloning inevitable: Future options for UN Governance.* United Nations University, Yokohama, Japan, 2007 (http://archive.ias.unu.edu/resource_centre/Cloning_9.20B.pdf).

5 The four functions of global bioethics are analysed by Ayo Wahlberg *et al.* (2013) From global bioethics to ethical governance of biomedical research collaborations. *Social Science & Medicine* 98: 293–300.

6 Maria Hvistendahl (2013) China's publication bazaar. *Science* 342: 1035–1039.

7 Lonneke Poort, Tora Holmberg and Malin Ideland (2013) Bringing in the controversy: Re-politicizing the de-politicized strategy of ethics committees. *Life Sciences, Society and Policy* 9: 11; doi: 10.1186/2195-7819-9-11.

8 The two forms of governance are distinguished by L.E. Paula (2008) *Ethics committees, public debate and regulation: An evaluation of policy instruments in bioethics governance.* Thesis Vrije Universiteit Amsterdam.

9 Alison Harvey and Brian Salter (2012) Governing the moral economy: Animal engineering, ethics and the liberal government of science. *Social Science & Medicine* 75: 198.

10 Helen Busby, Tamara Hervey and Alison Mohr (2008) Ethical EU law? The influence of the European Group on Ethics in Science and New Technologies. *European Law Review* 33: 803–824.

11 Calvin Wai Loon Ho, Leonardo D. de Castro, and Alastair V. Campbell (2014) Governance of biomedical research in Singapore and the challenge of conflicts of interest. *Cambridge Quarterly of Healthcare Ethics* 23: 289.

12 Brian Salter and Charlotte Salter (2007) Bioethics and the global moral economy: The cultural politics of human embryonic stem cell science. *Science, Technology & Human Values* 32(5): 555.

13 Robert Baker (2005) A draft model aggregate code of ethics for bioethicists. *The American Journal of Bioethics* 5(5): 38.

14 ASBH: *Core competencies in healthcare ethics consultation.*

15 ASBH: *Code of ethics and professional responsibilities for healthcare ethics consultants.* January 2014 (www.asbh.org/uploads/files/pubs/pdfs/asbh_code_of_ethics.pdf) (accessed 4 August 2015).

16 Peter M. Haas (1992) Epistemic communities and international policy coordination. *International Organization* 46(1): 1–35.

17 ASBH: *Code of ethics and professional responsibilities for healthcare ethics consultants*, 2014, page 1.

18 Stuart J. Murray and Adrian Guta (2014) Credentialization or critique? Neoliberal ideology and the fate of the ethical voice. *The American Journal of Bioethics* 14(1): 33–35; Jeremy R. Garrett (2014) Two agendas for bioethics: Critique and integration. *Bioethics*: doi: 10.1111/bioe.12116.

19 Global Bioethics Initiative: www.globalbioethics.org; Erasmus Mundus Master in Bioethics: https://med.kuleuven.be/eng/erasmus-mundus-bioethics (accessed 4 August 2015).

20 Fogarty International Center: www.fic.nih.gov/Programs/Pages/bioethics.aspx (accessed 3 August 2015).

21 Collaborative Institutional Training Initiative: www.citiprogram.org/ (accessed 3 August 2015).

22 The UNESCO bioethics core curriculum is downloadable at: http://unesdoc.unesco.org/images/0016/001636/163613e.pdf (accessed 3 August 2015).

23 WHO: Casebook on ethical issues in international health research. WHO, Geneva, 2009 (http://whqlibdoc.who.int/publications/2009/9789241547727_eng.pdf) (accessed 5 August 2015).

24 For international professional associations, see: IAB: http://bioethics-international.org/index.php?show=index; IALES: www.iales-aides.com/mission.html; SIBI: www.sibi.org/; ISCB: www.bioethics-iscb.org/; IAEE: www.ethicsassociation.org/ (accessed 3 August 2015).

25 Law, Ethics, Health Network in Senegal: http://rds.refer.sn/ (accessed 3 August 2015).

26 Bangladesh Bioethics Society: www.bioethics.org.bd/ (accessed 3 August 2015).

27 Universities Allied for Essential Medicines: https://uaem.org/ (accessed 3 August 2015).

28 Access to Medicine Index: www.accesstomedicineindex.org/(accessed 3 August 2015).

29 Global Health Impact Index: http://global-health-impact.org/aboutindex.php (accessed 3 August 2015).

30 NIH Bioethics Resources on the Web: http://bioethics.od.nih.gov/ (accessed 3 August 2015).

31 Ethics CORE (Collaborative Online Resource Environment): https://nationalethicscenter.org/(accessed 3 August 2015).

32 Bioethics and Law Observatory, Barcelona: www.bioeticayderecho.ub.edu/en (accessed 3 August 2015).

33 Global Ethics Observatory, UNESCO: www.unesco.org/new/en/social-and-human-sciences/themes/global-ethics-observatory/ (accessed 3 August 2015).

34 European Commission: International Dialogue on Bioethics, February 2009: www.comitedebioetica.es/documentacion/docs/national_ethics_councils.pdf (accessed 3 August 2015).

35 Global Summit of National Bioethics Advisory Bodies: www.who.int/ethics/globalsummit/en/ (accessed 3 August 2015).

36 Henk ten Have (2006) The activities of UNESCO in the area of ethics. *Kennedy Institute of Ethics Journal* 16(4): 333–351; Henk ten Have (2008) UNESCO's Ethics Education Programme. *Journal of Medical Ethics* 34(1): 57–59; Henk ten Have, Christophe Dikenou and Dafna Feinholz (2011) Assisting countries in establishing National Bioethics Committees: UNESCO's Assisting Bioethics Committee project. *Cambridge Quarterly of Healthcare Ethics* 20(3): 1–9.

11

GLOBAL PRACTICES AND BIOETHICS

This chapter will examine the question of how global practices are constituted and transformed. This is not simply a matter of applying ethical frameworks or implementing governance mechanisms. Practices are formed and transformed through interaction between global and local determinants. Rather than 'complying' with rules, regulations and rights, they are changing within the dialectics between these determinants. The major driving forces in these dialectics are social movements and NGOs, civil societies and media. Global bioethics directs these forces not towards individual actors but towards system issues, appealing to principles such as solidarity, justice, vulnerability and protection of future generations.

Practices

A practice is a set of activities governed by collectively shared rules. It combines normative views, theoretical knowledge and activities. This notion of practice is not opposed to theory, assuming that one first has to possess knowledge before it can be used, or, like in ethics, first identify the principles and then apply them. In reality, knowing and acting go together. Practices emerge because they focus on particular problems, and specify them with particular concepts; this specification commends what to do. Procedures and acts are guided by the values embedded in the practice. For example, when the risk of exploitation of research subjects, especially in developing countries, is problematic, the concept of vulnerability helps to clarify the problem and to indicate a solution. If the value of individual autonomy is fundamental to the practice, vulnerability is regarded as a deficit or weakness of autonomy; the main actions should focus on protection of the subjects and improvement of informed consent so that they will be able to protect their self-interest. However, if the value of justice is fundamental to the practice, vulnerability is regarded as the outcome of unequal social and economic conditions in which subjects are living. Actions should be performed to reduce dependency and inequality.

Practice as a 'form of life' that connects theoretical knowledge, activities and values is a useful notion for global bioethics. One reason is that values and moral ideals are embodied in a practice. Ethics is not added from the outside. Normative aspects are inseparable from the cognitive and operational dimensions of practices. In other words, what is done is influenced by what one knows and finds valuable, and what is valued is determined by how problems are conceptualized and addressed. Practices are furthermore collective and shared. One individual does not make a practice. Practices are not individual creations but common and cooperative activities; they are public by nature. Although they influence individual values, they are first of all the expression of shared values. Finally, practices are not isolated; they are always connected and confronted with other practices. They continuously change in response to changes in the surrounding 'world'. But changes can take place in various ways, through concepts, actions and values.

Present-day healthcare is a network of practices. The Danish philosopher Uffe Jensen has distinguished three practices in modern healthcare: the disease-orientated, situation-orientated and community-orientated practice.[1] The first practice is the dominant one. Here the basic problem is: How should the patient be treated? The fundamental concept is 'disease', i.e. the entity that causes organic dysfunction. Typical procedures aim at diagnosing diseases. If a disease is identified, specific treatment will be provided, preferably with the goal of cure. The situation-orientated practice emerged because many complaints and symptoms cannot be related to diseases. They have more to do with the particular life situations of individuals. Here the basic concept is 'illness'. Activities are not aimed at treatment but at understanding and teaching individuals to cope with their life situations. The community-orientated practice is concerned with the health of populations and communities rather than with individual health or disease. Its theoretical framework assumes that disease and illness are caused by social conditions. The basic concept therefore is 'sickness'. Interventions should aim at altering social and economic conditions so that the sources of problems are eliminated and future diseases prevented.

From the beginning, mainstream bioethics has been concentrating on the frictions and controversies between these practices. The example in Chapter 1 of the amputations during the Haiti earthquake illustrate that the focus on saving lives may conflict with the autonomy of patients and the social circumstances in which they continue to live. The other example of Tonga shows that collecting genetic data is promoted in a disease-orientated practice but conflicts with a community-orientated practice since genetic information can have serious social repercussions. The three practices continue to be relevant, also at a global level. But they are no longer sufficient to explain bioethical challenges. Dealing with global problems demands that the context of healthcare should be taken into account.

What Jensen did not identify are the healthcare practices that have emerged since the 1980s under the influence of neoliberal ideology. Nowadays, in most countries healthcare is dominated by market-orientated practices. The horizon in which bioethical problems emerge has become different from that of mainstream bioethics. This is due to mobility and interdependence as the characteristics of globalization. These two features however, are not equally balanced across the globe. In reality, there is asymmetry, inequality and exclusion. While the ethical problems confronting mainstream bioethics are associated with the power of science and technology, as well as professional power, the problems of global bioethics are related to economic and political power. That means that the source of global bioethical problems is different. Neoliberal globalization promotes a value system emphasizing rational choice, individual freedom, competition, personal responsibility and self-interest. Changing these market-orientated practices will require scrutiny and criticism of the underlying ideological framework.

Global practices

Healthcare practices across the world are similar in the sense that similar medical interventions, technologies and scientific knowledge are applied everywhere. At the same time, they are different since the context of application varies; costs are not the same, insurance systems differ, as well as cultural, political, legal and ethical determinants. Similarity and difference explain global phenomena such as health tourism, tissue trafficking, humanitarian aid and professional migration. Patients travel to other countries with the expectation of receiving the same medical care as in their own country but within another context, faster and with lower costs. Sometimes they make the journey to receive interventions that are not possible at home. Market-orientated practices at local levels can therefore differ. They are not equally developed everywhere. Commercial surrogate motherhood, for example, has been banned in China since 1994, while it is flourishing in India and Thailand. Health tourism was particularly promoted in South-East Asia as a response to the Asian financial crisis in the late 1990s (as discussed in Chapter 5). The constitution of global practices was not a coincidence but the result of deliberate economic and political decisions. Global practices are formed through a dialectic interaction of global and local determinants. This mutual influence implies that within the same global context, local manifestations of global practices are not the same.

How do global practices change? This is an important question since many will assume that the power of bioethics to change existing and ubiquitous global processes is minimal. How can abstract ethical discourse transform global practices? Practices are formed in dialectic interactions between global setting and local manifestations, as well as in common engagement on the basis of shared valued. These same two processes are vital for their transformation. However, these are not stable processes. Market-orientated practices are not the only ones. They are continuously confronted with other practices with different values, not only at the local level but also increasingly at the global level. Since values are embedded in a specific practice, they are often not discussed within the practice itself; since the practice is the local manifestation of a global practice, confrontations with other value systems are unavoidable; in these contestations other values are highlighted. The practice of commercial surrogate motherhood in Thailand is an example.

BABY GAMMY

Pattharamon Janbua has been surrogate mother for an Australian couple. When she gave birth to twins, the commissioning parents took one baby to Australia and left the other who was diagnosed with Down's syndrome and congenital heart disease behind. Six months later Janbua went to a Thai newspaper. She was no longer able to pay for the medical services needed for baby Gammy who also had a lung infection. The story was quickly picked up by international media in July 2014. The Thai military government fast-tracked legislation prohibiting paid surrogacy. In February 2015 laws were adopted to prohibit all paid surrogacy, to ban commercial surrogacy for foreigners, and to interdict mediating agencies.[2]

This international surrogacy scandal was not the first one. Since India, in 2013, tightened the rules, requesting special visas for foreigners commissioning surrogacy, Thailand has become the 'womb of Asia'. Top fertility clinics were offering the service. Although the Medical Council of Thailand had officially banned commercial surrogacy in 2011, there was no enforcement. It is not clear how the new legislation will make a change. Several clinics and agencies have moved to Nepal. This became evident when devastating earthquakes in April and May 2015 killed an estimated 8,000 people. Airplanes repatriated Israeli citizens, including 26 babies born to surrogate mothers in Nepal. Another 100 surrogate mothers with babies for single and same-sex Israelis remained in the ruins of Kathmandu. Domestic legislation will therefore be insufficient for global practices.

The Gammy case illustrates how practices can be influenced. First, it shows the importance of the media to connect local and global debates. The surrogate mother brought the case to a national journal but the message was disseminated in the international press. It quickly mobilized global civil society, putting pressure on the Thai government. The Australian government was embarrassed when it was detected that the Australian father had been in prison for accusations of sexual child abuse. The case also elicited a humanitarian movement. An Australian charity collected donations for the treatment of Gammy. In January 2015, baby Gammy was granted Australian citizenship.

The outcry over the case furthermore intensified the ethical debate. Commercial surrogacy is a global practice. But it thrives because of significant local differences. All states in Australia have prohibited commercial surrogacy; only a few states prohibit travelling to other countries to engage in surrogacy. These differences are used as an argument for international regulation. It is hypocritical to outlaw the practice in your own country and to permit citizens to go to another country to use the prohibited services. Another argument for regulation is that commercial surrogacy has now become more frequent than inter-country adoption. The practice of adoption has diminished because of human rights concerns, especially in regard to exploitation of women in low-income countries and concerns over the interests of the child. Similar concerns exist in regard to surrogacy. Ethical analysis should consider the interests of the baby, the surrogate mother, and the intending parents. In reality, however, the focus is primarily on the rights of commissioning parents, often assisted by specialized lawyers. Furthermore, there are ethical concerns about the broader context. Using notions such as vulnerability and exploitation it is argued that surrogate mothers do not have a real choice. Usually, like Janbua, they are poor, in debt, uneducated, and desperately in need of money. In this market-orientated practice, the surrogate is regarded as a worker or a 'carrier' who delivers a service for a fee. The baby is the product; if the baby is not healthy, the commissioning parents might request a refund for 'damaged goods'. Most parents are wealthy citizens from Western countries. Some have called this unequal transaction 'biological colonialism'.[3] Reproductive tourism, and health tourism in general, reinforces inequities. It helps to expand an unjust healthcare system: advanced specialist care available for 'tourists' and wealthy citizens, with basic care lacking for the majority of the population. The ethical principle of global justice is used to argue that more powerful and wealthier people have greater responsibilities when they use existing inequalities for their benefit. Engaging in commercial surrogacy is not a mutual transaction between two equal parties.

Changing practices

The case of baby Gammy and its global impact has instigated changes in the local practice of commercial surrogacy in Thailand but at the same time questioned global practices and accelerated initiatives for global regulation. The case shows that global practices are not stable and static but can change. What are the mechanisms of change?

Focus on lack of compliance

In global bioethics it is commonly assumed that the best way to influence and change practices is by developing and implementing global standards. When national governments are confronted with ethical challenges, their response is to introduce or strengthen regulation and legislation. The same response is taken at the global level: first, draft and adopt a normative instrument (preferably a Convention, otherwise a Declaration) so that there is agreement on the ethical principles that should guide global practices; second, create institutional arrangements that translate and enforce these principles within local contexts; this is essentially the purpose of global governance, as discussed in previous chapters; third, applying these principles, practices will transform and conform to the global framework.

This assumption should be criticized. In many areas, such as human rights, environment, development and healthcare, there is not a lack of normative frameworks but the main problem is that such frameworks are not implemented. It is possible to articulate ethical aspirations, but often impossible to put them into practice. This is the fifth gap in global governance: compliance. In international law, for example, there is limited enforcement of human rights, and no clarity about the responsibility to monitor commitments. In regard to human rights treaties, ratified by states, non-compliance with treaty obligations appears to be more common than compliance. The same weakness exists in global bioethics. The member states of UNESCO refused to mention any follow-up mechanisms in the UDBHR. They certainly did not like to have reporting duties. Some states even objected to the term 'implementation'. So it is not clear how the principles that have been adopted are translated into practices. This explains why international organizations have introduced a 'normative pause': no further development of normative instruments but first focus on the application of existing frameworks.

Recent research on how and why international law works shows that there is little correlation between ratification of human rights law and actual practices of respect for human rights.[4] At the same time there is not a lack of mechanisms for implementation in this area: oversight bodies, monitoring, reporting, special rapporteurs, periodic review of countries, international courts and tribunals. But at the global level (in distinction to the national level) there is no authority to make enforcement effective. It is up to states whether they wish to apply human rights in their territory, even if there is a substantial body of supra-territorial legislation. In global bioethics, such implementation mechanisms are completely absent. The UDBHR is unanimously adopted but its principles are ignored in a number of states; some obviously have no intention of doing anything in bioethics. What, therefore, is the practical importance of global frameworks?

Commitment is not compliance

There is also another point. When countries adopt a Declaration such as the UDBHR, they are fully aware that it is a non-binding normative instrument. Its adoption expresses a moral commitment. There can be many reasons for such adoption that have nothing to do with the intention to implement the document. International legal documents do not only have an instrumental role (creating a normative framework in order to address specific problems) but also an expressive role (making a statement on the position of the country). In 'declaring' global bioethical principles, states clarify what is acceptable in healthcare and medical research. They take a position concerning the principles that should guide international cooperation among civilized nations in these areas. These instrumental and expressive roles are not necessarily connected. Experiences with human rights treaties show that when there is minimal monitoring and enforcement the two roles are disconnected. In global bioethics, it seems easy to express a commitment as long as there is almost no monitoring of the effects of the position taken.

Globalization from below

The main lesson from human rights studies for global bioethics is that interpreting the lack of adherence to ethical principles in practical settings as primarily a compliance problem is wrong. It takes for granted that processes of globalization materialize in local contexts from above, and that states are the main actors. As argued in Chapter 9, many non-state actors are nowadays involved in globalization. There is intensive interaction between global and local values. Globalization is therefore not a one-sided influence but is operating within many diverse contexts. This view of 'globalization from below' is also in accordance with the notion of practice, used in this chapter. Human activities do not simply change because principles are imposed or theories are applied. Introducing and declaring a global framework will not in itself effectuate a change in practices. What is necessary for change is localization of implementation.

TWO PERSPECTIVES ON IMPLEMENTATION

1   Diffusion of transnational principles adopted by international organizations;
    –   implementation = 'compliance';
    –   there is a dichotomy between universal and local principles;
    –   this view requires teaching, awareness-raising and capacity-building by international agents.
2   Reinterpretation and construction of transnational principles to make them congruent with local practices and values;
    –   implementation = 'localization': a dynamic process of building convergence between global principles and local practices;
    –   there are reciprocal interactions between global and local principles;
    –   this view requires empowerment of domestic agents; deliberation, involvement, participation by local stakeholders.

Domestication

Improvements in human rights practices are more often the result of efforts of grassroots movements than accomplishment of global institutions. The institutions can create norms, but implementation is decentralized and domestic.[5] Actors and networks from civil society take up a cause (for example, access to healthcare), organize themselves, engage in contestation and struggle, and connect with similar movements and networks in other countries. They develop a practice around the right to health, but the practice is not simply the application of this right. Activities need to be adapted to the local circumstances and values, and can therefore be more successful in one setting (for example, South Africa) than in another. In this view, practices are constructed through collective labour within a specific context.

Implementation of global principles and values is therefore 'domestication'; they need to be transformed and internalized into domestic systems and local contexts. Usually, this is not done by governments but by non-governmental organizations and cooperating individuals.

Another aspect of localization of implementation is collective agency. Human rights are not just legal ideas or abstract principles but activities and processes of doing them and making them a reality. For bioethical principles it is important how they are conceived but even more how they can be realized; they require ethical-political work. The principles demand collective labour to convert moral asymmetry into socio-political symmetry. Sociologist Fuyuki Kurasawa has elaborated this view with the example of global justice.[6] He shows how struggling against global injustices produces transnational practices of bearing witness, forgiveness, foresight, aid and solidarity. The practice of bearing witness is fundamental for producing justice. It gives voice to abuses and structural violence, providing testimony of injustices and overcoming silence, incomprehension and indifference. It clears the way for the other practices of forgiveness, foresight (preventing harm) and humanitarian assistance. Finally, the social labour in response to injustice produces practices of solidarity. This requires the fostering of relationships across borders and growing global consciousness.

Practices will change if they localize global ethical frameworks through domestication and collective agency. These mechanisms of implementation of global principles at local levels will be successful under two conditions: dialogue and publicness. Dialogue is necessary to create the intercultural space within which diversity can be recognized and commonalities identified. This is not only information exchange but also sharing of experiences, approaches and challenges, forging political bonds, building alternative visions and participating in activities. Dialogical processes are facilitated by the growing global consciousness, and will further contribute to intensifying this consciousness. They create spaces of 'in-betweenness', envisioning the world no longer as a territorial location but as a condition for human existence. The second condition is that the practices are public. They should be spaces for participation and involvement of a wide variety of actors. They should encourage open debate and deliberation. In this way they can focus on commonalities among heterogeneous participants, so that the circle of moral concerns can further expand.

Global bioethics practices

The notion of practice discussed so far has consequences for our understanding of global bioethics. Like human rights cannot be abstracted from practices within specific settings, global ethical principles cannot be separated from their applications. The principles are necessary because they provide, what has been called in Chapter 6, the horizon of global bioethics. They point out that in order to address global problems we need a broader view of the individual person and richer concepts of society, relatedness, cooperation, responsibility and global commons than in mainstream bioethics. But outlining this horizon is not enough. Global bioethics practices require combining discourse with action. Principles cannot be articulated without a wide repertoire of activities: exposure and disclosure of problems and cases, awareness raising, analysis and critical examination of structural factors that underlie injustices, advancing arguments, pressuring important stakeholders, lobbying policy-makers, blaming and shaming. With this repertoire global bioethics aims to change practices so that they become more congruent with global ethical principles.

How are practices changing under the influence of ethical principles?[7] A similar question is asked in international law: how are human rights enforced? The sceptical answer is: they are not. Human rights law has limited enforcement mechanisms; it is up to states if they want to enforce them. Some scholars even doubt whether human rights practices in many states have changed at all. This view is reflected in global bioethics; ethical discourse is globalized but whether it leads to global practices depends on the local circumstances, and not on the principles or the discourse endorsing them. Other human rights scholars present a positive answer. They argue that views of compliance are often too simple. Practices are changing in conformity to principles in a long-term process. First, there is a long phase of interaction; principles are declared, defined, debated and negotiated. Second, principles need to be interpreted; they are often indeterminate. Principles are general and not defined; interpretation and specification are required to make them applicable in specific situations. Third, principles are internalized so that they become internal normative imperatives. The final phase is what has been called 'domestication'; global principles become incorporated in domestic systems (Figure 11.1).

This positive view is attractive for global bioethics. One reason is that it explains how practices are changing. Bioethical principles are not implemented in horizontal interaction between states that have adopted them. Principles are influencing practices because a range of non-state actors are discussing, interpreting and internalizing them. 'Domestication' does not so much mean that the government makes legislation but that institutions, organizations and citizens integrate principles into their value system. The other reason is that this view clarifies why practices become more congruent to principles. Compliance is not a matter of coercion. Principles are applied in practices because people are persuaded that this is the best

---

How are principles impacting on practices?

- power ——————————————→ coercion and sanctions
- self-interest ———————————→ rational choice, incentives
- normative considerations ———→ persuasion
  1. Interaction
  2. Interpretation
  3. Internalization: 'domestication'

FIGURE 11.1 How are principles impacting on practices?

way to proceed. The role of normative considerations is therefore emphasized, presenting a critique of two common explanations of compliance: power and self-interest. The first explanation argues that states comply with international law because they are forced by other states; doctors respect patient rights since they are obliged by the law and under scrutiny of patients' movements. The second explanation assumes that states and people chose to apply principles based on a rational calculation of self-interest. Both explanations do not account for normative motivations. They assume that practices are changing because of instrumental reasons, not because actors feel morally obliged to apply specific principles. As discussed in Chapter 8, management of the commons for a long time was interpreted with a similar false dilemma: the only choice is between the rational self-interest of the market and the authoritarian intervention of the state. Extensive research, however, showed that there is often responsible management of commons, based on shared values and a common sense of normative obligations (especially to future generations). The same goes for global practices. They may change, even if they are expensive or not congruent with the interests of states and individual policy-makers. They change because they are the right thing to do. The increased interest in global health can only partly be explained by self-interest. Particularly HIV/AIDS moved from being regarded as an issue of foreign aid to a moral calling.

A WORK OF MERCY

Billions of dollars have been made available for universal access to antiretroviral drugs. States engaged in expensive commitments not because of economic interests or security reasons but on the basis of moral motivations. When President Bush, in his 2003 State of the Union, launched the President's Emergency Plan for AIDS Relief (PEPFAR), he referred to the calling of the nation to make the world better. In an age of miraculous medicine, nobody should die because medicines are not available. The new relief plan will be a 'work of mercy': 'This comprehensive plan will prevent 7 million new AIDS infections, treat at least 2 million people with life-extending drugs and provide humane care for millions of people suffering from AIDS and for children orphaned by AIDS. I ask the Congress to commit $15 billion over the next five years, including nearly $10 billion in new money, to turn the tide against AIDS in the most afflicted nations of Africa and the Caribbean.'[8]

Driving forces for change

Global bioethics as practice is more than the application of theory or implementation of principles. It requires a repertoire of activities. Moral considerations can play a significant role in constituting and transforming practices. Although states and influential politicians can take initiatives, more often practices are influenced by a range of actors. More importantly, globalization from below not only refers to a variety of activities and actors but also to 'localization' or 'domestication' of global ideas. Global ethical frameworks are connected to local concerns. This has been called 'resonance'.[9] The challenge is to relate global values to existing local ones. Global principles have influence because they are filtered through domestic values, and on the other hand, domestic organizations can appeal to global principles to make a stronger argument. The right to health, for example, has been articulated at the global level. Countries such as Brazil and South Africa included this right in their constitutions and have specified it within their national health policies. Domestic organizations can then argue for expanding access to medication, and mobilize national and international actors to bring about change, as the example of TAC in South Africa demonstrated. Another example is the proposal for a Core Curriculum in Bioethics developed by UNESCO on the basis of the agreed principles of the UDBHR. It offers a flexible set of modules for a teaching programme but at the same time emphasizes that any programme should have minimum content and a basic number of teaching hours. This global proposal can be adapted by ethics teachers in specific countries, but they are able to convince their deans that setting up such a programme requires a core commitment in terms of time, resources and programming, not because it is their own preference but a recommendation of an international organization in the field of education.

If global bioethics can initiate changes, a further question is who drives these changes. Previous chapters have mentioned many of them by way of examples. Here, the role of three driving forces will be highlighted: social movements and NGOs, civil society, and media.

Social movements and NGOs

Social movements are 'organizations, groups of people and individuals, who act together to bring about transformation of society'.[10] They use a broad repertoire of activities, from media campaigns to public protest, boycotts, civil disobedience, demonstrations and legal action, but they emphasize non-violence. NGOs are more organized and institutional; they are voluntary, non-profit organizations that are value-driven; they gather around a specific cause (human rights for Amnesty International, environmental protection for Greenpeace, and humanitarian assistance for MSF). There are many differences between NGOs (in how they are organized and how they operate). In general, international NGOs have two types of activities: advocacy (lobbying, publicity, mobilizing public support, and campaigning) and service provision (emergency relief or healthcare). However, at the grassroots level NGOs are community-based; their members are united because they share a common cause, they interact on the basis of cooperation and trust, and are actively engaged not so much in advocacy or service but in social change.

At the global level, social movements and NGOs, although differences are noticeable, have three common features.[11] First, they are transnational networks, especially in areas such as human rights, environment and women's rights. These networks are voluntary, horizontal and reciprocal. They are based on self-organization. Historic examples are movements to abolish slavery, colonization, apartheid and dictatorships. More recently, the focus has been on global health and medical research. Second, they are organized around shared values and principled ideas. They bring people together on the basis of a common interpretation of reality and new visions of the world. Their global identity is forged on the view that the major problems of today are global and that they are caused by neoliberal globalization. This common perspective creates a platform for identification and solidarity across borders. Third, they engage in various forms of activism. This has two aspects. One is the challenge to existing practices. Social movements and NGOs have emerged because they seek change, for example better treatment of animals, increasing access to treatment, improving care for ill people. Social movements, more than NGOs, also aim at structural change; they want to address the root causes of global problems. They demonstrate what has been called the 'capacity to aspire' in Chapter 6: imagining possibilities of different worlds rather than merely probabilities. The second aspect of activism is collective action. Changes cannot be effectuated by individuals but require cooperation and mutual commitment. Action should be rooted in everyday practice including and giving voice to all people concerned. TAC united marginalized people around a common interest and moral concern; most of its membership was poor, black people without access to healthcare. The previous example of self-organizing homeless people in Mumbai (in Chapter 6) illustrates these aspects. Grassroots activism is connected with cross-national cosmopolitanism, building horizontal as well as vertical solidarities between people who are marginalized in processes of globalization. Their social movement engaged in resistance, reform, restoration and transformation of collective social life.

Social movements and NGOs can be effective in changing practices. They demonstrate what has been called 'the power of the powerless'.[12] TAC transformed the access to antiretrovirals for AIDS patients. The social movement in the Bolivian city of Cochabamba reversed the privatization of water supplies and later energized the Bolivian government to propose access to water as a human right (Chapter 8). A broad coalition of advocacy groups appealed to the Supreme Court of India to reject the patent on cancer drug Glivec, which the Court did in April 2013. However, not all NGOs are influential. Effectiveness does not only depend on ideas and values but also on organizational structure. NGOs have an important role as sources of information that is factual (and different from other, more partisan sources) and also testimonial; they give voice to victims and vulnerable stakeholders. With information provided, the debate can be structured in a specific way, and the agenda for the discussion can be set. NGOs can furthermore put pressure on actors to change behaviour; they apply moral leverage, for example, by using the media to mobilize shame.

The most effective NGOs in human rights operate with centralized proposal and enforcement powers and decentralized agenda implementation. They do not simply appeal to global principles but acknowledge local differences in application and they integrate contextual knowledge in the global framework.

INFLUENCE OF ADVOCACY NETWORKS

Types of network influence:

'(1) issue creation and agenda setting;
(2) influence on discursive positions of states and international organizations;
(3) influence on institutional procedures;
(4) influence on policy change in 'target actors' which may be states, international organizations like the World Bank, or private actors ...,
and (5) influence on state behavior.'[13]

Social movements and NGOs are nowadays under critique.[14] First, they are sometimes more powerful than states, especially in the developed world. With larger budgets than the health ministries, they can distort priorities in healthcare, focusing for example on diseases that do not have the biggest impact on the disease burden of a country. They are also generally criticized for not being transparent and accountable. International organizations, though bureaucratic, have at least clear mechanisms of decision-making and accountability. Another critique is that the multitude of NGOs is often competing; they use media coverage to create compassion and generate donations. Finally, NGOs are increasingly co-opted by the actors they are challenging. Instead of resisting and providing alternatives to neoliberalism, many NGOs have adopted the same neoliberal market language. Through partnering with businesses they intend to make consumers more ethical but avoid criticizing the underlying inequalities. By offering micro-solutions that do not challenge the domination of neoliberalism, activism is effectively pacified. Examples abound. Environmental activist organizations are funded by commercial enterprises that pollute the environment. Mental Health America, a NGO advocating for mental health as a fundamental social justice issue, receives three-quarters of its budget from medical firms. The International Alliance of Patients' Organizations was founded and is funded by a consortium of 30 major companies. The sources of funding are not published.

DISEASE MONGERING AND ADVOCACY GROUPS

Defining problems in medical terms (as illness or disorder) and using medical interventions to treat them is known as 'medicalization'. Hyperactivity, shyness, anxiety, child abuse and menopause are transformed into new medical categories. Today, this process is driven by commercial and market interests. Fabricating new diseases will create new markets for existing drugs. Pharmaceutical companies often seek cooperation with patient advocacy groups to promote their drugs. Ritalin for ADHD was approved for use in children since the 1970s. Industry started to promote its use in adults. It funded the advocacy group Children and Adults with Attention Deficit and Hyperactivity Disorder that strongly advocated the treatment of 'adult ADHD'.[15]

Civil society

The view of implementation from below implies that local actors play an important role in the diffusion of global principles. They build congruence ('resonance') between global principles and existing local frameworks through the dynamic process of 'domestication'. The role of individual citizens and groups of citizens is expressed in the concept of 'civil society'. Active citizenship means that individual citizens can unite and take initiatives. The change from medical ethics to bioethics in the 1960s and 1970s (Chapter 2) was the result of a movement of emancipation among citizens. The medical profession was increasingly criticized; citizens were claiming control over the power of science and technology, and claiming rights as patients. Civil society was mobilized around issues of health, disease, life and death. It obligated the governments and the medical profession to change existing practices.

Nowadays, civil society is no longer restricted to a particular territory. Public debate and political action cross the borders. Citizens in one state can link up with others in other countries, and organize around a common cause or issue. The growing interconnectedness and the emerging sense of global community have created global civil society. This includes social movements and NGOs, discussed above, but is wider since it applies to every citizen. Global civil society is considered as a sphere of interaction between state and market. Especially with the new media it gives room to discourses that are not controlled by governments or commercial forces (even if they try to influence them). It is also a sphere of public conversation and reasoning, of common deliberation and participation, of contestation and conflict. Finally, it is a sphere of public engagement; self-organizing groups of individuals can undertake collective action.

The role of civil society in global bioethics is demonstrated in the debate about vertical and horizontal health interventions. Vertical programmes are preferred by international agencies since they have clear targets and focus on technological solutions. Horizontal programmes focus on health systems. They require grassroots participation; programmes are community based. Without the involvement of civil society basic social and economic needs that produce health problems cannot be addressed. Healthcare services are not discrete interventions but demand a systemic approach, guided by local knowledge. Another example is the Declaration of Istanbul about organ trade. WHO estimates that each year 5–10 per cent of all 70,000 transplanted kidneys are from illegal trafficking. The organs are usually sold by poor vendors in countries such as Pakistan, the Philippines and Moldova. Many countries have adopted legislation to prohibit commercial transplantation. But in most cases, enforcement is difficult or absent. The increasing concern about organ trade has mobilized scientists, policy-makers, health insurance companies and patient organizations. They convened in 2008 and adopted the Declaration of Istanbul. Because kidney transplantation is impossible without the involvement of physicians, professional medical organizations and prestigious surgeons have appealed to public opinion and have put pressure on colleagues in countries to stop cooperating with the kidney trade. The Declaration brought together two groups of advocates of different ethical positions: prohibition of the sale of organs, and regulation of the organ market. Both groups agreed that unregulated commercial organ exchange at global level should not be allowed. The proposed solution is localization. While organ trafficking emerged as a result of globalization of transplantation medicine, it can only be eradicated through de-globalization. Each country should become self-sufficient in organ donations; the shortage of organs in the country needs to be eliminated through donations within that country, whatever the system used.

THE DECLARATION OF ISTANBUL ON ORGAN TRAFFICKING AND TRANSPLANT TOURISM

'Organ trafficking and transplant tourism violate the principles of equity, justice and respect for human dignity and should be prohibited ...

a   Prohibitions on these practices should include a ban on all types of advertising ..., soliciting, or brokering for the purpose of transplant commercialism, organ trafficking, or transplant tourism ...

c   Practices that induce vulnerable individuals or groups (such as illiterate and impoverished persons, undocumented immigrants, prisoners, and political or economic refugees) to become living donors are incompatible with the aim of combating organ trafficking, transplant tourism and transplant commercialism.'[16]

Media

The third driving force to change global bioethics practices is the media – not only traditional media such as newspapers, radio and television but increasingly new social media. The baby Gammy case illustrates the role of the media. In fact, the emergence and development of bioethics was very much promoted by stories and news in the media. The committee to determine who would qualify for kidney dialysis (see Chapter 2) was the subject of a landmark publication in 1962 in *Life*. The scandal of the Tuskegee syphilis study was revealed in the *Washington Star* and the *New York Times* in 1972 after a whistle-blower contacted a reporter. The Karen Ann Quinlan case in the US was a big media event in 1975. A similar string of media attention is now focused on global bioethics. Media frenzy broke out after a university professor uncovered syphilis experiments in Guatemala, carried out in 1946–1948 by the US Public Health Service and sponsored by NIH. In 2010 the government apologized for these unethical experiments. The Trovan case in Nigeria became an international scandal after reports in *The Washington Post* in 2006. In fact, all examples in Chapter 1 have become known through publication in various media around the world.

In bioethics, the role of popular media is often criticized: they simplify, sensationalize, reduce and distort complex issues as sound or print bites. But a more positive view underlines that they have helped to constitute and expand bioethics.[17] Without stories in the media bioethics would have probably never been born and matured. Nowadays, new scientific developments (e.g. stem cell research or face transplantation) are often presented as bioethical issues. Media presentations bring ethical concerns into the public arena. In doing so, they affirm that such concerns are legitimate; they are reasons for public debate and policy-making. At the same time, communicating these concerns articulates dominant values. If people are used without their knowledge as guinea pigs in experiments that are harmful, viewers and readers are not merely outraged but they are acutely aware that informed consent and non-maleficence are important values that need to be defended. This affirmative role of media is particularly important for global bioethics. Media make the local immediately global. They help to further global consciousness and to expand the circle of moral concern. It is important that the media report what is going on in the world. They have more public outreach than bioethics publications. They raise awareness and function as an early warning system or watchdog. The need for information is clear. In a recent US survey 93 per cent of respondents had never heard of the Universal Declaration of Human Rights.[18] But popular media do more than transmit information. They also explore ethical issues, present them in a broader context, and rearrange stories in particular directions so that practices are going to change. When surrogate mother Janbua went to the press, her story was not a neutral report but a complaint, even accusation, about the abandonment of her disabled son. The individual story was located in a global context of inequality and exploitation. Ethics was mobilized to effectuate changes. Especially the new media can be used to publicize causes and to raise support for putting pressure on relevant actors ('blaming and shaming'). The examples of the Global Health Impact Index and the Access to Medicines Index (see Chapter 10) provide publicly accessible information about the efforts of pharmaceutical companies to improve access to medication in developing countries.

In global bioethics popular media raise specific concerns. One is that they often reinforce stereotypes. Africa is presented as a continent of poverty, famine, disease and violence. It is pictured as a reservoir of infection, a dirty place where people consume monkeys and bats.

BUSHMEAT

In August 2014 *Newsweek* featured a cover story that African bushmeat could be a backdoor of Ebola to the United States. It stated that meat from wild animals such as bats and chimpanzees is a delicacy in Africa. According to the story it is also a deadly threat since it can transmit viruses like Ebola. Since tons of African bushmeat are smuggled into the US the country is at risk. *The Washington Post* criticized this story as reinforcing the image of Africans as 'savage animals'. Everybody hunting deer in the US and eating it as venison is consuming bushmeat. The suggestion associates immigrants with disease.[19]

Stories from other countries (e.g. Thailand) tend to convey the message, often implicitly, of rampant corruption, exploitation and lack of regulation. Another concern is that competition for fundraising induces NGOs to 'sell' the suffering of others, or to 'market' feelings of empathy to raise donations for humanitarian assistance. People are portrayed as helpless victims in need of assistance. These images of misery not only reinforce stereotypes but also place anecdotes and individuals in the foreground. Underlying structures that produce vulnerability and injustice are rarely highlighted. Responsibility for suffering is shifted away from states and corporations to individual persons. On the other hand, the viewers and readers of this type of media coverage are equally stereotyped. They are appealed to as saviours; with a few dollars they can keep starving children alive. Humanitarian assistance is a matter of charity or compassion rather than obligation or justice. Again, the suggestion is that immediate needs rather than structural causes should be alleviated. The increasing commercialization of NGOs furthermore appeals to citizens interested in global problems as consumers. The more they buy the products of the commercial partners of an NGO, the more they contribute to the eradication of poverty. The suggestion is that one can change the world by consuming specific merchandise ('ethical' or 'charitable' shopping when a company donates an item for each one bought). Change is the result of individual efforts (riding a bike against climate change, or running a marathon against cancer). The individual consumer does not have to participate in collective action or to make significant changes in lifestyle. Systemic problems are approached with micro-solutions. The market is the primary mechanism of change rather than the underlying problem.

Normative tools for change

Global practices are changing through processes of localization. Global ethical frameworks are not simply applied or rejected but 'domesticated'. Global practices are the result of dialectic interaction between the global domain where principles are formulated, declared and disseminated by international organizations, and the local contexts where principles are diffused since they are shaped and integrated into particular conditions. Global principles are more often than not contested because they are frequently in tension with existing practices. Contestation means intensive interactions between the global and the local. It also means that global principles need to be interpreted so that they will fit to the particular circumstances. Localization builds what earlier has been called 'convergence' (Chapter 4). The interaction of global and local not only emphasizes and reiterates differences but also uncovers areas of agreement and discloses commonly shared values. Global bioethical discourse provides the concepts to facilitate the dialectical interaction, interpretation and internalization of principles into practices. This ethical discourse will be discussed in the next chapter. But before this, the question can be asked: How have normative concepts had an impact on global practices? The notion of practice used in this chapter assumes that normative views and values are already embedded in practices. Normativity is not an add-on but constitutive for practices. How then can normative concepts lead to changing practices?

Horizon

In earlier chapters it is argued that global bioethics expands the perspective of mainstream bioethics. It provides a broader background in which phenomena are interpreted and perceived as global problems. The term 'horizon' has been used to explain this broader perspective. Global bioethics introduces different language and conceptual viewpoints. It has a focus on connectedness and interdependency. It also has a focus on the conditioning powers that produce inequality and injustice (such as the regime of patent rules). Global bioethics discourse therefore shifts the perspective from the individual to the common. This shift opens up other perspectives as alternatives to the dominant one. For example, HIV/AIDS is usually regarded as a medical challenge. But it can also be interpreted as a human rights issue, a justice issue, a security issue, or an issue of intellectual property rights. Health, as discussed in the previous chapter, can be considered as a global common good, a human right or a tradable commodity. Each interpretation has different consequences and leads to different approaches and solutions.

Framing

Social scientists have pointed out the importance of framing.[20] Frames are schemes of interpretation. They have two characteristics. Like practices, they are not individual but common accomplishments. They help us to make sense of what is happening; they create community because they provide meaning by structuring and organizing experiences. Secondly, they facilitate involvement so that common activities will be possible. Frames not only explain how phenomena are produced but also what responses and solutions will be possible. First of all, frames define problems; they highlight certain aspects as most relevant and problematic within a specific context. They also diagnose causes, identifying what has created the problem. Next, they evaluate the problem and its causes, so that a moral judgement is provided. Finally, they recommend a treatment or suggest remedies. The example of PEPFAR shows how the framing of HIV/AIDS relief as a religious obligation and as part of the American moral tradition has mobilized enormous funds for assistance. The importance of framing is also illustrated in the case of female genital mutilation (see Chapter 4).

FEMALE GENITAL MUTILATION (FGM)

Early campaigns to eradicate FGM in Kenya failed. It was regarded by the population as a traditional cultural practice. Efforts to suppress this practice symbolized colonialism, the imposition of Western values upon traditional culture. The usual name, 'female circumcision', also suggested that like male circumcision it was not really risky and harmful. In the 1980s, the practice was framed as violation of human rights, and renamed as 'mutilation'. The new frame subsumed the practice in a broader category (violence against women and child abuse) that could be supported by a larger range of actors and populations.

Three different frames are applied to the practice of FGM: cultural diversity, human rights, and health. The difference is reflected in the names: female circumcision, female genital mutilation, or female genital cutting. In all cases, the procedures are not different: partial or total removal of the external female genitalia. What differs is the interpretation as a problem and the normative evaluation. Female circumcision is a practice that has existed for centuries in a limited number of countries in Africa and the Middle East. In these countries it is a rite of initiation for female members of society; it is an act of purity and a source of cultural identity. The implication is that it should be respected as a cultural tradition. In the 1970s this framing became increasingly contested. From a human rights perspective, the practice was regarded as a violation of women's rights and discrimination of women. Since it is most commonly performed on girls between 4 and 10 years of age, it is also a violation of the rights of children. This framing of the problem encouraged legal action. More and more countries prohibited female circumcision. However, legislation often had little effect. Against this background, another frame emerged, emphasizing women's health rather than women's rights. More data became available about the short-term and long-term effects on health. It was argued that removal of anatomical structures without medical necessity is mutilation, so that the name of the practice should change. This perception of the problem generates a solution: eradication. In a health frame, FGM is like an epidemic disease. Nowadays, 125 million women and girls have undergone FGM, and more than 3 million girls each year are 'at risk'. As a health problem, FGM is now under the mandate of WHO. However, when the UN asked WHO to study the practice in 1958, the organization refused because FGM was regarded as a cultural issue.

Successful frames

The example of FGM illustrates the usefulness of framing for changing practices. First, it provides a conceptual platform for building alliances. The human rights and health frames unite NGOs and activists, medical professionals, teachers, social workers and religious leaders. Especially younger generations of women are campaigning against the practice. Several media have joined these campaigns. The UN has declared 6 February as the International Day of Zero Tolerance for Female Genital Mutilation/Cutting. Second, framing facilitates matching with local values, and thus promotes domestication. The number of local NGOs campaigning against FGM has increased rapidly. The majority of African countries where the practice is prevalent have now outlawed FGM. Particularly, the health frame is useful for local activists. Pointing out the health effects does not imply a moral judgement on tradition or culture, but appeals to commonly shared concerns. At the same time, it has become clear that FGM is a global problem, not merely a problem of specific countries. Due to immigration, Western countries have a growing population of women and girls subjected to FGM. Third, framing helps to make a balanced assessment of a practice. There are always different frames or even counter-frames so that normative evaluations have to be weighted. The health frame seems the most powerful now. Appeals to cultural diversity and accusations of bioethical imperialism are less convincing with growing evidence and awareness of harmful effects. Health is a common value; in this frame there are no benefits, only harms. Legal approaches based on the rights frame are necessary but ineffective, as long as they do not address systemic determinants of the practice in culture and society.

The UN General Assembly adopted in December 2012 a resolution calling for the worldwide elimination of FGM.[21] It was the first time that the organization explicitly supported a ban. The practice is in decline in several countries. However, it will not be easy to change a long-standing practice. A frequently mentioned success story is the eradication of the practice of foot binding in China which succeeded in the early twentieth century after almost 200 years of campaigning. But not all framing is successful. The example in Chapter 10 of transgenic animals shows that the frame of intrinsic value of animals was not successful in competition with the frame of scientific progress and the frame of commercial opportunity.

The success of framing is determined by three factors. The first factor, as mentioned above, is 'resonance'. Frames that create a broad alliance of actors, facilitate a balanced assessment and are connected with the local context will be more successful. They relate global principles to contextual values. The second factor is the normative claims of the frame. Frames that emphasize moral concerns that transcend the specific context and refer to common humanity are more appealing than frames that are less inclusive. Particularly, accentuating bodily harm to the vulnerable, and injustice have been powerful normative ideas in transforming the nature of debates and in shaping policies.[22] The third factor is a systemic approach. The practice of FGM, for example, is affecting the health and human rights of individual girls and women but the health and human rights frames should be careful to locate the determinants of the practice in social and cultural traditions, not in individual persons. Influencing these traditions will require a long-term common effort. Framing an issue in terms of human rights is necessary but it is only a first step in changing practices. A similar shift in attention from individuals to systems is noticeable in other areas, for example end of life care. In the US, after 40 years of efforts to improve end of life care, there is still a big gap between theory and practice. Although patients' rights have been established and clear ethical guidelines promulgated, patient preferences at the end of life are often not followed. Securing individual rights is important but not sufficient to change practices. This is also the result of relative neglect of social and economic rights such as the right to health, which implies the obligations of governments and communities to provide health to citizens. Attention is now more focused on the healthcare system, especially its institutions, organizations and finance, and on possibilities for systemic reform.[23]

Another example is the area of disaster relief. Humanitarian aid is traditionally aimed at addressing individual needs; victims' lives have to be saved. Disasters are natural events. The innocent victims call for sympathy, solidarity and generosity. The frame of vulnerability, however, has introduced a broader perspective. Many disasters are in fact man-made, the result of violence, negligence and exploitation. The focus should therefore be on the conditions that have made individuals vulnerable. The new language of humanitarianism is based on the idea of common humanity and is the expression of cosmopolitanism; it shows that the circle of moral concern is expanding. But in order to have a longer-term impact it must move beyond the moral imperative of rescuing and protecting individual human lives and must address the normative concerns of justice. Many humanitarian agencies are now shifting their attention from emergency and temporary assistance to root causes such as poverty and violence.[24]

One of the most successful activist movements has been the AIDS community. They succeeded in transforming the existing regime of access to essential medicines.[25] But this accomplishment came only after a transnational business network had successfully advocated the globalization of intellectual property rights, realized in the 1994 TRIPS Agreement. Before the 1980s, patents were regarded as privileges and monopolies, impediments to free trade. The business network changed this perception by arguing that piracy and counterfeiting were undermining the economic competitiveness of the US. Patents were in fact essential for innovation, free trade and economic growth. This framing was also normative: theft can never be justified. The TRIPS Agreement was a victory for business interests. The HIV/AIDS pandemic made this new policy framework problematic. Various social movements were initially concerned with individual behaviour and stigmatization of categories of people but moved from emphasizing individual rights to socio-economic rights, particularly since more effective treatments became available after 1996. A transnational network of NGOs emerged that argued that public health concerns are more important than business interests. IPR protection makes drugs unaffordable for many people in developing countries. The frame of public health enabled the linking of patents and death. The normative message was that life-saving treatment should not depend on the ability to pay but should be universally accessible. The framing also depicted pharmaceutical companies as greedy and immoral: they make astronomical profits at the expense of millions of people dying. The Doha Declaration of 2002 was a victory for the campaigns for access to medication. The framing by NGOs was supported by countries such as Brazil and South Africa that emphasized the right to health. At the same time, the US, as the main supporter of IPR, was discredited when confronted in 2001 with anthrax bioterrorism: the government argued that it would override the patent for the available medication since it was too expensive. Obviously, health is more important than protecting property rights. But if this normative assessment is valid for one government it should be allowed to all others.

Normative entrepreneurs

The emphasis on localization and framing as mechanisms for changing global practices rejects the view that implementation of global ethical frameworks is application of principles and compliance with the frameworks in practical settings. Instead, implementation requires sustained work: building convergence through 'domestication'; dialogue, debate and interaction; and involvement of local stakeholders. This work is not only practical but includes discourse. Persuasion and learning are basic instruments for changing values at the global level. They demonstrate the power of ideas. In this context, the role of so-called 'transnational moral entrepreneurs' is highlighted.[26] They are agents that promote specific principles in the global system, mobilize support and inspire others to accommodate these principles to their own value systems. They can be prominent individuals, epistemic communities or NGOs. Frequently mentioned examples are Henri Dunant who established the International Committee of the Red Cross in 1863, Eleanor Roosevelt who was a driving force in the adoption of the Universal Declaration of Human Rights, Czech dissident and later President Vaclav Havel, and Kofi Annan when he was Secretary-General of the UN, promoting the universality of human rights and humanitarian intervention.

Not only individuals can have moral authority and inspire global community building. An example in bioethics is the National Commission for the Protection of Human Subjects of Biomedical and Behavioral Research. Its Belmont Report issued in 1978 initiated collective action in the field of research ethics, promoting principles, mobilizing support and inspiring legislation and regulation of practices, at first in the United States. The advocated normative approach was put in a larger context so that it could be accepted more broadly. This dynamic was promoted in the 1990s by CIOMS that acted as global normative entrepreneur. In global bioethics, Doctors without Borders is another example. When it received the Nobel Peace Prize in 1999, the award money was used to start the Campaign for Access to Essential Medicines to increase access to medication in developing countries. The same entrepreneurial role can be performed by professional organizations. The Transplantation Society and the International Society of Nephrology convened in 2008 the Summit that adopted the Declaration of Istanbul on Organ Trafficking and Transplant Tourism.

Collective action

The framing of issues in normative terms in order to influence practices is not an individual affair. Even when normative entrepreneurs operate as catalysts to put an issue on the global agenda, individual action will not have much effect unless popular opinion and political support are mobilized. Frames are common and action-oriented. They bring people together because they share the same understanding of a problem as well as its proposed solution, and they motivate people to engage in collective action. In the recent Ebola epidemic, MSF has acted as agent to elicit a structural response. Epidemic diseases can only be controlled when there is joint action of states, international organizations, NGOs and individuals. Environmental degradation cannot be addressed by individual action and by making 'green' consumer choices. It will require the cooperation of citizens in order to change the institutional arrangements and lifestyles that contribute to deterioration of the environment; it also implies criticizing the responsibilities of governments and corporations for promoting such arrangements and lifestyles. Only collective agency could change the system of apartheid in South Africa or abolish slavery. Action was motivated not by self-interest but by the global normative ideals of justice and equality. It illustrates the main characteristic of collective action: it is not the result of calculations of rational individuals but driven by the pursuit of common goals and the contribution to the common good. It is a realm of activism situated between the interventions of governments and the individual decisions of consumers in the market. Actors are cooperating because they are citizens, not consumers.

Conclusion

In this book an intermediate version of global bioethics is developed that considers global bioethics not as a finished product that can be applied in various circumstances but as a process, an ongoing activity, aimed at convergence between global principles and local practices. This view implies that global bioethics requires intellectual as well as practical work: it is continuous scrutinizing, analysing, debating, exchanging, interpreting, applying, modifying, transforming, negotiating and interacting between the global and the local. This continuous work is possible when moral diversity as well as universality are recognized and taken seriously. The notion of 'interculturality' is used to explain the possibilities for cultivating common ground. Global bioethics as an intercultural process is not only the work of international organizations and agencies but it requires the involvement and engagement of many actors at various levels. Implementation of global principles in practices is not a matter of compliance but of 'domestication': the integration and internalization of principles in local value systems. In this way, global principles are 'localized'. But on the other hand, these local processes feed back into the global framework so that global responses can be formulated to problems of organ trafficking, surrogate motherhood and access to medication. This chapter has discussed how the dialectic interaction between the global and the local constitutes and changes practices. Social movements and NGOs, civil society and media are the driving forces of this interaction. Normative considerations play a major role in these dialectics. They transition and translate principles into practices because they provide arguments for global action. But this again is work, not simple rational deduction and practical application. It demands deliberating, learning, persuading, blaming and shaming. Processes of translation are facilitated by framing. Frames organize experiences and guide action. They mobilize support since they articulate specific values. Framing a global problem as a human rights issue for example is challenging the authority of states over its citizens (freedom from torture or inhuman treatment) but it can also emphasize the responsibility of states for providing basic healthcare (right to health). Frames bring people together and motivate them to act.

Dominant frames in contemporary societies are derived from the neoliberal ideology. These frames are often reflected in mainstream bioethics as argued in Chapter 5. Global bioethics, however, operates with a different horizon. It emphasizes interdependency, interconnectedness, shared values and common perspectives. It therefore can provide alternative frames based on arguments that focus on systemic transformation rather than individual interests. Global principles such as solidarity, justice, vulnerability, social responsibility and protecting future generations have inspired discursive practices that promote a different way of globalization, not based on market ideology and economic growth but on respect for human interaction and communication, and on the need to create a social, cultural and material environment that makes flourishing possible for all human beings. The next chapter will examine this global moral discourse.

CHAPTER SUMMARY

- The main question of this chapter is: How are global practices influenced by global bioethical frameworks?
- A practice is a form of life that combines theoretical knowledge, activities and values. Ethical views are embedded in practices.
- Healthcare is a network of different practices orientated on disease, situation, community or market.
- The case of commercial surrogate motherhood is used to illustrate that global practices are not stable but can change.
- Global practices are changing in dialectic interaction between global principles and local activities.

- Compliance with global ethical principles can be the result of power (coercion), interests (short-term and long-term benefits) and normative considerations (what ought to be done). This chapter focuses on normative issues.
- Implementation of global principles means 'domestication': global principles and local practices are aligned in a dynamic process of building convergence.
- Implementation is therefore a long-term process with three phases:
  - Interaction: principles are declared, debated, negotiated.
  - Interpretation: principles are interpreted and specified.
  - Internalization: principles are incorporated in local value systems.
  Normative views and arguments play a role in all phases.
- Driving forces; global principles are translated into local settings by:
  - Social movements and NGOs
  - Civil society
  - Media.
- The influence of normative considerations on practices is facilitated by framing. Frames define problems, diagnose causes, suggest solutions and motivate action.
- Frames are successful if:
  - there is 'resonance'
  - they appeal to common moral concerns
  - they promote a systemic approach.
- Individual agency can inspire and energize the change of practices through (re)framing ('normative entrepreneurs') but change will only happen through collective agency aimed at structural conditions.

Notes

1 For the notion of practice, see Uffe Juul Jensen (1987) *Practice & progress: A theory for the modern health-care system.* Blackwell Scientific Publications: Oxford. Also Alasdair MacIntyre (1985) *After virtue: A study in moral theory.* Duckworth: London, p. 187.
2 Claire Achmad (2014) How the rise of commercial surrogacy is turning babies into commodities. *The Washington Post,* 31 December 2014 (www.washingtonpost.com/posteverything/wp/2014/12/31/how-the-rise-of-commercial-surrogacy-is-turning-babies-into-commodities/) Accessed 4 August 2015.
3 The expression 'biological colonialism' is from Abby Lippman in: Amel Ahmed (2014) Offshore babies: The murky world of transnational surrogacy. Aljazeera America, 11 August 2014 (http://america.aljazeera.com/articles/2014/8/11/offshore-babies-thebus inessoftransnationalsurrogacy.html). Accessed 4 August 2015.
4 Thomas Risse, Stephen C. Ropp and Kathryn Sikkink (eds.) (2013) *The persistent power of human rights: From commitment to compliance.* Cambridge University Press: Cambridge,

UK; Emilie M. Hafner- Burton (2013) *Making human rights a reality*. Princeton University Press: Princeton and New York.

5 Harold Koh (1999) How is international human rights law enforced? *Indiana Law Journal* 74(4): 1397–1417; Joshua W. Busby (2010) *Moral movements and foreign policy*. Cambridge University Press: Cambridge (UK).

6 Fuyuki Kurasawa (2007) *The work of global justice: Human rights as practices*. Cambridge University Press: Cambridge (UK).

7 Andrew P. Cortell and James W. Davis (1996) How do international institutions matter? The domestic impact of international rules and norms. *International Studies Quarterly* 40: 451–478; Wayne Sandholtz and Kendall Stiles (2009) *International norms and cycles of change*. Oxford University Press: Oxford and New York; Mark P. Lagon and Anthony Clark Arend (eds) (2014) *Human dignity and the future of global institutions*. Georgetown University Press: Washington (DC).

8 John W. Dietrich (2007) The Politics of PEPFAR: The Presidents' Emergency Plan for AIDS Relief. *Ethics & International Affairs* 21(3): 277–292.

9 See: Andrew P. Cortell and James W. Davis (1996) How do international institutions matter? The domestic impact of international rules and norms. *International Studies Quarterly* 40: 451–478; Andrew P. Cortell and James W. Davis (2000) Understanding the domestic impact of international norms: A research agenda. *International Studies Review* 2(1): 65–87; Amitav Acharya (2004) How ideas spread: Whose norms matter? Norm localization and institutional change in Asian regionalism. *International Organization* 58(2): 239–275.

10 Mary Kaldor (2003) *Global civil society: An answer to war*. Polity Press: Cambridge (UK) and Malden (USA), p. 82.

11 Margaret E. Keck and Kathryn Sikkink (1998) *Activists beyond borders: Advocacy networks in international politics*. Cornell University Press: Ithaca and London.

12 Vaclav Havel *et al.* (1985) *The power of the powerless: Citizens against the state in central-eastern Europe*. Armonk: New York: M. E. Sharpe, Inc.

13 Keck and Sikkink (1998) *Activist beyond borders*, p. 25.

14 Peter Dauvergne and Genevieve Lebaron (2014) *Protect Inc. The corporatization of activism*. Polity Press: Cambridge (UK) and Malden (USA); Andrew Herxheimer (2003) Relationship between the pharmaceutical industry and patients' organisations. *British Medical Journal* 326: 1208–1210.

15 Peter Conrad (2005) The shifting engines of medicalization. *Journal of Health and Social Behavior* 46: 3–14. See also: Joseph Dumit (2012) *Drugs for life: How pharmaceutical companies define our health*. Duke University Press: Durham and London.

16 Declaration of Istanbul, see http://multivu.prnewswire.com/mnr/transplantationsociety/33914/docs/33914-Declaration_of_Istanbul-Lancet.pdf (accessed 15 May 2015).

17 Peter Simonson (2002) Bioethics and the rituals of media. *Hastings Center Report* 32(1): 32–39.

18 Emilie M. Hafner-Burton (2013) *Making human rights a reality*. Princeton University Press: Princeton and New York, p. 91.

19 *Newsweek:* A back door for Ebola: Smuggled bushmeat could spark a U.S. epidemic. 29 August 2014 (www.newsweek.com/2014/08/29/smuggled-bushmeat-ebolas-back-door-america-265668.html); *The Washington Post*: The long and ugly tradition of treating Africa as a dirty, diseased place. 25 August 2014 (www.washingtonpost.com/

blogs/monkey-cage/wp/2014/08/25/othering-ebola-and-the-history-and-politics-of-pointing-at-immigrants-as-potential-disease-vectors/). Accessed 5 August 2015.

20 Robert D. Benford and David A. Snow (2000) Framing processes and social movements. An overview and assessment. *Annual Review of Sociology* 26: 611–639; Ronald Labonté and Michelle L. Gagnon (2010) Framing health and foreign policy: Lessons for global health diplomacy. *Globalization and Health* 6: 15; doi: 10.1186/1744-8603-6-14.

21 UN General Assembly: Intensifying global efforts for the elimination of female genital mutilations. November 2012: www.unfpa.org/sites/default/files/resource-pdf/67th_UNGA-Resolution_adopted_on_FGM_0.pdf (accessed 5 August 2015). See also: Audrey Ceschia (2015) FGM: The mutilation of girls and young women must stop. *The Lancet* 385: 483–484.

22 Margaret E. Keck and Kathryn Sikkink (1998) *Activists beyond borders: Advocacy networks in international politics.* Cornell University Press: Ithaca and London. They particularly mention bodily harm to vulnerable individuals and legal inequality of opportunity as powerful normative frames (Keck and Sikkink 1998, p. 27).

23 Susan M. Wolf, Nancy Berlinger and Bruce Jennings (2015) Forty years of work on end-of-life care – From patients' rights to systemic reform. *New England Journal of Medicine* 372(7): 678–682.

24 Hugo Slim (2002) Not philanthropy but rights: The proper politicisation of humanitarian philosophy. *The International Journal of Human Rights* 6(2): 1–22; Thomas G. Weiss (2013) *Humanitarian business.* Polity Press: Cambridge, UK.

25 Susan K. Sell and Aseem Prakash (2004) Using ideas strategically: The contest between business and NGO networks in intellectual property rights. *International Studies Quarterly* 48: 143–175; Ethan B. Kapstein and Joshua W. Busby (2013) *AIDS drugs for all: Social movements and market transformation.* Cambridge University Press: Cambridge, UK.

26 Stacie E. Goddard (2009) Brokering change: Networks and entrepreneurs in international politics. *International Theory* 1(2): 249–281.

12

GLOBAL BIOETHICAL DISCOURSE

Van Rensselaer Potter introduced the term 'global bioethics' to give voice to the need for a broader approach to ethics in relation to health, disease, life and death. This approach affirms interconnectedness (involving a broad set of disciplines and activities), comprehensiveness (presenting a perspective beyond borders based on what is common to all human beings), independence (criticizing the social, environmental and political context in which problems arise), and a strategic focus (aiming at changing this structural setting with inclusion and participation of all relevant stakeholders). To address the problems of humanity, global bioethics advances a moral discourse that emphasizes views and perspectives that differ from mainstream bioethics. This chapter will examine this global discourse. First, it will explain why a different discourse is necessary. It will then elaborate several ethical principles that are crucial in this discourse. Finally, the relationship between ethics and politics will be discussed. Global bioethics is often blamed for being political rather than ethical. The chapter will conclude that this is precisely the advantage of global bioethics: it connects ethics and politics within a broad, critical discourse of globalization.

Need for another bioethical discourse

The basic reason why there is a need for a bioethical discourse that is different from the mainstream one is that today's bioethical problems are not merely associated with the phenomenon of globalization. That would be a too superficial diagnosis. Ethical problems are in fact produced by a specific kind of globalization that is dominated by neoliberal ideology. Bioethics is often captured within the ethical framework of this ideology. Therefore, it cannot adequately address current global problems since it does not critically examine their source. Like neoliberalism, mainstream bioethics has a practical focus: it intends to promote individual well-being. But it does not have a strategic focus trying to question and improve the structural settings in which individuals exist.

An additional reason for another moral discourse is that human rights law is not sufficient to criticize neoliberal globalization. The argument is that in theory human rights offer a different perspective but in practice they are often subsumed within the neoliberal approach. Theoretically, human rights are based on a distinct ethical framework. They do not presuppose an isolated, self-interested individual; they do not separate individual freedom rights from subsistence rights. The Universal Declaration on Human Rights refers to the 'human family', a 'spirit of brotherhood' (Article 1), and 'duties to the community' (Article 29).[1] Human rights also envision a role of the state as implementer of human rights obligations, while neoliberal policies reduce the social responsibilities of the state.

In practice, human rights discourse conflicts with neoliberal globalization. The introduction of user fees, for instance, turns health into a commodity rather than a right that is independent of the ability to pay. In this case, neoliberal policies directly conflict with the protection of human rights, and they take priority over human rights. In practice, rights focus on the individual who can claim them; they less often articulate who is responsible to provide them. Rights also tend to highlight the individual opposed to a violent and oppressive system; they are less often used to criticize these systemic conditions in which individuals exist. If human rights are recognized, it is frequently the civil and political rights which receive attention, rather than the social and economic rights which are especially important for developing countries. Articulating human rights is therefore indispensable to define a baseline; they refer to what is necessary for a decent existence of human beings. But in order to apply these requirements in practice, an expanded ethical discourse is needed. Addressing the sources or root causes of global bioethical problems requires more than articulating rights. It calls for what innovative global health scholar Solomon Benatar has called 'moral imagination'. Bioethical discourse is not simply language that evokes rights or appraises the world. On the contrary, it opens the world, it creates community, and it provides access to what makes us different as well as common.

MORAL IMAGINATION IN GLOBAL HEALTH

'The ability to empathise with others requires the critical examination of our individual lives and of our nations' actions, the capacity to see ourselves as bound to all other human beings, and the sensitivity to imagine what it might be like to be a person living a very deprived and threatened life.'[2]

Furthermore, two practical considerations underline the need for a different bioethical discourse. One is that neoliberal globalization is not a natural event or inevitable process, but man-made. It is deliberately manufactured and promoted by political decisions and actions. This ideology can be changed. A new discourse that on the one hand rejects the language of profitability, privatization and commodification in basic areas as education, health, water and social security, and on the other hand takes the viewpoint of the vulnerable and marginalized, criticizes inequality and exclusion, and highlights solidarity and ecological sustainability, shows that other perspectives exist. It also demonstrates that globalization and neoliberalism are not necessarily linked. The second consideration is related to the importance of implementation, examined in the previous chapter. Rights and principles are not simply applied (from above) but must be internalized (from below). This demands collective work and dialogue with a crucial role for interaction and persuasion. But it assumes that an ethical discourse is available to inspire and motivate action.

Global responsibilities

Global bioethics is inspired by the discourse of human rights as well as the moral ideals of cosmopolitanism. These ideals posit that all people belong to the global community. They share the same dignity and equality. Developing global bioethics as a normative approach that can be shared expands the circle of moral concern by accentuating common perspectives and a sense of common humanity. The implication is that as global citizens, human beings have responsibilities to each other, and not only to those with whom they share national citizenship.

The focus on responsibilities indicates that ethical discourse goes beyond the language of rights. It is not sufficient to formulate and claim rights. It is also necessary to specify responsibilities. In the early days of bioethics, the philosopher Hans Jonas advanced the 'imperative of responsibility'.[3] Like Potter, he argued that there is a need for a new planetary macro-ethics. An ethics of proximity is not enough; we have common responsibilities for the planet. This idea of global responsibility was picked up at the international level. The Parliament of World's Religions (1993), for example, calls for 'a new consciousness of ethical responsibility'.[4] The Commission on Global Governance (1995) underlines shared responsibilities, joined with common rights. The first responsibility mentioned is the responsibility to contribute to the common good. In 1997, a Universal Declaration of Human Responsibilities was proposed by a group of former state leaders but has not resulted in further action.[5] The notion of shared responsibility is furthermore a basic principle in the United Nations Millennium Declaration (see Chapter 7).

UNITED NATIONS MILLENNIUM DECLARATION (2000)

'We recognize that, in addition to our separate responsibilities to our individual societies, we have a collective responsibility to uphold the principles of human dignity, equality and equity at the global level. As leaders we have a duty therefore to all the world's people, especially the most vulnerable and, in particular, the children of the world, to whom the future belongs.'[6]

These examples illustrate in another way the need for different discourse. Responses are needed to the poverty and suffering of so many people, the injustices in care and treatment, and the unequal chances of health and well-being across the world. While human rights language emphasizes 'recipience', clarifying to what everyone is entitled, responsibility focuses on what must be done to secure these rights and who has obligations to act.[7] Traditionally, the concept of responsibility is applied to an individual towards specific other individuals; responsibility emerges within a personal or professional relationship. In a cosmopolitan perspective, the concept is extended in two directions. First, we have special obligations to people close to us or related to us but we have also obligations to other human beings, regardless of affiliations and borders. Responsibility applies to distant people and future generations. Second, responsibilities are individual but also collective or institutional. Confronted with global problems, individuals have the responsibility to help if they can. And in fact many do. If a disaster takes place far away, people donate money or assist as volunteer to aid fellow human beings who suffer. Philanthropy, charity and personal sacrifice, however, do not address the underlying structures of suffering and violence. For this reason, global problems require collective responsibility. They need the action of collective agents, first of all states. In many cases individual states are unable or unwilling to do the work. Also non-state actors such as global institutions (e.g. World Trade Organization), NGOs and multinational corporations have global responsibilities. But their efforts will not be very effective if they do not cooperate.

The discussion of global responsibilities as a more encompassing moral context for human rights refers to ethical principles that are relevant for global bioethics. It points in particular to several principles 'declared' in the UDBHR: respect for human vulnerability; solidarity and cooperation; equality, justice and equity; social responsibility; sharing of benefits; protecting future generations; and protection of the environment, the biosphere and biodiversity. These principles serve as 'pointers' to highlight how global responsibilities should be materialized and made operational. Since they are formulated in general terms, they show a particular direction without specifying actions and policies. That direction is the perspective of commonalities, shared by all global citizens.

Respect for human vulnerability

Globalization has significantly increased human vulnerability. While it has improved existence for some, it has made human life more precarious for many others. Neoliberal policies are associated with increasing inequality. Examples such as the 10/90 gap in global health research are given in Chapter 5. A recent IMF study recognizes that economic growth is lower if inequality in society increases.[8] There is no 'trickle-down' effect as argued in neoliberalism. Half of total global wealth is now owned by 1 per cent of the world population. Even worse, for 90 per cent of the population the share in global wealth has only diminished; neoliberal globalization has made the rich only richer. Global phenomena such as disasters and pandemics have also contributed to the increase of vulnerability. Another aspect is that it is more difficult to deal with vulnerability since protective and coping mechanisms have been eroded. Neoliberal policies have emphasized innovation, profitability, privatization and protection of property rights at the expense of public welfare and public health services. In order to promote the global market, rules and regulations protecting society and the environment have been weakened. Lack of safety and security have become crucial characteristics of present-day existence. 'People everywhere are more vulnerable', concluded the United Nations Development Programme (UNDP) in 1999.[9] One of the most vulnerable populations is irregular migrants.

IRREGULAR MIGRANTS

Nowadays there are approximately 214 million cross-border migrants (3.1 per cent of the world population). Many of them receive asylum in host countries. Irregular migrants do not have legal status; they have been denied refugee status. In many countries they are excluded from healthcare. Estimations are that 15–20 per cent of international migrants are irregular (30–40 million people). Their number is rapidly growing. At the close of 2014 almost 60 million people were forced to leave their homes due to violence, war and persecution; 8.3 million more than one year earlier. One in every 122 human beings is now a refugee.[10]

The notion of vulnerability is relatively new in bioethical discourse. The majority of publications on the subject are since 2000. In mainstream bioethics, vulnerability is primarily interpreted as a lack of individual autonomy. It is defined in the 1993 CIOMS Guidelines as 'substantial incapacity to protect one's own interests'.[11] The implication is that vulnerable subjects need special protection, for example researchers should use stricter requirements of consent and should limit the risks of exposure to harm. But the concept of human vulnerability has two faces; neither of them is recognized by the emphasis on individual autonomy. One type is general vulnerability. People are inherently vulnerable because they are human beings. The human condition is always fragile. The other type is special vulnerability. Due to social, political and economic conditions some people, especially in developing countries, are more exposed to harm than others. The difference between being and making vulnerable is ethically significant. The first type of vulnerability is given and hard to change, the second type can be influenced through ameliorating or removing the underlying conditions. The discourse of mainstream bioethics ignores this distinction through framing vulnerability as lack of individual autonomy. It neglects why the notion of vulnerability has emerged in the context of neoliberal globalization.

In order to recapture the significance of vulnerability for global bioethics it is important to reflect on the two types of vulnerability.[12] As a general characteristic of being human, vulnerability is shared among human beings. It is a condition that precedes individual agency; it already exists before we are rational, self-interested and acting individuals. Rather than protection, it demands respect, care, compassion and solidarity. Special vulnerability on the other hand is produced by circumstances that affect entire groups and populations. It implies that social and political action is needed. Special vulnerability demands specific positive action based on dignity, respect and social responsibility. In this view, research with vulnerable populations requires more than stricter informed consent procedures; it calls for post-trial access and benefit-sharing. The conclusion is that it is not sufficient to frame vulnerability in terms of individual incapacities. People living in poverty, hunger, deprivation and corruption are not vulnerable as a result of individual decisions. Vulnerability refers to commonality and solidarity. It can only be addressed through a systemic approach, changing the conditions that produce injustice and inequality. Assuming that vulnerability can be reduced or eliminated through protecting and empowering autonomous decision-makers and neglecting its social dimension, mainstream bioethics evades the confrontation with the neoliberal ideology that produces vulnerability.

Solidarity and cooperation

As argued previously, bioethics is expanding into global bioethics because global problems can no longer be addressed by separate states and organizations. This expansion reflects the growing recognition that human beings are citizens of the world, belonging to a global community with common values, shared commons and responsibilities. The first factor leads to the need for international cooperation, the second emphasizes the importance of global solidarity. The UDBHR combines solidarity and cooperation in one principle (Article 13).

Solidarity

Solidarity is an ancient concept. It refers to social bonds between groups of people that prevent a society from breaking down. It expresses that people are connected because they have common goals and a shared identity. Many scholars argue that solidarity nowadays is diminishing due to neoliberal policies.[13] At the same time, the concept of solidarity is receiving increasing attention in the search for different ways of globalization.

HUMANITARIAN ACTION

The earthquake in 2010 in Haiti (Chapter 1) produced an enormous global response. Over 900 NGOs provided help. More than $9 billion was donated by governments, foundations and individual citizens from all over the world. Humanitarian assistance is based on solidarity with victims of disasters, war, violence, and oppression. One of its basic principles is that of humanity, stating that human suffering must be addressed regardless of where it is found. Underlying is the cosmopolitan view of common humanity. In practice, humanitarian action faces many new ethical challenges.

That solidarity plays a fundamental role in global bioethics is visible in many ways. The interconnectedness of the world brings distant suffering nearby; it calls for action to help. Organizations of homeless people in Mumbai (Chapter 6) and TAC in South Africa (Chapter 9) elicited solidarity across the world. They illustrate that new forms of solidarity have arrived ('network solidarity' or 'cosmopolitan solidarity').[14] These forms are achieved 'from below', not through existing political organizations and structures. Local networks are formed around a specific cause; they are connecting to networks in other countries and areas so that global networks arise, not because people have a moral duty but because they can identify with the cause, and share common values and goals. This global solidarity is based on the cosmopolitan ideal of world citizenship, but global solidarity itself also fosters the building of a global moral community.

Why is global solidarity necessary? One argument is that in addressing global problems more is needed than aid and generosity. The objectives of foreign aid are usually defined by donors and humanitarian organizations. Recipients of aid are regarded as helpless victims. Aid and donations are dependent on specific causes (victims of earthquakes generate more response than malaria patients) and are usually not sustained in the long run. Solidarity introduces another mindset than charity, altruism and philanthropy. The main difference is that solidarity signifies a symmetrical relation; it is a relationship between equals; it necessarily means inclusion as well as cooperation.

A second argument refers to commonalities of the human condition. If global health is considered as a common good, the health of all citizens in the world is a shared concern. Particularly, health inequities should be addressed from the perspective of the world community with global solidarity as the main inspiration for action. The concern for commons, as argued previously, demands collective action. This is why global solidarity is important: each individual person is powerless in the face of global problems; but together they can have an impact. Solidarity therefore motivates people to undertake collective action. The notion of solidarity is crucial for the moral discourse of global bioethics. It demonstrates that human beings are primarily social beings. They (thus we) can only live and flourish among other people with whom they (we) are connected. Solidarity cannot be explained in the language of self-interest. It is not coalition-building of selfish individuals. It is far from the rational egoism of Ayn Rand. Solidarity demonstrates the idea of the world as *mundus*: it is situated in what Hannah Arendt calls the 'in-between', the intercultural public space between human beings in which they interact and constitute the world through collaborative work and action.

Often a difference is made between strong and weak solidarity. The first requires some kind of action (even if it is only joining a group or cause). Solidarity is not a pious intention but shows itself in supporting a specific cause. It is understood as a shared practice. Common action is therefore typical for strong solidarity. It is the 'pragmatic solidarity' advocated for by people like Paul Farmer. On the other hand, weak solidarity refers to the openness to the perspective of others and the willingness to make sacrifices. Many argue that this is not enough. Solidarity means joining and sharing action.

A related debate concerns the value of solidarity: is it instrumental or intrinsic? Many argue that global solidarity is an instrument to accomplish a particular goal, for example health equity. Others conceive solidarity as a value in itself. Although health equity is a valuable end, the process of achieving that end is more important than the outcome. Solidarity is valuable because it shows that ultimately all human beings should be included in addressing global problems. Citizens manifesting solidarity with distant others convey the message that they share common concerns. Their solidarity is with specific people in specific places but they demonstrate that global justice is not a challenge for particular populations or particular places but a universal concern with a global issue.

The principle of global solidarity is connected to the notion of responsibility. But it differs from this notion because it is not associated with particular capacities and consequences. People who do not show solidarity cannot be held accountable while they can if they have certain responsibilities. Solidarity is furthermore connected to vulnerability. Often vulnerable subjects, groups and populations are the object of solidarity but, basically, solidarity recognizes that all human beings are intrinsically vulnerable. Finally, the principle of solidarity is related to that of cooperation.

Cooperation

One of the purposes of the United Nations is international cooperation in order to solve global problems. Without cooperation global governance will not be possible. Human rights cannot be realized without cooperation. Particularly, social and economic rights, such as the right to health, require joint action and cooperation; they can only be realized in the longer run (progressively) and as far as resources are available. This need for global cooperation is not contested but in the real world it is often difficult and fragile. The reason is that two different views of cooperation are at work, reflecting the different value of solidarity: cooperation as instrumental and as an end in itself. In the first view, cooperation is an instrument to achieve specific ends. In the second view, cooperation itself is worthwhile; whether or not it is accomplished, achieving an end in a cooperative manner is valuable; rather than the product it delivers, the experience and process of cooperating is what counts. An analogy can be made with playing in a music band. Its value is not merely in the outcome but also in the process of playing together.

These different views of cooperation are used in neoliberalism and global bioethics. In the neoliberal perspective, competition rather than collaboration determines social interactions. If it occurs, cooperation is the interaction between self-interested, rational individuals for a defined purpose. There is no value in cooperation itself. The decision to work together is based on the expectation of maximum individual gain. Cooperation in this perspective is based on self-interest of individuals or national interest of states. It can be short term but also long term. Many global problems require long-term cooperation; they bring short-term sacrifices but when the long-term advantages override these costs, parties can still decide to work together because it is in their interest (reframed as 'deferred' or 'enlightened' self-interest). For neoliberalism, cooperation has nothing to do with ethics; it is always instrumental.

In the perspective of global bioethics, human relations cannot be reduced to self-interest. Individuals are not only connected with each other but also concerned with common goods. People cooperate because they share common interests, for example global health or the survival of the planet. They do not expect that working together delivers benefits to themselves; it may even bring costs. Cooperation can deliver results but its moral motivation is not self-interest but global concern for humankind. In the global bioethics perspective, cooperation is a value in itself. It demonstrates horizontal associations between human beings, replacing vertical, top-down interactions. It is a manifestation of equality among partners. It will imply that humanitarian action, as an example, is not supporting helpless victims but a collaborative effort to engage all relevant parties. It also implies an approach to global governance 'from below' (as described in Chapter 9). Based on global solidarity, cooperating in this perspective prioritizes negotiation over application; incorporation over exclusion and expulsion. Another example in global research ethics is joint ethical review.

JOINT ETHICAL REVIEW IN RESEARCH

Indiana University in the US and Moi University in Kenya collaborate in health research and bioethics training programmes located in both countries. They launched a proposal to establish a joint, independent research ethics committee. International guidelines require review of research proposals in host countries. In practice many committees in the global North act paternalistically and do the review themselves, assuming that committees in the global South are not sufficiently capable. The proposal for a joint committee was based on the notion of partnership that recognizes cultural differences and at the same time searches for common perspectives. Ironically, despite the support of both universities and the researchers involved, the proposal was rejected by the Kenyan National Bioethics Committee.[15]

Cooperating in this ethical perspective is not driven by self-interest but by concern for common goods. It is argued that this is too idealistic. Why should pharmaceutical companies cooperate with WHO and the Global Fund to increase access to medication? It is not in their interest to reduce the price of essential medication in order to increase access. As the argument goes, they will cooperate for opportunistic reasons, for example to enhance their reputation, or because the market for their products will expand. Nonetheless, cooperation itself can effectuate changes. It shows shared responsibility regardless of the initial motivation to work together. This can foster the evolution of common perspectives and interests; it can generate more concern for ethical norms. The role of self-interest in cooperation as articulated in neoliberalism is seriously questioned in recent research.[16] In real life human beings are disposed to cooperate for other reasons than self-interest. They are 'a cooperative species'; they share common interests and work together because they value ethical behaviour for its own sake. The same conclusions were drawn from studies about the commons. As discussed in Chapter 8, communities are very well able to manage commons in a sustainable manner to the benefit of all. Through cooperation and collective agency they are self-organizing and self-governing. In such cases there is no need for state intervention or private markets. The lesson is that social sharing is not an anomaly.

Equality, justice and equity

Human rights and cosmopolitan discourse both emphasize that human beings have equal moral worth. However, in several chapters it has been pointed out that major differences in health exist within and across countries. In the real world people do not have equal health, due to genetic constitution, poverty or lifestyle. In many cases health inequalities are not the result of choices and conduct of individuals with poor health. Chapter 5 gave the example of the 10/90 gap in global health research. Also, people with diseases and disabilities have no access to care because it is not available or because they are discriminated against. Groups of people are therefore systematically disadvantaged. Global differences in health are not just inequalities but inequities. If people are equal in a moral sense then justice should apply to all; everybody has a right to health and should have the opportunity to be healthy and enjoy life. The principle of equity expresses the idea that everyone should have a fair opportunity to attain health.

HEALTH INEQUITY

'Equity is the absence of avoidable or remediable differences among groups of people, whether those groups are defined socially, economically, demographically, or geographically.'[17]

Inequity exists when health differences are avoidable and unnecessary. Asymmetries in social, political and economic power that produce vulnerability cause health inequity. It is therefore not sufficient to remedy particular inequities. Systemic changes are necessary to do justice to vulnerable populations.

Global justice is a much debated notion.[18] Some argue that the principle of justice is applicable within the state; it cannot be extended to the global level since there are no institutions to implement it. From a cosmopolitan perspective others point out that we have responsibilities to other people, not only to people in our own community or state; global justice is based on the framework of human rights; there are global governance mechanisms, and institutions to implement this principle. These two interpretations, however, are not incompatible. States have domestic as well as global responsibilities.

Whether the principle of justice applies at the global level has implications for the scope of the resulting obligations. In the first interpretation, we only have duties to our own community, not to outside and distant people. Duties are not impartial because we always have special relationships. In the second perspective, we have duties to all human beings. These are negative duties (to avoid deprivation and not to cause suffering) as well as positive duties (to provide assistance). Since harming others is worse than not preventing harm, negative duties are morally stronger than positive ones. Thomas Pogge argues on this basis that people in high-income countries have a duty not to impose a harmful global order on people in low-income countries (see Chapter 4). The current global order is a major cause of poverty and violation of human rights while it should be to the benefit of all. People in rich countries contribute and participate in an unjust structured world through the global IPR regime. They therefore violate the negative duty not to harm other people. The second, cosmopolitan perspective furthermore criticizes the emphasis on charity and aid. Though in the first perspective there are no duties to outsiders, providing assistance is morally recommendable. But this is not a moral duty but charity. This point of view is criticized because it does not address the injustice of social structures; many inequalities are created by root causes that cannot be removed or remediated by individual sacrifices regardless of how much individuals donate to relieve the needs of others. The earthquake in Haiti was especially devastating because of basic deprivation, poverty and corruption in the country after centuries of colonial exploitation. In the capital Port-au-Prince nine in ten people lived in slums without basic services while building regulations were non-existent. Another example is international food relief; it often damages the local food production in the longer run. The emphasis on aid and humanitarian action therefore does not acknowledge that the proper focus should be on structural injustice, on rights and obligations. Disadvantaged people are regarded as passive recipients, not moral agents themselves.

The principle of global justice, if accepted, engenders debates about its content and consequences. Most of them focus on the notion of basic human needs. These needs such as food, water, shelter, education are fundamental for the right to health. Basic needs also have value that transcends cultures. Every human being should be able to meet basic needs; otherwise he or she cannot function as a human being. Policies and practices should therefore focus on providing for needs through negative and positive duties (regardless of how near or distant people are). Different theoretical approaches have been suggested:

- maximin principle: priority should be given to the worst-off populations so that the benefits for those with unmet basic needs will be maximized;
- principle of equality of opportunity: everybody should have the same chance to realize a healthy life through satisfying basic needs;

- capabilities approach:policies should promote and sustain capabilities that are necessary for human flourishing; and
- minimum floor principle: a minimum level of provision for basic needs should be guaranteed.

The notion of basic needs is furthermore used to articulate the core content of the right to health. This right includes the provision of essential health services but also the promotion of the preconditions of health (food, water, housing and security). The WHO has estimated that a basic package of health services will cost $60 per person a year.[19] Thus, providing for the basic needs of all people in the world will cost only 0.1 per cent of the GDP of rich countries. Redressing health inequities with a conception of global justice as meeting basic human needs is feasible.

Social responsibility

The principle of social responsibility explicitly addresses the socio-economic determinants of health. It requests that progress in science and technology should advance access to quality healthcare and essential medicines, access to adequate nutrition and water, reduction of poverty and illiteracy, improvement of living conditions and the environment, and elimination of marginalization and exclusion of persons.

Social responsibility and health combine two basic ideas. First, many actors are responsible for health; not just states (that committed themselves to the right to health) but also individuals as well as private and public organizations. Responsibility here refers not to the personal responsibility of each individual but to the responsibility of an individual as a member of society. The physician has professional responsibility that includes a social role. He or she should not only provide good patient care but should furthermore contribute to the welfare of society. The AMA Code of Medical Ethics, for example, states: 'Each physician has an obligation to share in providing care to the indigent.'[20] Scientific responsibility equally includes social responsibility. Scientists invent knowledge and produce technologies that can be used for the benefit of humankind. But the outcomes of scientific work can have negative impact on the environment, health, labour and food. They can deliberately be misused. Scientists need to be aware of these negative consequences so that proactive prevention and retroactive remediation will be possible. Scientists should be conscious that knowledge will not only be used for peace, justice, environmental sustainability and social welfare. They should be attentive to possible misuse. Nowadays, scientific organizations have taken action to prevent and reduce the risk of misuse and abuse. New concerns, such as dual use, bio-security, and responsible conduct of research have therefore been added to the agenda of global bioethics.

DUAL USE IN SCIENCE

Dual use means that vaccines, biotechnical products and micro-organisms can be applied as bio-weapons. A famous case is the creation of a new form of the avian flu virus that is transmissible between mammals. In 2011, a Dutch researcher submitted the results of his experiments to the journal *Science*. The US National Science Advisory Board for Biosecurity decided that the manuscript should be redacted so that the details of the experiments would not be publicly known and could not be used by bioterrorists.[21]

The innovation of the principle of social responsibility in healthcare is that the protection and promotion of health is regarded as a shared responsibility. It is not just a concern for states and individuals but also of business organizations. Policies and practices of transnational corporations can affect millions of people. The normative argument that companies should prevent or remediate negative effects of their activities for health puts emphasis on the notion of 'corporate social responsibility'. An important landmark is the UN Global Compact, launched in 2000.[22] It brings together 8,320 companies and 170 countries committed to doing business in a responsible way based on ten principles regarding human rights, labour, environment and anti-corruption. Many pharmaceutical companies now have special units and programmes for corporate social responsibility. Their efforts to increase access to medicines are more often publicly monitored and independently assessed. Investments in research for diseases in developing countries, aiming to diminish the 10/90 gap, have increased.

The second basic idea included in the principle of social responsibility is that global problems reflect common challenges and should be addressed through common action. The principle presupposes therefore the principle of solidarity and cooperation. It furthermore presupposes that health is a common good. Access to care should be guaranteed but healthcare is only one determinant of health. Other common goods (e.g. the environment, adequate nutrition and safe drinking water) that determine health should be protected. Promoting global health involves cooperation of many stakeholders, not merely governments. New forms of global governance are necessary in order to enhance this type of cooperation, especially engaging transnational corporations that are under-regulated at the global level. Emphasizing social responsibility therefore is clearly associated with new forms of governance. The underlying idea is that trade and health are not incompatible; it is possible to have ethical globalization that benefits all global citizens and protects the common good.

The notion and particularly the practices of social responsibility are disputed.[23] First, the principle is rejected by some with the argument that health is the responsibility of governments. The aim of companies is to increase profit for its shareholders. As long as a company fulfils its legal obligations there is no moral requirement to contribute to the common good. This argument is not plausible for pharmaceutical companies; their activities clearly have a direct impact on health.

A second argument holds that if corporate responsibility exists, it is best realized on a voluntary basis and through 'self-regulation' rather than through external or legal regulation. The problem with this argument is that voluntariness is a weak incentive for real changes. Codes of conduct have been adopted for various types of business but examples of effective changes in business practices are rare. The Global Compact is presented as a 'learning network'. It seems more interested in sharing experiences than in compliance with its principles.

Third, social responsibility is criticized as an opportunistic, not a moral strategy. Companies may not regard it as a moral obligation but as a matter of charity with donations and 'responsible' conduct, motivated ultimately by self-interest. It is an important matter for companies because it makes them more competitive. Research shows that big pharmaceutical companies are engaged in social responsibility with motives such as reputational benefits, employee satisfaction, or creating new markets. They rarely mention that it is a moral obligation.

A more critical argument is that social responsibility is a cover up for neoliberal globalization. It is a strategy to pacify the increasing critique of disastrous impacts of corporate power. For example, the collapse of a garment factory in Bangladesh killing many people (in April 2013) pointed to the behaviour of Western clothing brands (like Gap, since 2003 a member of Global Compact). Consumers in developed countries put pressure on the companies. Global activism necessitated them to respond and to underline their social responsibility for workplace safety and labour rights. Another example is the outsourcing of clinical trials. This is usually justified because of lower costs, faster ethical review and data generation, easier and quicker recruitment of research subjects. But companies hardly use the argument that priority is given to researching diseases relevant for the, often vulnerable populations from which subjects are recruited. Social responsibility can be used as rhetorical language to conceal that outsourcing is, in fact, reinforcing existing inequalities. The health needs of countries are not addressed since the benefits go to the companies and the people in Western countries. Appeals to social responsibility can express sincere moral convictions but they can also be an exercise in public relations. How useful the principle of social responsibility will be depends on how its role is conceptualized: as problem-solving or critical transformation. This raises the question of the social responsibility of bioethics itself: does it use this notion to help manage the neoliberal agenda, or to critically redress the agenda because global health is more important than trade and profit?

Sharing of benefits

One of the principles that follow from those of global justice and social responsibility is benefit-sharing. Global exchanges in healthcare often involve inequities. International clinical trials can be more beneficial for sponsors, researchers and potential patients in developed countries than for research subjects in developing countries. Genetic resources are patented and sold by pharmaceutical companies to countries with rich biodiversity which have been their original source. A recent controversy concerns virus sharing.

VIRUS SHARING

In 2007, the Indonesian government decided not to share avian flu virus samples with WHO. These samples are used to research the virus, manufacture vaccines or antiviral medication. Countries like Indonesia, where flu epidemics often start, are the first to provide materials to prepare preventive and therapeutic responses for other countries. But the exchange is unequal. The virus sample is given by WHO to private companies. The produced vaccine is patented by these companies. The countries that donated the sample have to buy the vaccine. The benefits of international cooperation therefore go to pharma enterprises that receive biological and genetic materials for free, and to populations of developed countries that are wealthy enough to secure vaccines before the epidemic shows up within their borders.[24]

Previously, with the 2005 avian influenza, Indonesia had provided virus samples. Later it discovered that WHO had transferred the sample to a company that had patented the resulting vaccine. This made the vaccine unaffordable for most countries. While the system of sharing was built on the principle of global solidarity, in practice it was commercialized and turned into a system that further increased health inequality, notably by WHO itself. Another negative experience was that while Indonesia was hit hard by this earlier avian flu and had provided the materials to make the vaccine, it was unable to buy the vaccine since wealthy countries had reserved and bought all the available stock. Because of flagrant injustice and inequality, the decision was made to stop virus sharing until balanced benefit-sharing was accomplished (no vaccine, no virus). The Indonesian decision initiated a long and heated process of negotiation, opposing the views of developing and developed countries. In May 2011, an agreement was reached in order to have an equitable distribution of benefits (Pandemic Influenza Preparedness Framework). Countries were encouraged to share; recipients of the virus would be obliged to participate in benefit-sharing.

The principle of sharing benefits is currently used in an increasing number of contexts. The adoption of the Convention for Biological Diversity (CBD, 1992) applies it to genetic resources.[25] The CBD has three purposes: conservation of biological diversity; sustainable use of its components; and fair and equitable sharing of benefits from the use of genetic resources. Medical research is another area of application. The Declaration of Helsinki introduced in 2000 the obligation of post-trial access by study participants. A third context is migration of healthcare professionals. Globalization is associated with mobility. Health professionals have freedom of movement, like everybody else. Many migrate to developed countries because of attractive salaries or better work conditions. At the same time, medical education has been provided and paid for by the home countries while the host countries benefit to address their health shortages without investment in education. The benefits of migration are unequal and unjust.

BRAIN AND CARE DRAIN

Many physicians and nurses migrate in search of a better life. Healthcare organizations in developed countries have recruitment agencies to deliberately encourage migration, while the home countries have shortages. These practices are increasingly criticized. They are incompatible with the global ethics discourse of solidarity and justice. They also do not comply with the principle of benefit-sharing. Benefits for one actor are obtained through harming another actor. In order to balance benefits, the World Health Assembly adopted the WHO Global Code of Practice on the International Recruitment of Health Personnel in 2010. However, the Code is voluntary.[26]

One of the challenges to the principle of benefit-sharing is that it is not clear what 'benefits' are. There are not many good examples of successful sharing. It is important not to identify benefits with profit. Monetary benefits (access fees, fees per sample, research funding or joint ventures) should be distinguished from non-monetary benefits (sharing of research results, participation in teaching and training, capacity building). Furthermore, what counts as 'benefit' is not the same in all countries but is dependent on the social and cultural context and varies according to local needs. Sharing of benefits is a theoretical principle based on the principles of justice and solidarity. Its aim is to protect vulnerable populations through countering inequality and exploitation. It furthermore underlines that the environment should be protected. Benefits must be shared because biosphere and biodiversity are common goods. The practical challenge is how to do this justly.

Protecting future generations

One of the new features of global bioethics is the expansion of ethical concerns to future generations. This broadening of concerns, demonstrating the growth of global bioethics as advocated by Potter, became increasingly important because of the interdependency of global problems, for example environmental disasters in one region will affect other regions and other generations. Technology has altered the nature of human activity. Technological innovations have an impact on current as well as future generations. The increasing awareness that human existence depends on the survival of the planet and the preservation of the common heritage reinforced the conviction that global responsibility not only should be intra-generational (current generations) but also inter-generational (future generations).

One of the first to promote this idea was Hans Jonas. He argued that we have duties to the future. These duties are non-reciprocal. We have the power to determine how future generations will live; but they have no power over us. Intra-generational responsibility on the other hand is reciprocal. We share similar concerns and assist each other to protect common goods. This assumes that there is a symmetrical relationship and thus shared responsibility. But when relationships are asymmetrical there should be responsibility for the party that is most vulnerable, e.g. future people, because it is most important to protect the common good. This leads Jonas to formulate a new ethical imperative: 'Act so that the effects of your action are not destructive for the future possibility of such [genuine human] life.'[27]

The principle of protecting future generations is particularly applied in two contexts: the impact of new technologies on healthcare and on the environment. In the area of healthcare, the principle has been used in regard to xeno-transplantation, gene-line genetic interventions, and GM food. In these cases it is not exactly known whether and which adverse effects result from interventions. There is not sufficient scientific evidence to conclude that harm for future generations will not occur. In such uncertain cases precautionary policies should be employed in order to protect these generations. On the other hand vaccinations are effective means to protect individuals without harming future generations. The second context in which the principle is applied is the environment. The World Commission on Environment and Development linked present and future generations, arguing that sustainability is only possible if the focus in policies is no longer only on the people living now but includes future people.[28] The responsibility for future generations was endorsed in 1992 in the Rio Declaration on Environment and Development. A few years later UNESCO adopted the Declaration on the Responsibilities of the Present Generations towards Future Generations.

PRESERVATION OF LIFE ON EARTH

Article 4: 'The present generations have the responsibilities to bequeath to future generations an Earth which will not one day be irreversibly damaged by human activity. Each generation inheriting the Earth temporarily should take care to use natural resources reasonably and ensure that life is not prejudiced by harmful modifications of the ecosystems and that scientific and technological progress in all fields does not harm life on Earth.'[29]

This Declaration connects intra-generational and inter-generational responsibility. The major problems of today require global cooperation in order for humanity and the planet to survive. Protection of the environment, preservation of natural resources, safeguarding the biological, genetic, and cultural diversity of humankind are calling for inter-generational justice. On the one hand, present generations use the common heritage of humankind. They enjoy the benefits of the achievements of previous generations that have preserved and sustained basic resources for the continuation of human life. On the other hand, they have the responsibility to transmit this heritage to the future, precisely because it is a shared responsibility and because it concerns basic resources that are common property.

The concept of inter-generational justice is challenging. How can we have responsibilities towards persons who do not yet exist? What do we mean by 'future' generations: children or grandchildren who are just born; human beings not yet born; distant generations? One answer is that we do not have obligations to possible people of the future. Responsibilities can only exist between real actors who are in reciprocal relationships. This reciprocity is fictional with future generations.

Other answers argue that generations are in moral relations to each other. The implications of these relations are stronger as the impact of our current acting is more imaginable and predictable. One position therefore is that we do have moral responsibility but primarily to one or two future generations. Another position argues that all distant generations can claim our responsibility because concepts such as common heritage and commons apply to all generations. The last two arguments produce another query: what kind of obligations do we have to people who do not yet exist or might never exist? The problem is that we do not know what will be the needs of future generations. Human existence is changing. The needs of people one century ago were different from today, and they could not have imagined the needs of our generation. Future generations are, per definition, not there to explain what their needs are.

Many efforts have been made to give voices to future generations. A long-standing practice in health research is that special institutions and mechanisms have been created to protect vulnerable people that cannot protect their own interests, and to speak on their behalf. In a similar way, offices of guardian have been established to represent posterity at national, regional and internationals levels. In 1993, France established the Council for the Rights of Future Generations, Finland its Committee for the Future. The Hungarian Ombudsman for Future Generations has been active since 2007. In April 2015, the Well-Being of Future Generations Act became law in Wales. It establishes a Future Generations Commissioner to act as an advocate.[30]

Protection of the environment, the biosphere and biodiversity

Potter and Jonas share the same concern for the future. This concern is associated with environmental degradation and disasters. The link between human behaviour today and the well-being of people in the future, as well as the conviction that human beings are part of nature motivated Potter to coin the term 'bioethics' meant to include environmental ethics. The first part 'bio' indicates that all living beings should be taken into account since humanity cannot survive without the biosphere and biodiversity. Potter was disappointed that bioethics as it developed did not regard environmental issues as part of its agenda.

This separation between environmental ethics and bioethics is impossible to maintain. In a global perspective it can no longer be denied that loss of biodiversity and climate change are affecting health and raising ethical concerns.

The term 'biodiversity' was used for the first time in the 1980s. It refers to the variety of life on Earth. At the level of genes it means the variety of genes within and between species. At the level of species it refers to the diversity of animals, plants and micro-organisms. More than 1.7 million species are identified out of an estimated 10 million. At the level of ecosystems (such as deserts and tropical rainforests) the focus is on the environment in which species live and develop. Continuation of life on Earth depends on the interactions between these three levels of biodiversity. Biodiversity is currently under threat. One-third of all plant and animal species will be extinguished in 2030. Brazil has an enormous biodiversity; 20 per cent of all biodiversity on Earth. It has the largest tropical rainforest in the world with one-quarter of all known plant species. No wonder that the UN organized an Earth Summit in 1992 in Rio de Janeiro, adopting the CBD as well as the Framework Convention on Climate Change. Over 150 countries have signed the CBD. But in 2014 they were forced to conclude that none of the 2010 targets have been met. Biodiversity has decreased by 40 per cent since 1970. Not even the rate of biodiversity loss has been reduced.[31]

Loss of biodiversity raises serious ethical questions. Biological diversity is a resource for food and new medication. Most species are unknown and they are extinguished in a fast way. We do not even know what genetic potentiality we could have available for medicines. Because of this potential, pharmaceutical companies are prospecting genetically diverse areas. Biodiversity loss also presents threats. New diseases such as Ebola emerge when tropical forest is reduced and interactions between humans and animals increase with unknown viruses spilling over from wild animals. Biodiversity is a source of conflict. It is often the basis of traditional knowledge of indigenous populations. Living in close contact with nature in a sustainable way, these populations protect the environment as a common good and common heritage; they reject the notion of patenting. Biodiversity therefore is associated with health and medical science. It makes an appeal to ethical principles, particularly solidarity, cooperation, sharing of benefits, and protecting future generations.

Climate change has been denied for a long time. Many people contradict that it relates to human behaviour. But it can no longer be ignored that its effects are negative for global health.

CLIMATE CHANGE

The WHO estimates that 'climate change will cause approximately 250,000 additional deaths per year, before the middle of the current century'. Important effects are:

- many determinants of health affected: clean air, drinking water, shelter, food;
- health risks of heat waves;
- higher levels of ozone and aeroallergens;

- higher risks of water-borne diseases;
- changing patterns of infection such as malaria and dengue;
- natural disasters and rising sea levels impacting health and health services.[32]

Biodiversity and climate change are associated; both are manifestations of a fundamental ecological crisis. Both have negative effects on health. Both phenomena necessitate cooperation, common approaches and goals. They are therefore quintessential problems for global bioethics, explaining why protection of the environment, the biosphere and biodiversity is regarded as one of its principles in contrast to mainstream bioethics which focuses on domestic or regionalized challenges and could therefore be separated from environmental ethics. Addressing these problems will be an almost insurmountable challenge. The lack of progress is depressing. The abundance of hypocrisy is upsetting.

ETHICAL CHOCOLATE

Cacao del Peru Norte has carried out deforestation of thousands of hectares of primary rainforest in Peru in order to create a monoculture of cacao plantations. The company is owned by an international consortium, United Cacao. On its website the company promotes itself as providing large-scale, 'ethically' produced cacao. With an annual global market of almost $100 billion, the chocolate industry has a long-standing history of slavery, child labour, corruption and exploitation. Companies have set up their own rating systems where you select the most 'ethical' chocolate bar.[33]

Another example concerns the company that dumped toxic waste in Abidjan and which joined Global Compact in 2015 (see Chapter 9). It is now advertising on its website that it operates a robust governance framework focused on health, safety, environment and communities. Until today the company denies any wrongdoing in Côte d'Ivoire while the number of victims has grown to more than 110,000; they have hardly been compensated. Imagine what would have happened if the toxic waste dumping had occurred in a European country.

The examples illustrate that talking about ethics can be deceptive. It reflects the criticism on Global Compact. Ethical concerns are voluntary. It is not clear what is verbal and what is really done in practice. Accountability is low. Serious and sustainable efforts to protect the environment with a worldwide impact are scarce.

At the same time, over the last few decades increasing awareness, collective action, activism, new policies, legal frameworks and governance structures, and mostly targeted and specific changes can be witnessed. Climate change is high on the international political agenda. Activism is growing, as well as 'green' products. There is also more theorizing. Notions such as global commons, sustainability, inter-generational solidarity and vulnerability are increasingly applied in global bioethics. The fundamental ethical debate confronts the anthropocentric environmental perspective with non-anthropocentric ones. The first emphasizes that ethics is human centred. Human beings have moral duties only towards each other. Human interests therefore prevail over the interests of other species. This perspective is more related to Western culture (in which nature often has an economic value). Non-anthropocentric perspectives give a broader scope to human duties. Biocentric ethics assume that living organisms other than humans have intrinsic value. All life forms are 'moral patients', i.e. subjects that are entitled to moral consideration. It is therefore an ethical imperative to respect all life forms. This view is more related to non-Western cultural traditions. Ecocentric ethics argues that ecosystems have intrinsic value as well. Nature as a whole is a 'moral patient'. This means that all organisms and entities in the ecosphere are part of the interrelated whole and equal in intrinsic value. The prosperity of human beings depends on the prosperity of nature. Human beings are part of nature. They have, therefore, the duty to conserve and protect the integrity of the ecosystem and its biodiversity.

The environmental crisis is a fundamental challenge for global bioethics. It certainly inspired many individuals to change their lifestyle and diminish pollution. But the crisis is not the result of individual behaviour. It is produced by collective agency and ways of life at a global scale. As a global problem the solution has to be found at this level. Rather than influencing individual choices it will be necessary to develop an ethical discourse that promotes another way of life and counters the overwhelming priority given to economic values over the value of health.

The Rio Declaration stresses that harmony with nature and the planet should be promoted to achieve a just balance among economic, social and environmental needs of the present and future generations of humanity. A new vision of human existence is necessary. This does not mean going back to a romanticized past and applying traditional ways of life. As the concept of Buen Vivir (Chapter 8) shows, one can learn from the past and revitalize, for example, indigenous practices that have preserved biodiversity for thousands of years. The central notion of these practices is harmony. Another way of life protecting biodiversity, the biosphere, and the environment requires a collective effort to live in harmony with nature.

AN ETHICS OF HARMONY

Symbiosis between human beings and nature includes:

- emphasis on relatedness: not exploitation and domination;
- different model of development: focus on human needs and durability;
- global solidarity and responsibility;
- good living for all is more important than better living for some;
- the subject of good living is the individual but also the community, both intimately connected to nature.

Contrary to the current way of life that is thoroughly impacted by the neoliberal ideology and the problems produced by this ideology, a transformation of values is required through the horizon of global bioethics. The main input in this transformation will come from the recognition that human beings are embedded in communities and cultures, societies and nature. This is expressed in the 'we' of Ubuntu, or the fullness of life in Buen Vivir. Globalization creates tremendous opportunities but its benefits currently accrue to a minority of human beings; many experience harms, disadvantages. Global bioethics should criticize and reject the conditions and processes that impede many people to accomplish good living and particularly good health.

Biopolitics

Will global bioethics be able to provide answers to the ethical problems of today's health, healthcare and health technologies? Critics have argued that there is such pervasive disagreement about ethical issues that it is a failed project; it is biopolitics rather than bioethics (Chapter 6). For answers and solutions political compromise is decisive, not ethical arguments and justifications. This critique is intended to discredit global bioethics. However, as the critique is often advanced from the perspective of neoliberalism and is assuming the priority of individual, national and economic self-interest, it is political itself.

It is true that global bioethics (as well as its critique) obliterates the distinction between ethics and politics. With neoliberalism as the dominant political ideology and as the source of many global bioethical problems, how can bioethics not be political? As argued in Chapter 5, ethics and politics are intimately connected in neoliberalism. Neoliberal projects promote ethical principles such as personal autonomy, individual responsibility and self-support; have particular visions on cooperation and justice; and reject or minimize the importance of most of the principles discussed in this chapter. This connection between ethics and politics is not surprising. Normative considerations are central to both ethics and politics. What is surprising is that the development of mainstream bioethics has mirrored the neoliberal values while at the same time maintaining that it is critically reflecting on medical and scientific progress in health and healthcare. Bioethics has entered into a 'double bind'. It has been born because of the moral problems engendered through such progress. On the one hand, it aspires to assist in addressing these problems, for example articulating patients' rights and the value of personal autonomy and responsibility. On the other hand, it cannot really address the issues as long as it is using the same values that produce the problems. As long as it is employing the underlying value system of neoliberalism, it will not fundamentally challenge the neoliberal ideology. More so, it will be useful to this ideology since it can appease and neutralize the most conflicting disagreements. Against this backdrop, it is understandable that mainstream bioethics will not be interested in global bioethics as new discourse. It flourishes in the maelstrom of continuous medical, scientific and technological controversies. It needs disagreements to pacify them. But at the same time, it prefers to minimize the risk that pacification leads to transformation of the underlying value system that produces the conflicts. This is the biopolitical programme of mainstream bioethics.

Nowadays it is difficult to deny that bioethics is biopolitics. Many issues discussed in this book testify to this interconnection.

- The political determinants of health are manifested in the negative effects of the structural adjustment measures of the IMF and World Bank in developing countries on population health since the 1980s.
- Humanitarian action is political rather than technical. Some countries receive more aid than others even if their needs are lower. Aid can be misused and diverted at the expense of some parties. Aid can prolong conflicts but still continue to be provided for political reasons. The main objective of humanitarianism is saving lives but divorced from the context that produces vulnerability. The political choice is not to analyse unjust power structures.
- Global governance is political, as the examples in Chapter 9 illustrate.
- Social movements, NGOs, and civil society are increasingly entangled in the logic of the market. They are criticized for becoming a component of this logic instead of being a critical change agent.

The focus in these examples is on the promises of science and technology and the challenges for individual decision-makers. The concern is not with the social and cultural implications of biotechnology and medical science, and certainly not with the economic context dominated by neoliberal discourse. Mainstream bioethics argues that such concerns are political, not ethical. But in fact, this precisely *is* a political argument. It removes the social context from the domain of critical analysis. Individualizing analysis and reflection is the preferred approach of bioethics since it results in de-politicization. This approach continues to assume that the promises of medical and scientific progress are primarily individual challenges. This is observable in the most recent stage of biopolitics: bioeconomy. International trade organizations are promoting the idea that all living beings are sources of renewable energy. Human beings themselves are regarded as economic objects as well as subjects. Their biological bodies and body parts are tradable commodities. Bio-objects should therefore be recycled, as in the case of tissue trade (Chapter 1). Furthermore, those bodies can be perfected with the latest biotechnologies. Humans are also economic subjects; as responsible bio-citizens they should invest in their biological capital. The implication is that human beings should take care of their body and bodily health; there is no need to improve the social conditions in which they live.

The conclusion of these observations is that mainstream bioethics has become a particular biopolitics adapted to the neoliberal value system. Bioethics originated from the criticism of medical paternalism and the power of medical science and technology, as well as the rise of patients' rights (Chapter 2). Its rapid development, however, did not result in a broader approach beyond the narrow biomedical, individual and short-term concerns. Little attention was paid to social, economic and environmental issues that impact on health (Chapter 3). As a broader approach, global bioethics emerged in the 1990s because global ethical problems became more apparent. This new global bioethics is considered a response to the need to analyse, moderate, transform, resist neoliberal globalization, and to return to human values and human rights (Chapters 4–5). But global bioethics runs the same risks to be adapted and incorporated into expanding neoliberal policies and practices, and be applied to facilitate and pacify potential disagreements and conflicts, as mainstream bioethics. However, global bioethics presents a different horizon (Chapter 6). It aims to get out of the neoliberal ideology, critically analyse it, and present alternative ways of thinking and different practices that will enhance the health and well-being of the global population beyond the privileged. This is certainly a political project. The question is whether it is possible. Can global bioethics escape from the dominant ideology?

Global bioethics as social ethics

The first answer is: acknowledge that ethics and politics cannot be separated. Bioethics is not just an academic exercise. It is not about abstract issues but concerns real human life and its flourishing. Furthermore, bioethics is a normative endeavour that starts with moral dissatisfaction. Certain situations and practices are unacceptable and need to change, thus inviting activism. This activism should be reflective, not spontaneous or intuitive but guided by ideas and principles. The power of ideas should not be underestimated. Moral ideas reflect existing conditions but also inspire individuals, groups and populations to change those conditions. With a different horizon, global bioethics points to new destinations. At the same time, it should actually move because it is practically concerned about the world. Biopolitics cannot be avoided.

The second answer is that global bioethics should articulate a different biopolitics. Philosopher Simon Critchley defined politics recently as '... an ethical practice that is driven by a response to situated injustices and wrongs.'[34] The question is: What ethical practice? The theoretical and practical approaches of global bioethics, as discussed in this book, provide the following perspectives.

a   *Broader view of the human person.* There is no abstract and de-contextualized human being; he or she is necessarily socially connected. Individuality is produced by social conditioning. For global bioethics, personal autonomy is as important as in mainstream bioethics but it recognizes that the context of individual existence (hence, human vulnerability) should necessarily be considered.

b   *Positive notion of society.* Bioethics should focus on the social, economic, cultural and political conditions that make flourishing in health possible. Governments should provide for those conditions that determine population health; it is not the role of the market. Ethical debate should centre on the notions of cooperation (rather than competition), social responsibility (rather than individual responsibility), solidarity (rather than private interests) as well as global justice (rather than increasing inequity).

c   *Focus on the common good.* Living together means that human beings are sharing heritage and common goods. They interact with each other in the public sphere. Common interest is not simply the sum of private interests. Global bioethics should reject the neoliberal assumption that the human person is primarily driven by self-interest. Individuals are not consumers acting on the basis of benefit and profit, but citizens concerned with the common good.

d. *Emphasis on collective agency.* Individual action is important but cannot bring social transformation. Engaged individuals planting trees and eating organic food will not change the world. In this way, the global distribution of power will not change. Other forms of collective engagement will be necessary to influence systemic conditions that produce global problems. This is precisely what the logic of neoliberalism tries to prevent.

These perspectives produce a broader and richer moral discourse. Global problems are viewed in a way that directs attention to the structural causes and the underlying neoliberal value framework that used to be seen as untouchable and unchangeable.

The third answer to the question of how global bioethics can escape from being co-opted into the biopolitical framework of neoliberalism is that it has developed a broader repertoire of theoretical and practical activities. Further expansion and strengthening is needed, but as of now it includes the following:

a   *Global research.* There is a growing information base that is broader than official reports. A good example is the Global Health Watch, an initiative of NGO People's Health Movement that follows closely the work of WHO and produces alternative World Health Reports.[35] Many other examples have been giving in this book of sources of information, data, and cases which complement scientific journals and studies.

b   *Public education and communication.* The possibilities for sharing information and experiences, contacting and cooperating with colleagues elsewhere are nowadays almost unlimited; more opportunities could be exploited in global bioethics.

c   *Building networks and coalitions.* Some bioethics NGOs as well as global organizations exist and the number and activities are growing, so that global ethical issues will be increasingly disputed and contested, and experiences and theories exchanged.

d   *Advocacy and activism.* These activities were until recently not condoned in bioethics (as political, not academic). Now they are necessary if global bioethics wants to be more than studies and books. They are often initiated by a few individuals (like most NGOs have started). They help to transform moral dissatisfaction into movements and organizations that structurally challenge existing practices. Systemic failures cannot be addressed by individuals alone. Sometimes, advocacy and activism require blaming and shaming, leaving aside nuanced and subtle language, to identify the root causes of global problems. This motivates research and examination of hitherto neglected and avoided subjects because they are 'political'. For example, identifying the international trade system, in other words the neoliberal ideology, as 'the rot at the core of global governance today' will call attention to an area of research and reflection that is seriously underdeveloped in today's bioethics.[36] Activism in global bioethics should therefore be 'reflective activism', inspired and based on research and theory, and should itself be motivating to further research and reflection.

e.   *Capacity-building.* This now fashionable idea in bioethics is redefined in global bioethics. It should not be understood as 'empowerment' because this puts emphasis on the individual as agent of change. That reflects the neoliberal view that, for example the poor, should be encouraged to find solutions themselves. The underlying assumption is that poverty is the result of irresponsibility, and that finding the solution is a matter of individual capacities. In the perspective of global bioethics, a global problem like poverty can only be resolved by addressing the root causes. It is a matter of global injustice that requires '*moral* structural adjustment' and not individual empowerment. Capacity-building should thus be based on promoting the common good, much more than on enhancing individual capacities.

The fourth answer to the above question of biopolitics is that global bioethics should be conscious that it is at risk of being transformed from a critical point of view into a practical tool in neoliberal biopolitics. It should always be alert that incorporation and adaptation are continuously possible. A different global biopolitics needs to be sustained, developed and expanded in the face of the efforts to neutralize and co-opt global ethics discourse, and reduce its horizon and moral imagination. Global bioethics should be mindful of the type of biopolitics that is at stake in order to remain true to what Socrates has proposed as the roles of the philosopher: 'gadfly', an uncomfortable louse in the skin of society; and 'midwife', delivering new ideas and bringing them to life.

This mindfulness will not be difficult. Every day we are reminded that 2.8 billion people live on less than $2 a day; 1 billion people do not have safe drinking water; 2.5 billion people have no access to sanitation facilities. Four children die each minute; 1 billion children do not receive services essential to survival and development. The number of people with access to essential medicines is between 1.3 and 2.1 billion people. While a Japanese citizen has an overall life expectancy of 84 years, one in Sierra Leone has only 46 years. Every year, 2 to 3 million people die of tuberculosis; 8 million develop active infections. Numbers are rising. Almost 95 per cent of cases occur in poor countries. Most of these patients, however, could be treated but at the global level 79 per cent of them do not have access to appropriate medicines.

This data reminds us that philosophy does not start with wonder but, as Simon Critchley points out, with disappointment, indignation, the experience of failure and injustice. The same is true for ethics. Chapter 1 argues that medical ethics was transformed into bioethics because of disturbing experiences such as scandals of medical research and challenges of technological interventions that could bring great benefits but also serious harm and impersonal, dehumanizing care. Chapter 2 explains that the rise and expansion of global bioethics is stimulated by disturbing cases such as people dying from treatable diseases, the use of different standards of care in research in developing countries, women exploited as commercial wombs, and the Trovan case in Nigeria. We are continuously confronted with a world that is thoroughly unjust and exploitative. Critchley argues that we need a motivating ethics that 'empowers subjects to political action'.[37] The moral dissatisfaction that confronts us daily motivates action because the ethical subject faces not abstract notions like justice or solidarity but concrete demands of other people, not in general but as particular human beings: strangers, marginalized, vulnerable and excluded. Because of our shared interconnectedness and vulnerability we are committed to the demands of the other, near or distant. Ethical commitment gives rise to a different biopolitics because it makes universal claims to address situations of resistance. This is the same point made by Alain Badiou: confronted with inhumanity, we encounter a universal address that makes us search for new possibilities within a particular context. Universality is situated. The singular is always related to the universal. This is not just ethics; it is simultaneously politics; in the words of Badiou: politics is 'the local creation of something generic'.[38]

In this line of thinking, global bioethics is not the imposition of a value system. It is engaged in a dialectical and intercultural process of interaction between global principles and local practices, a contentious intercourse between 'above' and 'below'. Neoliberal globalization is resisted at the local level, in a particular situation, but with the appeal to universality. Global bioethics therefore is not a ready-made product but in process. It is the aspiration to realize the universal in the local. But it is first of all a social ethics that goes beyond the view that ethics is primarily a matter of personal commitment and individual lifestyle. Global bioethics presents a horizon of reflection, analysis and action that brings ethical principles associated with commons, cooperation, future generations, justice, protection of the environment, social responsibility, and vulnerability into the debate of globalization.

CHAPTER SUMMARY

The discourse of global bioethics operates from a horizon presenting different perspectives and principles than are used in mainstream bioethics.

- Why is another bioethical discourse necessary?
  - Mainstream bioethics is too closely aligned to neoliberal discourse.
  - Human rights discourse is not sufficient to scrutinize the neoliberal framework.
  - Practical considerations: neoliberalism is not a fact of nature but a political construct so that ideas can change it.

- What are the ethical principles of global ethical discourse?
  Basic to this discourse is the notion of global responsibilities. Including the mainstream ethical principles of respect for autonomy, benefit and non-harm, global bioethics, as social ethics, emphasizes:
  - Respect for human vulnerability
    - ☐ General: characteristics of being human
    - ☐ Specific: due to external conditions
  - Global solidarity
    - ☐ Strong: resulting in action
    - ☐ Weak: willingness to support
  - Cooperation
    - ☐ Instrumental: motivated by self-interest
    - ☐ End in itself: a value motivated by the common good
  - Global justice: focus on basic human needs
  - Social responsibility: focus on socio-economic determinants of health
    - ☐ Shared responsibility: range of actors responsible for health
    - ☐ Common problems require common action
  - Sharing of benefits: vulnerability requires solidarity and justice which implies sharing of benefits
  - Protecting future generations:
    - ☐ Inter-generational justice complements intra-generational justice
    - ☐ Focus on the commons ('sustainability')
  - Protection of the environment, the biosphere and biodiversity
    - ☐ Global bioethics includes environmental ethics
    - ☐ Need for an ethics of harmony.
- Bioethics and biopolitics cannot be separated; the question is how a different bioethics and biopolitics can be developed beyond the neoliberal ideology.
  - Global bioethics is social ethics
    - ☐ Broader view of the human person
    - ☐ Positive notion of society
    - ☐ Focus on the common good
    - ☐ Emphasis on collective agency
  - Broad repertoire of theoretical and practical activities.
  - Confrontations with global injustices demand action in situations. Global problems are not abstract but localized in particular contexts. In these contexts they are addressed from a universal point of view. This dialectic is the job of global bioethics.

Notes

1 *Universal Declaration of Human Rights*, 1948: www.ohchr.org/EN/UDHR/Documents/ UDHR_Translations/eng.pdf (Accessed 4 August 2015).

2 Solomon R. Benatar (2005) Moral imagination: The missing component in global health. *PLos Medicine* 2(12): 1209.

3 The 'imperative of responsibility' was the title of the English translation of Hans Jonas's book *Das Prinzip Verantwortung: Versuch einer Ethik für die technologische Zivilization* (Insel Verlag, Frankfurt am Main, 1979 (*The imperative of responsibility: In search of ethics for the technological age.* University of Chicago Press: Chicago, 1984).

4 Parliament of World's Religions (1993) *Toward a Global Ethic*, p. 14 (www. parliamentofreligions.org/_includes/fckcontent/file/towardsaglobalethic.pdf) (accessed 4 August 2015).

5 InterAction Council (1997) *Declaration on Human Responsibilities* (http:// interactioncouncil.org/universal-declaration-human-responsibilities). (Accessed 5 August 2015).

6 United Nations General Assembly A/RES/55/2: *United Nations Millennium Declaration*, 18 September 2000 (www.un.org/millennium/declaration/ares552e.pdf). (Accessed 4 August 2015).

7 The focus of human rights 'on recipience rather than on action and obligations' is elaborated in Onora O'Neill (2005) Agents of justice (p. 38) in Andrew Kuper (ed.): *Global responsibilities: Who must deliver on human rights?* Routledge: New York and London, pp. 37–52.

8 Jonathan D. Ostry, Andrew Berg and Charalambos G. Tsangarides (2014) *Redistribution, inequality and growth.* International Monetary Fund, February 2014 (www.imf.org/ external/pubs/ft/sdn/2014/sdn1402.pdf). (Accessed 4 August 2015).

9 UNDP (United Nations Development Programme) (1999) *Human Development Report 1999.* New York: Oxford University Press, p. 90.

10 UNHCR Global Trends 2014: World at war (www.unhcr.org/556725e69.html).

11 CIOMS (1993) *International ethical guidelines for biomedical research involving human subjects.* Geneva: CIOMS (www.codex.uu.se/texts/international.html) (quotation on page 10).

12 Henk ten Have (2015) Respect for human vulnerability: The emergence of a new principle in bioethics. *Journal of Bioethical Inquiry*, 12(3): 395–408.

13 Patricia Illingworth and Wendy E. Parmet (2012) Solidarity for global health. *Bioethics* 26(7): ii–iv; Julio Frenk, Octavio Gomez-Dantes, Suerie Moon (2014) From sovereignty to solidarity: A renewed concept of global health for an era of complex interdependence. *The Lancet* 383: 94–97.

14 The term 'network solidarities' is from Carol Gould (2007) Transnational solidarities. *Journal of Social Philosophy* 38: 148–164. Pensky has introduced the term 'cosmopolitan solidarity' (Two cheers for cosmopolitanism: Cosmopolitan solidarity as second-order inclusion. *Journal of Social Philosophy* 2007; 38: 165–184). For the notion of 'pragmatic solidarity' see Paul Farmer (2004) *Pathologies of power: Health, human rights, and the new war on the poor.* Berkeley/Los Angeles/London: University of California Press.

15 Eric M. Meslin, Edwin Were and David Ayuku (2013) Taking stock of the ethical foundations of international health research: Pragmatic lessons from the IU-Moi Academic Research Ethics Partnership. *Journal of General Internal Medicine*; 28 (Suppl 3): S639–645.

16 Samuel Bowles and Herbert Gintis (2011) *A cooperative species: Human reciprocity and its evolution*. Princeton and Oxford: Princeton University Press; Jennifer Prah Ruger (2011) Shared health governance. *The American Journal of Bioethics* 11(7): 32–45.

17 WHO, www.who.int/healthsystems/topics/equity/en/ (accessed 4 August 2015).

18 Gillian Brock (2009) *Global justice: A cosmopolitan account*. Oxford: Oxford University Press.

19 Jeffrey D. Sachs (2012) Achieving universal health coverage in low-income settings. *The Lancet* 380 (9845): 944–947.

20 AMA Code of Medical Ethics is in Opinion 9.065 (www.ama-assn.org/ama/pub/physician-resources/medical-ethics/code-medical-ethics/opinion9065.page). (Accessed 3 August 2015).

21 Michael Tu (2012) Between publishing and perishing? H5N1 research unleashes unprecedented dual-use research controversy. 3 May 2012: www.nti.org/analysis/articles/between-publishing-and-perishing-h5n1-research-unleashes-unprecedented-dual-use-research-controversy/ (accessed 4 August 2015).

22 John Gerard Ruggie (2013) *Just business: Multinational corporations and human rights*. New York/London: W.W.Norton & Company.

23 Susanne Soederberg (2007) Taming corporations or buttressing market-led development? A critical assessment of the Global Compact. *Globalizations* 4(4): 500–513.

24 Siti Fadilah Supari (2008) *It's time for the world to change: In the spirit of dignity, equity, and transparency*. Penerbit Lentera: Jakarta.

25 Convention on Biological Diversity (1992) www.cbd.int/doc/legal/cbd-en.pdf (accessed 4 August 2015).

26 World Health Assembly (2010) *WHO Global Code of Practice on the International Recruitment of Health Personnel* (www.who.int/hrh/migration/code/code_en.pdf?ua=1). (Accessed 4 August 2015).

27 Hans Jonas (1984) *The imperative of responsibility: In search of an ethics for the technical age*. University of Chicago Press: Chicago, p. 11.

28 Report of the World Commission on Environment and Development: *Our common future*, p. 41 (www.un-documents.net/our-common-future.pdf) (accessed 3 August 2015).

29 *Declaration on the Responsibilities of the Present Generations towards Future Generations*. Paris, UNESCO, 1997 (http://portal.unesco.org/en/ev.php-URL_ID=13178&URL_DO=DO_TOPIC&URL_SECTION=201.html). (Accessed 3 August 2015).

30 Welsh Government: The Well-being of Future Generations (Wales) Act 2015: http://gov.wales/legislation/programme/assemblybills/future-generations/?lang=en (accessed 4 August 2015).

31 For data, see Secretariat of the Convention on Biological Diversity (2010) *Global Biodiversity Outlook 3*. Montréal, Canada (www.cbd.int/doc/publications/gbo/gbo3-final-en.pdf). (Accessed 5 August 2015).

32 World Health Organization: *Conference on Health and Climate Change*. Geneva: Switzerland, 22–29 August 2014, p. 6 (www.who.int/globalchange/mediacentre/events/climate-health-conference/whoconferenceonhealthandclimatechangefinalreport.pdf?ua=1). (Accessed 5 August 2015).

33 David Hill: Can Peru stop 'ethical chocolate' from destroying the Amazon? *The Guardian* 18 April 2015 (www.theguardian.com/environment/andes-to-the-amazon/2015/

apr/17/can-peru-stop-ethical-chocolate-destroying-amazon). (Accessed 3 August 2015).

34 Simon Critchley (2012) *Infinitely demanding: Ethics of commitments, politics of resistance.* London and New York, Verso, p. 132.

35 Global Health Watch. *An alternative World Health Report*; four editions (2005, 2008, 2011 and 2014). www.ghwatch.org/who-watch/about). (Accessed 3 August 2015).

36 The statement 'the rot at the core of global governance today' is from Jennifer Chan (2015) *Politics in the corridor of dying: AIDS activism and global health governance.* Johns Hopkins University Press: Baltimore, p. 177.

37 Critchley (2012) *Infinitely demanding*, p. 8.

38 Alain Badiou (2015) *Philosophy for militants.* London and New York: Verso, p. 56.

GLOSSARY

Biodiversity: '… the variability among living organisms from all sources … terrestrial, marine and other aquatic ecosystems and the ecological complexes of which they are part; this includes diversity between species, between species and of ecosystems.' (Convention on Biological Diversity)

Bioethical imperialism: The view that global bioethics is in fact Western bioethics imposed on the rest of the world (also: Moral colonialism).

Biopiracy: '… the appropriation of the knowledge and genetic resources of farming and indigenous communities by individuals or institutions who seek exclusive monopoly control (patents or intellectual property) over these resources and knowledge.' (Action Group on Erosion, Technology and Concentration; www.etcgroup.org/en/issues/biopiracy.html)

Buen vivir: Social philosophy of 'living well', adopted in the constitutions of Bolivia and Ecuador, based on indigenous traditions of harmony between human beings and nature (also Sumak Kawsay, in Quechua language).

Codification: Statements of rules and prescriptions for the behaviour of professionals, expressed in codes of conduct.

Common heritage of humankind: The notion that certain material and immaterial entities are the property of the global human population; these entities cannot be legally owned by individuals or states.

Commons: Natural and cultural resources that are accessible to all members of a society, and can be used and shared by them as common property for which they are responsible (e.g. sea, air and water).

Convention: A binding agreement between states (also Treaty or Covenant).

Cosmopolitanism: The philosophical, political and moral view that basically all people everywhere are, or should, understand themselves as citizens of the world.

Creative Commons: A non-profit organization that enables the sharing and use of creativity and knowledge through free legal tools.

Declaration: A document that states agreed upon standards but which is not legally binding.

Domestication: The internalization and integration of global principles in local value systems.

Epistemic community: '… a network of professionals with recognized expertise and competence in a particular domain and an authoritative claim to policy-relevant knowledge within that domain or issue-area.' (Haas, 1992: 3)

Global bioethics: The study of global ethical problems related to health, healthcare, health science and research, and health technologies and policies, and the activities, practices and policies to influence and resolve these global problems.

Global burden of disease: The burden (mortality, disability, injuries and risk factors) of all diseases around the world.

Global commons: Domains that are the property of humanity and to which all nations have access (e.g. outer space, and ocean floors).

Global Compact: A voluntary initiative, launched in 2000 by the UN, to bring together businesses and civil society on the basis of ten principles for human rights, labour, environment and anti-corruption.

Global Fund: Global Fund to Fight AIDS, Tuberculosis and Malaria, established in 2002.

Global governance: 'collective efforts to identify, understand, or address worldwide problems that go beyond the capacities of individual states to solve.' (Weiss, 2013: 32)

Intellectual property: Any creative work or invention that can be protected by an intellectual property right (copyright, patent, design or trademark).

Intellectual Property Right (IPR): Legal protection for intellectual property that for a given period of time excludes others from using it without the permission of the owner.

Interculturality: 'a dynamic process whereby people from different cultures interact to learn about and question their own and each other's cultures.' (Baring Foundation)

Mainstream bioethics: Bioethics as it has developed during the last half century, starting in the US and expanding to mainly Western countries.

Medical deontology: Theory of medical duties of physicians.

Multiculturalism: The theory that multiple cultures exist and that they merit equal respect.

National Commission: National Commission for the Protection of Human Subjects of Biomedical and Behavioral Research, established in 1974 in the United States.

Neoliberalism: '… theory of political economic practices that proposes that human well-being can best be advanced by liberating individual entrepreneurial freedoms and skills with an institutional framework characterized by strong private property rights, free markets, and free trade...' (Harvey, 2005: 2).

Oviedo Convention: European Convention on Human Rights and Biomedicine, adopted by the Council of Europe in 1997; signed in Oviedo, Spain.

Patent: A temporary grant of the exclusive right to make, use, offer for sale, or import an invention; a form of intellectual property right that protects scientific and technical innovations for a period of 20 years from the filing date.

Principlism: Methodology in practical ethics that starts with the formulation of principles and then applies these principles to clarify and solve practical problems.

Rio Declaration: UN Declaration on Environment and Development, adopted in Rio de Janeiro in 1992.

Ubuntu: African philosophy of the individual as member of a group or community ('I am who I am because of who we are').

FURTHER READING BY CHAPTER

Chapter 1: Bioethics reality check

For the case of Marlise Muñoz see: David Usborne (2014) Marlise Muñoz: Brain-dead pregnant Texas woman removed from life-support. *The Independent*, 26 January 2014 (www.independent.co.uk/news/world/americas/marlise-munoz-braindead-pregnant-texas-woman-removed-from-lifesupport-9086489.html).

The story of Rhonda and Gerry Wile is told in Leslie Morgan Steiner (2013) *The baby chase: How surrogacy is transforming the American family*. St. Martin's Press: New York.

The global tissue trade is described in Kate Willson, Vlad Lavrov, Martina Keller, Thomas Maier and Gerard Ryle (2012) Human corpses are prize in global drive for profits. *Huffington Post*, 17 July 2012 (www.huffingtonpost.com/icij/human-corpses-profits_b_1679094.html).

Disaster bioethics is discussed in: Donal P. O'Mathuna, Bert Gordijn and Mike Clarke (eds) (2014) *Disaster bioethics: Normative issues when nothing is normal*. Springer: Dordrecht.

For the Tonga case, see: Bob Burton (2002) Proposed genetic database on Tongans opposed. *British Medical Journal* 324: 443.

Chapter 2: From medical ethics to bioethics

The most extensive overview of the history of medical ethics is: Baker, R.B. and McCullough, L.B. (eds) (2009) *The Cambridge world history of medical ethics*. Cambridge University Press: New York.

The emergence of bioethics is covered in several historical studies: David J. Rothman (1991) *Strangers at the bedside: A history of how law and bioethics transformed medical decision making*. Basic Books: New York; Albert R. Jonsen (1990) *The new medicine and the old ethics*. Harvard University Press: Cambridge (Mass) and London (England); Albert R. Jonsen (1998) *The birth of bioethics*. Oxford University Press: New York/Oxford.

Percival's work is often regarded as a milestone in the history of medical ethics. See: Thomas Percival (1803) *Medical ethics, or a code of institutes and precepts adapted to the professional conduct of physicians and surgeons*. S. Russell: Manchester (http://books.google.com/book

s?hl=nl&lr=&id=tVsUAAAAQAAJ&oi=fnd&pg=PR7&dq=Thomas+Percival:+Medi
cal+ethics&ots=qUQ8BdY15j&sig=bzS_Zi0akiF8yPIMHuuLsHoZFZA#v=onepage
&q=Thomas%20Percival%3A%20Medical%20ethics&f=false).
More information about the European tradition of anthropological medicine can be found
in: Henk ten Have and Gerlof Verwey (eds) (1995) Anthropological medicine. *Theoretical
Medicine* 16(1): 3–114.

Chapter 3: From bioethics to global bioethics

The two main publications of Van Rensselaer Potter are: *Bioethics: Bridge to the future*
(Prentice Hall: Englewood Cliffs, NJ, 1971) and *Global bioethics: Building on the Leopold
legacy* (Michigan State University Press: East Lansing, 1988). Another source for Potter's
ideas is his address to the American Association for Cancer Research: Humility with
responsibility – A bioethic for oncologists: Presidential address. *Cancer Research* 1975; 35:
2297–2306.
For the development of Potter's ideas, see: Henk ten Have (2012) Potter's notion of
bioethics. *Kennedy Institute of Ethics Journal* 22(1): 59–82.
The recent history of bioethics is described in Albert R. Jonsen (1998) *The birth of bioethics*.
Oxford University Press: New York/Oxford. The development in European countries
is presented in a thematic issue of the journal *Theoretical Medicine* (1988; issue 3). The
development in Latin America is discussed in a thematic issue of *The Journal of Medicine
and Philosophy* (1996; issue 6).
For the methodological paradigm of bioethics, see Tom L. Beauchamp and James F.
Childress (1978) *Principles of biomedical ethics*. Oxford University Press: New York/
Oxford (the book has been subsequently revised several times; the seventh edition was
published in 2013). For the critical debate on principle-based bioethics, see: Edwin R.
DuBose, Ron Hamel and Laurence J. O'Connell (eds) (1994) *A matter of principles?
Ferment in U.S. bioethics*. Trinity Press International: Valley Forge.
The claim about Jahr is elaborated by Hans-Martin Sass: Fritz Jahr's 1927 concept of
bioethics. *Kennedy Institute of Ethics Journal* 2008; 17(4): 279–295. All articles on bioethics
and ethics published by Jahr between 1927 and 1947 are available in English translation
in: Amir Muzur and Hans-Martin Sass (eds) (2012) *Fritz Jahr and the foundations of global
bioethics*. Lit Publishers: Berlin.

Chapter 4: Globalization of bioethics

The literature on globalization is abundant. In this chapter, the following publications are
used: Ulrich Beck (2000) *What is globalization?* Polity Press: Cambridge; Jan Aart Scholte
(2000) *Globalization: A critical introduction*. Palgrave: Houndmills; Manfred B. Steger
(2003) *Globalization: A very short introduction*. Oxford University Press: Oxford/New
York.
For globalizing bioethics in general, the work of Daniel Callahan is useful, in particular:
Minimalist ethics. On the pacification of morality, in Arthur L. Caplan and Daniel
Callahan (eds) (1981) *Ethics in hard times*. Plenum Press: New York and London,
pp. 261–281. See also: Daniel Callahan (2012) *The roots of bioethics, health, progress,
technology, death*. Oxford University Press: Oxford, New York.
Interesting comparative studies in bioethics are Kazumasa Hoshino (ed.) (1997) *Japanese and
western bioethics.: Studies in moral diversity*. Kluwer Academic Publishers: Dordrecht/
Boston/London; Angeles Tan Alora and Josephine M. Lumitao (eds) (2001) *Beyond a*

western bioethics: Voices from the developing world. Georgetown University Press: Washington DC.

The case of female genital mutilation is discussed in: Ruth Macklin (1999) *Against relativism: Cultural diversity and the search for ethical universals in medicine.* Oxford University Press: New York/Oxford. For the Trovan case, see: Ruth Macklin (2004) *Double standards in medical research in developing countries.* Cambridge University Press: Cambridge (UK), p. 99 ff.

Thin versions of global bioethics are, among others, presented by Heather Widdows, Donna Dickenson and Sirkku Hellsten (2003) Global bioethics. *New Review of Bioethics* 1(1): 101–116; Leigh Turner (2005) From the local to the global: Bioethics and the concept of culture. *Journal of Medicine and Philosophy* 30: 305–320; Miltos Ladikas and Doris Schroeder (2005) Too early for global ethics? *Cambridge Quarterly of Healthcare Ethics;* 14: 404–415; Søren Holm and Bryn Williams-Jones (2006) Global bioethics – myth or reality? *BMC Medical Ethics* 7: 10; doi: 10.1186/1472-6939-7-10; Sirkku K. Hellsten (2008) Global bioethics: Utopia or reality? *Developing World Bioethics* 8(2): 70–81; Roberta M. Berry (2011) A small bioethical world? *HEC Forum* 23: 1–14. The expression 'everyday bioethics' is introduced by Giovanni Berlinguer (Bioethics, health, and inequality. *Lancet* 2004; 364: 1086–1091). Maura Ryan (2004) argues for 'bioethics from below' (Beyond a western bioethics? *Theological Studies* 65: 158–177).

Thick versions of global bioethics are elaborated in various theories.

For cosmopolitanism, see Nigel Dower (2007) *World ethics: The new agenda.* Edinburgh University Press: Edinburgh (2nd edition); David Held (2010) *Cosmopolitanism: Ideals and realities.* Polity Press: Cambridge (UK) and Malden (MA).

For the utilitarian theory, see Peter Singer (2003) *One world: The ethics of globalization.* Yale University Press: New Haven & London.

For the capabilities approach, see Martha C. Nussbaum (2011) *Creating capabilities: The human development approach.* The Belknap Press of Harvard University Press: Cambridge (MA) and London (UK).

For human rights-based approaches, see Jonathan Mann (1997) Medicine and public health, ethics and human rights. *Hastings Center Report* 37(3): 6–13; Lori P. Knowles (2001) The lingua franca of human rights and the rise of a global bioethic. *Cambridge Quarterly of Healthcare Ethics* 10: 253–263.

For contractarian approaches, see Thomas Pogge (2013) *World poverty and human rights: Cosmopolitan responsibilities and reforms.* Polity Press: Cambridge (UK) and Malden (MA), 2nd edition.

For multiculturalism and interculturality, the following publications are used: Charles Taylor (1992) *Multiculturalism and 'The politics of recognition.'* Princeton University Press: Princeton (NJ); Will Kymlicka (1995) *Multicultural citizenship: A liberal theory of minority rights.* Clarendon Press: Oxford; Bhikhu Parekh (2006) Rethinking multiculturalism. *Cultural diversity and political theory.* Palgrave Macmillan: Houndmills (UK), 2nd edition; François Levrau and Patrick Loobuyck (2013) Should interculturalism replace multiculturalism? A plea for complementariness. *Ethical Perspectives* 20(4): 605–630.

Labelling bioethics as 'rich man's ethics' is from Erich Loewy (2002) Bioethics: Past, present, and an open future. *Cambridge Quarterly of Healthcare Ethics;* 11: 388–397; see also Howard Brody: Bioethics should side with the powerless and the oppressed. Howard Brody (2009) *Future of bioethics.* Oxford University Press: New York and Oxford.

Chapter 5: Global bioethical problems

The analysis of problems has used the works of John Dewey, in particular his *Logic: The theory of Inquiry* (New York: Henry Holt and Co., 1938).

For the concept of 'horizon' Saulius Geniusas (2012) *The origins of the horizon in Husserl's phenomenology*. Springer: Dordrecht is useful. Adam Hedgecoe's distinction between consequent and antecedent dimensions of bioethical problems has been used (Critical bioethics: Beyond the social science critique of applied ethics. *Bioethics* 2004; 18(2): 120–143).

Data on child mortality (2012) UN Inter-agency Group for Child Mortality Estimation: *Levels & Trends in Child Mortality. Report 2012*. New York: United Nations Children's Fund (www.childmortality.org/files_v16/download/Levels%20and%20Trends%20in%20Child%20Mortality%20Report%202012.pdf) (accessed 20 July 2015).

Thomas Pogge's arguments are presented in *World poverty and human rights: Cosmopolitan responsibilities and reforms*. Polity Press: Cambridge (UK) and Malden (MA), 2013, 2nd edition.

The example of suicide rates in India is from: Jonathan Kennedy and Lawrence King (2014) The political economy of farmers' suicides in India: Indebted cash-crop farmers with marginal landholdings explain state-level variation in suicide rates. *Globalization and Health* 10: 16; doi: 10.1186/1744-8603-10-16.

The literature on 'health tourism' is abundant. A recent overview is Jill R. Hodges, Leigh Turner, and Ann Marie Kimball (eds) (2012) *Risks and challenges in medical tourism: Understanding the global market for health services*. Praeger: Santa Barbara. See further: Meghani, Zahra (2013) The ethics of medical tourism: From the United Kingdom to India seeking medical care. *International Journal of Health Services* 43(4): 779–800; Smith, Kristen (2012) The problematization of medical tourism: A critique of neoliberalism. *Developing World Bioethics* 12(1): 1–8; Turner, Leigh (2013) Transnational medical travel: Ethical dimensions of global healthcare. *Cambridge Quarterly of Healthcare Ethics* 22: 170–180.

The reference to the book connecting 'global' and 'local' is: Hakan Seckinelgin (2008) *International politics of HIV/AIDS. Global disease – local pain*. Routledge: Abingdon (UK). The dialectics of global and local is elaborated by Saskia Sassen (2014) *Expulsions: Brutality and complexity in the global economy*. The Belknap Press of Harvard University Press: Cambridge (Mass) and London (England).

A useful analysis of neoliberalism is Taylor Boas and Jordan Gans-Morse (2009) Neoliberalism: From new liberal philosophy to anti-liberal slogan. *Studies in Comparative International Development* 44: 137–161; David Harvey (2005) *A brief history of neoliberalism*. Oxford University Press: Oxford, New York; Jamie Peck (2010) *Constructions of neoliberal reason*. Oxford University Press: Oxford. For Ayn Rand see her *The virtue of selfishness: A new concept of egoism*. Signet/Penguin: New York, 1964. For the ideas of Friedrich Hayek (1944) *The road to serfdom*. University of Chicago Press, Chicago. See also: James G. Carrier (ed.) (1997) *Meanings of the market: The free market in Western culture*. Berg: Oxford/New York.

For the negative impact of neoliberal policies on healthcare, see: Sara E. Davies (2010) *Global politics of health*. Polity Press: Cambridge (UK) and Malden (MA); Nuria Homedes and Antonio Ugalde (2005) Why neoliberal health reforms have failed in Latin America. *Health Policy* 71: 83–96; Rene Loewenson (1993) Structural adjustment and health policy in Africa. *International Journal of Health Services* 23(4): 717–730.

Chapter 6: Global responses

Critical views of global bioethics are presented in many ways. For global bioethics as nothing new, see: Catherine Myser (ed.) (2011) *Bioethics around the globe*. Oxford University Press: Oxford/New York. A quantitative study of international publications in bioethics is done by: Borry, Pascal, Schotsmans, Paul and Dierickx, Kris (2006) How international is bioethics? A quantitative retrospective study. *BMC Medical Ethics* 7: 1; doi: 10.1186/1472-6939-7-1.

For the view that global bioethics is not possible: H. Tristram Engelhardt (ed.) (2006) *Global bioethics: The collapse of consensus*. M&M Scrivener Press: Salem. See also: Alan Petersen (*The politics of bioethics*. Routledge: New York/London, 2011).

For global bioethics as not desirable: Tao, J. (ed.) (2002) *Cross-cultural perspectives on the (im)possibility of global bioethics*. Kluwer Academic Publishers: Dordrecht/Boston/London.

That it is not necessary to have agreement on moral principles in order to agree on what to do in practice is famously explained in: Jonsen, Albert R. and Toulmin, Stephen (1988) *The abuse of casuistry: A history of moral reasoning*. University of California Press: Berkeley/Los Angeles London.

Finally, for global bioethics as suffering from hubris: Joseph Boyle (2006) The bioethics of global medicine: A natural law reflection, in: H. Tristram Engelhardt, T. (ed.) (2006) *Global bioethics: The collapse of consensus*. pp. 303–4). The example of war as bioethical problem is given by: James Dwyer (2003) Teaching global bioethics. *Bioethics* 17(5–6): 432–446.

The section on 'New context – different answers' has made use of Amartya Sen (2006) *Identity and violence: The illusion of destiny*. W.W.Norton & Company: New York and London, and Arjun Appadurai (2013) *The future as cultural fact: Essay on the global condition*. Verso: London/New York. For the debate on Asian values, see the interview with Singapore's leader Lee Kuan Yew (1994) (Fareed Zakaria: Culture is destiny: A conversation with Lee Kuan Yew. *Foreign Affairs* 73(2): 109–126). Fuyuki Kurasawa presents the view that cultures are processes, 'actively created and recreated on the basis of appropriation, imposition, and negotiation over time and in different places' (see: *The ethnological imagination: A cross-cultural critique of modernity*. University of Minnesota Press: Minneapolis/London, 2004, p. 172).

The section on 'Answers are unavoidable and necessary' draws on the work of advocates of global bioethics. Especially the publications of Heather Widdows are helpful here. See: Heather Widdows (2011) *Global ethics: An introduction*. Acumen: Durham (UK); Heather Widdows (2011) Localized past, globalized future: Towards an effective bioethical framework using examples from population genetics and medical tourism. *Bioethics* 25(2): 83–91; Heather Widdows (2007) Is global ethics moral neo-colonialism? An investigation of the issue in the context of bioethics. *Bioethics* 21(6): 305–315. The connection between global problems and 'systemic risk' is elaborated in: Ian Goldin and Mike Mariathasan (2014) *The butterfly defect: How globalization creates systemic risks and what to do about it*. Princeton University Press: Princeton and Oxford. The idea of philosophy as a way of life plays an important role in Pierre Hadot (1995) *Qu'est-ce que la philosophie antique?* Gallimard: Paris. The notion of 'cultural aspiration' is introduced by Arjun Appadurai (2013) *The future as cultural fact: Essays on the global condition*. Verso: London, New York, p. 195.

For a positive reading of the history of ethics and the issue of moral progress, see Kenan Malik (2014) *The quest for a moral compass: A global history of ethics*. Atlantic Books: London. Malik argues that the idea of a universal community has been developed in various civilizations. A detailed study about the decline of violence is: Steven Pinker

(2011) *The better angels of our nature*. Penguins Books: London. The theory that the circle of ethics has expanded has been developed by philosopher Peter Singer (2011) *The expanding circle: Ethics, evolution, and moral progress*. Princeton University Press: Princeton and Oxford (original 1981).

Critique of mainstream bioethics is elaborated by Alan Petersen (2011) *The politics of bioethics*. Routledge: New York/London and Jan Helge Solbakk (2013) Bioethics on the couch. *Cambridge Quarterly of Healthcare Ethics* 22: 319–326.

For a critique of neoliberal ideology. See: Jürgen Habermas (2001) *Die Zeit* (www.zeit.de/2001/27/Warum_braucht_Europa_eine_Verfassung).

The section 'Expanding the horizon' has benefited from Susan Braedley and Meg Luxton (eds) (2010) *Neoliberalism in everyday life*. McGill-Queen's University Press: Montreal & Kingston/London/Ithaca) and Fiona Robinson (2011) *The ethics of care: A feminist approach to human security*. Temple University Press: Philadelphia.

Chapter 7: Global bioethical frameworks

General orientation regarding human rights is provided by: Michael Ignatieff (2001) *Human rights as politics and idolatry*. Princeton University Press: Princeton and Oxford; Lynn Hunt (2007) *Inventing human rights: A history*. W.W.Norton & Company: New York/London; Aryeh Neier (2012) *The international human rights movement: A history*. Princeton University Press: Princeton and Oxford. That universality is the chief novelty of human rights is strongly emphasized by René Cassin, member of the Human Rights Commission that drafted the UDHR at the General Assembly adopting the Declaration (General Assembly United Nations: Meetings records 180th plenary session, 9 December 1948, A/PV.180) (www.un.org/ga/search/view_doc.asp?symbol=A/PV.180).

For the connection between human rights and medicine, see: David J. Rothman and Sheila M. Rothman (2006) *Trust is not enough: Bringing human rights to medicine*. New York Review Books: New York.

For the search for common values, see Sissela Bok 1995 (2002) *Common values*. University of Missouri Press: Columbia and London. See also: CIOMS: A global agenda for bioethics (1995) Declaration of Ixtapa. *Canadian Journal of Medical Technology* 57: 79–80; Parliament of the World's Religions (1993) *Toward a global ethics*. Chicago: Council for a Parliament of the World's Religions. See also: Karl-Josef Kuschel and Dietmar Mieth (eds) (2001) *In search of universal values*. SCM Press: London.

For the section on declaring global bioethics: Allyn L. Taylor (1999) Globalization and biotechnology: UNESCO and an international strategy to advance human rights and public health. *American Journal of Law & Medicine* 25: 479–541; Henk ten Have and Michèle S. Jean (eds) (2009) *The UNESCO Universal Declaration on bioethics and human rights: Background, principles and application*. UNESCO Publishing: Paris; Adèle Langlois (2013) *Negotiating bioethics: The governance of UNESCO's bioethics programme*. Routledge: London and New York. For other UNESCO Declarations (1997) *Universal Declaration on the Human Genome and Human Rights*. UNESCO, Paris. http://portal.unesco.org/en/ev.php-URL_ID=13177&URL_DO=DO_TOPIC&URL_SECTION=201.html (accessed 1 October 2014). *International Declaration on Human Genetic Data*. UNESCO, Paris, 2003. http://portal.unesco.org/en/ev.php-URL_ID=17720&URL_DO=DO_TOPIC&URL_SECTION=201.html (accessed 1 October 2014).

The two-level model of global ethics, discussed in 'Components of global bioethics' is presented by William M. Sullivan and Will Kymlicka (eds) (2007) *The globalization of ethics*. Cambridge University Press: New York: 4, 207 ff; David Held (2010)

Cosmopolitanism: Ideals and realities. Polity Press: Cambridge (UK) and Malden (MA): 80 ff. For a philosophical analysis of the relations and distinctions between the notion of 'universal', 'uniform', and 'common', as the notion of post-universal, see François Jullien (2014) *On the universal, the uniform, the common and dialogue between cultures.* Polity Press: Cambridge (UK) and Malden (MA).

The relation of bioethics and human rights is examined in: Henk AMJ ten Have: Future perspectives. In: Henk ten Have and Bert Gordijn (eds) (2014) *Handbook of global bioethics.* Springer Publishers: Dordrecht, pp. 829–844. Other informative publications on the connections between human rights and bioethics: Robert Baker (2001) Bioethics and human rights: A historical perspective. *Cambridge Quarterly of Healthcare Ethics* 10: 241–252; Lori P. Knowles (2001) The lingua franca of human rights and the rise of a global bioethic. *Cambridge Quarterly of Healthcare Ethics* 10: 253–263; Richard E. Ashcroft (2010) Could human rights supersede bioethics? *Human Rights Law Review* 10(4): 639–660.

The argument that human rights discourse provides an alternative to the neoliberal ideology that views health systems and services as commodities is elaborated in: Audrey R. Chapman (2009) Globalization, human rights, and the social determinants of health. *Bioethics* 23(2): 97–111.

There is a wide range of literature on cosmopolitanism. For interesting overviews, see: Kwame Anthony Appiah (2006) *Cosmopolitanism: Ethics in a world of strangers.* Allen Lane (Penguin Books): London; Robert Fine (2007) *Cosmopolitanism.* Routledge: London and New York; Gerard Delanty (2009) *The cosmopolitan imagination: The renewal of critical social theory.* Cambridge University Press: Cambridge (UK); David Held (2010) *Cosmopolitanism: Ideals and realities.* Polity Press: Cambridge (UK) and Malden (MA). Peter Kemp (2011) *Citizen of the world: The cosmopolitan ideal for the twenty-first century.* Humanity Books: New York; Louis Lourme (2014) *Le nouvel âge de la citoyenneté mondiale.* Presses Universitaires de France: Paris.

Chapter 8: Sharing the world: common perspectives

For the section 'Global moral community', see Henk ten Have (2011) Global bioethics and communitarianism. *Theoretical Medicine and Bioethics* 32: 315–326. For biopiracy, see: Vandana Shiva (1997) *Biopiracy: The plunder of nature and knowledge.* South End Press: Boston (MA); Vandana Shiva (2001) *Protect or plunder? Understanding intellectual property rights.* Zed Books: London and New York; Daniel F. Robinson (2010) *Confronting biopiracy: Challenges, cases and international debates.* Earthscan: London/New York.

Sources used for the section 'Common heritage', are: Arvid Pardo (1968) Who will control the seabed? *Foreign Affairs* 47: 123–137; Kemal Baslar (1998) *The concept of the common heritage of mankind in international law.* Martinus Nijhoff Publishers: The Hague; Jasper Bovenberg (2006) Mining the common heritage of our DNA: Lessons learned from Grotius and Pardo. *Duke Law & Technology Review* 5(8): 1–20; Alexandre Kiss (1985) The common heritage of mankind: Utopia or reality? *International Journal* 40(3): 423–441. The application of the notion of common heritage to the human genome is discussed in: HUGO Ethical, Legal and Social Issues Committee (1995) *Statement on the Principled Conduct of Genetics Research* (www.hugo-international.org/img/statment%20 on%20the%20principled%20conduct%20of%20genetics%20research.pdf) (accessed 20 July 2015). See further: Christian Byk (1998) A map to a new treasure island: The human genome and the concept of common heritage. *Journal of Medicine and Philosophy*

23(3): 234–246; Bartha N. Knoppers and Yann Joly (2007) Our social genome? *Trends in Biotechnology* 25(7): 284–288.

The best introduction to the concept of interculturality is: Ted Cantle (2012) *Interculturalism: The new era of cohesion and diversity*. Palgrave Macmillan: New York. See further: Ram Adhar Mall (2004) The concept of an intercultural philosophy. In: Fred E. Jandt (ed.): *Intercultural communication. A global reader*. Thousand Oaks, London, New Delhi: SAGE Publications, pp. 315–327; Darla K. Deardorff (ed.) (2009) *The SAGE handbook of intercultural competence*. Los Angeles: SAGE Publications; Clara Sarmento (ed.) (2010) *From here to diversity: Globalization and intercultural dialogues*. Cambridge Scholars Publishing: Newcastle upon Tyne; Nasar Meer and Tariq Modood (2011) How does interculturalism contrast with multiculturalism? *Journal of Intercultural Studies* 33(2): 175–196; Michele Lobo, Vince Marotta and Nicole Oke (eds) (2011) *Intercultural relations in a global world*. Common Ground Publishing: Champaign (Ill).

The section on Commons has benefited from: Michael Goldman (ed.) (1998) *Privatizing nature. Political struggles for the global commons*. Rutgers University Press: New Brunswick (NJ); Pranab Bardhan and Isha Ray (eds) (2008) *The contested commons: Conversations between economists and anthropologists*. Blackwell Publishing: Malden (MA); David Bollier and Silke Helfrich (eds) (2012) *The wealth of the commons: A world beyond market and state*. Leveller Press: Amherst (MA); Béatrice Parance and Jacques de Saint Victor (eds) (2014) *Repenser les biens communs*. CNRS Éditions: Paris; Pierre Darlot and Christian Laval (2014) *Commun. Essai sur la révolution au XXIe siècle*. Éditions La Découverte: Paris.

'Anticommons' are discussed in: Michael Heller and Rebecca Eisenberg (1998) Can patents deter innovation? The anticommons in biomedical research. *Science* 280: 698–701; Michael Heller (2008) *The gridlock economy: How too much ownership wrecks markets, stops innovation, and costs lives*. Basic Books: New York. The UN Commission on Global Governance (1995) discussed the global commons in: https://humanbeingsfirst.files. wordpress.com/2009/10/cacheof-pdf-our-global-neighborhood-from-sovereignty-net. pdf (especially pp. 251–253 and 357).

For water and ethics, see: COMEST (World Commission on the Ethics of Scientific Knowledge and Technology) (2004) *Best ethical practice in water use*. UNESCO, Paris (http://unesdoc.unesco.org/images/0013/001344/134430e.pdf). See also: Oscar Olivera (2004) *Cochabamba! Water war in Bolivia*. South End Press: Cambridge (MA); Saskia Sassen (2014) *Expulsions: Brutality and complexity in the global economy*. The Belknap Press of Harvard University Press: Cambridge (MA) and London (UK), pp. 191–198.

A recent critical analysis of the intellectual property rights regime is: Peter Baldwin (2014) *The copyright wars: Three centuries of trans-atlantic battle*. Princeton University Press: Princeton and Oxford. Among other critical studies are: Peter Drahos (1999) Intellectual property and human rights. *Intellectual Property Quarterly* 3: 349–371; Peter Drahos (2002) Developing countries and international intellectual property standard-setting. *Journal of World Intellectual Property* 5: 765–789; Michele Boldrin and David K. Levine (2012) *The case against patents*. Working paper. Research Division, Federal Reserve Bank of St. Louis. St. Louis (http://research.stlouisfed.org/wp/2012/2012-035.pdf). Alternative approaches are elaborated in: Dan L. Burk and Mark A. Lemley (2009) *The patent crisis and how the courts can solve it*. The University of Chicago Press: Chicago and London. For the connection to medicine and healthcare see: Sixty-first World Health Assembly: Global strategy and plan of action on public health, innovation and intellectual property. WHA61.21, 24 May 2008 (http://apps.who.int/gb/ebwha/pdf_files/A61/A61_ R21-en.pdf); Cynthia M. Ho: Beyond patents: Global challenges to affordable medicine. In I. Glenn Cohen (ed.) (2013) *The globalization of health care: Legal and ethical issues*.

Oxford University Press: Oxford/New York: 302–317. The argument that property rights endanger the freedom of culture is made by Lawrence Lessig (2004) *Free culture: The nature and future of creativity.* Penguin Books: New York, p. 170.

The concept of Buen Vivir is elaborated in: Alberto Acosta (2014) *Le Bien Vivir: Pour imaginer d'autres mondes.* Les Éditions Utopia: Paris. See also: David Cortez and Heike Wagner (2010) Zur Genealogie des Indigenen 'Guten Lebens' ('Sumak Kawsay') in Ecuador. In: Leo Gabriel and Herbert Berger (eds): *Lateinamerikas Demokratien im Umbruch.* Verlag Mandelbaum: Vienna: 167–200; Marlene Brant Castellano (2014) Ethics of aboriginal research. In: Wanda Teays, John-Stewart Gordon and Alison Dundes Renteln (eds): *Global bioethics and human rights: Contemporary issues.* Rowman & Littlefield: Lanham (Maryland), pp. 273–288.

Sources for the connection between bioethics and commons are: Danish Council of Ethics (2005) *Patenting human genes and stem cells.* Copenhagen; Lori B. Andrews and Jordan Paradise (2005) Gene patents: The need for bioethics scrutiny and legal change. *Yale Journal of Health Policy, Law, and Ethics* 5(1): 403–412; The Myriad case is analysed in: E. Richard Gold and Julia Carbone (2010) Myriad Genetics: In the eye of the policy storm. *Genetics in Medicine* 12(4): S39–S70. DOI: 10.1097/GIM.0b013e3181d72661.

Sharing of clinical trials data is discussed by: Marc A. Rodwin (2012) Clinical trial data as a public good. *JAMA* 308(9): 871–872; Trudo Lemmens and Candice Telfer: Clinical trials registration and results reporting and the right to health. In: I. Glenn Cohen (ed.) (2013) *The globalization of health care: Legal and ethical issues.* Oxford University Press: Oxford/New York: 255–271; Peter Doshi, Tom Jefferson and Chris Del Mar (2012) The imperative to share clinical study reports: Recommendations from the Tamiflu experience. *PLoS Medicine* 9(4): e1001201.

Academic patenting and the role of universities is a central issue in: Dave A. Chokshi (2006) Improving access to medicines in poor countries: The role of universities. *PLoS Medicine* 3(6): e136. DOI: 10.1371/journal.pmed.0030136.

Publications on open science and science commons are: David Weatherall (2000) Academia and industry: Increasingly uneasy bedfellows. *The Lancet* 355: 1574; Merryn Ekberg (2005) Seven risks emerging from life patents and corporate science. *Bulletin of Science, Technology & Society*; 25(6): 475–483; Robert Cook-Deegan (2007) The science commons in health research: Structure, function, and value. *Journal of Technology Transfer* 32(3): 133–156.

The notion of 'common good' is elaborated in: Michèle Stanton-Jean: *La Déclaration universelle sur la bioéthique et les droits de l'homme: Une vision du bien commun dans un contexte mondial de pluralité et de diversité culturelle?* [The Universal Declaration on Bioethics and Human Rights: A vision of the Common Good in a pluralistic and culturally diverse global context?]. PhD thesis in Applied Human Sciences. Montreal. Montreal University. Online: www.bnds.fr and at: https://papyrus.bib.umontreal.ca/xmlui/handle/1866/5181.

Chapter 9: Global health governance

Sources for global governance: Antonio Franceschet (2009) *The ethics of global governance.* Lynne Rienner Publishers: Boulder and London; Timothy J. Sinclair (2012) *Global governance.* Polity Press: Cambridge (UK) and Malden (MA); Thomas G. Weiss (2013) *Global governance: Why? What? Whither?* Polity Press: Cambridge (UK) and Malden (MA).

For global health governance, see: Mark W. Zacher and Tania J. Keefe (2008) *The politics of global health governance: United by contagion.* Palgrave Macmillan: New York; Kelley Lee (2009) *The World Health Organization (WHO).* Routledge: London and New York; Sophie Harman (2012) *Global health governance.* Routledge: London and New York; Jeremy Youde (2012) *Global health governance.* Polity Press: Cambridge (UK). The positive role of WHO in the governance of the SARS outbreak in 2003 is analysed by David P. Fidler (2004) *SARS, governance and the globalization of disease.* Palgrave Macmillan: Houndsmills (UK).

Infectious diseases are examined as the 'dark side of globalization' in Geoffrey B. Cockerham and William E. Cockerham (2010) *Health and globalization.* Polity Press: Cambridge (UK) and Malden (MA), p. 62. For the Ebola case: Anthony S. Fauci (2014) Ebola – Underscoring the global disparities in health care resources. *New England Journal of Medicine* 371(12): 1084–1086; Margaret Chan (2014) Ebola virus disease in West Africa – No early end to the outbreak. *New England Journal of Medicine* 371(13): 1183–1185; Thomas R. Frieden, Inger Damon, Beth P. Bell, Thomas Kenyon and Stuart Nichol (2014) Ebola 2014 – New challenges, new global response and responsibility. *New England Journal of Medicine* 371(13): 1177–1180; 45(1): 5–6. For the military background, see: Kathleen Raven (2012) Stop-work order creates uncertainty for Ebola drug research. *Nature Medicine* 18(9): 1312. Lessons from Ebola are provided in: *Save the Children: A wake-up call. Lessons from Ebola for the world's health systems.* London, March 2015. (www. savethechildren.org/atf/cf/%7B9def2ebe-10ae-432c-9bd0-df91d2eba74a%7D/ WAKE%20UP%20CALL%20REPORT%20PDF.PDF) (accessed 20 July 2015).

Problems of governance are examined by Thomas G. Weiss (2013) *Global governance: Why? What? Whither?* Polity Press: Cambridge (UK) and Malden (MA). The inadequacy of global institutions is analysed in: David Held (2010) *Cosmopolitanism: Ideals and realities.* Polity Press: Cambridge (UK) and Malden (MA), p. 186 ff. Diverging normative perspectives and policies are analysed in Kelley Lee (2009) *The World Health Organization (WHO).* Routledge: London and New York (p. 126 ff) and Colin McInnes and Kelley Lee (2012) *Global health & international relations.* Polity Press: Cambridge (UK), pp. 18–19. See also: Raphael Lencucha (2013) Cosmopolitanism and foreign policy for health: Ethics for and beyond the state. *BMC International Health and Human Rights* 13: 29; doi: 10.1186/1472-698X-13-29.

For the distinction between globalization from above and from below, see: Jeremy Brecher, Tim Costello and Brendan Smith (2000) *Globalization from below: The power of solidarity.* South End Press: Cambridge (MA). See also: Fuyuki Kurasawa (2004) A cosmopolitanism from below: Alternative globalization and the creation of a solidarity without bounds. *Archives of European Sociology* 45: 233–255; Gilbert Leung (2013) Cosmopolitan ethics from below. *Ethical Perspectives* 20(1): 43–60.

For the example of TAC, see: Mark Heywood (2009) South Africa's Treatment Action Campaign: Combining law and social mobilization to realize the right to health. *Journal of Human Rights Practice* 1(1): 14–36. See also: Leslie London (2004) Health and human rights: What can ten years of democracy in South Africa tell us? *Health and Human Rights* 8(1): 1–25; Steven Friedman and Shauna Mottiar (2005) A rewarding engagement? The Treatment Action Campaign and the politics of HIV/AIDS. *Politics & Society* 33(4): 511–565.

For new forms of governance: Richard Falk (1995) The world order between inter-state law and the law of humanity: The role of civil society institutions. In: Daniele Archibugi and David Held (eds): *Cosmopolitan democracy: An agenda for a new world order.* Polity Press: Cambridge (UK), pp. 163–179. Proposals for improving global governance for health have been made by the Commission on Global Governance for Health: The political origins of health inequity: prospects for change. *The Lancet* 2014; 383: 630–667.

Chapter 10: Bioethics governance

Sources for bioethics governance: Brian Salter and Mavis Jones (2002) Human genetic technologies, European governance and the politics of bioethics. *Nature Reviews Genetics* 3: 808–814; Brian Salter (2007) The global politics of human embryonic stem cell science. *Global Governance* 13: 277–298; Alison Harvey and Brian Salter (2012) Governing the moral economy: Animal engineering, ethics and the liberal government of science. *Social Science & Medicine* 75: 193–199; Brian Salter and Charlotte Salter (2013) Bioethical ambition, political opportunity and the European governance of patenting: The case of human embryonic stem cell science. *Social Science & Medicine* 98: 286–292.

The example of the Committee on Animal Biotechnology in the Netherlands is studied by L.E. Paula (2008) *Ethics committees, public debate and regulation: An evaluation of policy instruments in bioethics governance.* Thesis Vrije Universiteit Amsterdam.

Bioethics governance in the European Union is discussed in: Commission of the European Communities (2001) *European governance. A white paper.* Brussels (http://eur-lex.europa.eu/legal-content/EN/TXT/PDF/?uri=CELEX:52001DC0428&rid=2); Alison Mohr, Helen Busby, Tamara Hervey and Robert Dingwall (2012) Mapping the role of official bioethics advice in the governance of biotechnologies in the EU: The European Group on Ethics' Opinion on commercial cord blood banking. *Science and Public Policy* 39: 105–117.

For 'Bioethics governance at the global level': Allyn L. Taylor (1999) Globalization and biotechnology: UNESCO and an international strategy to advance human rights and public health. *American Journal of Law & Medicine* 25: 479–541. For the global impact of the Genome Declaration, see: Brian Salter and Charlotte Salter (2013) Bioethical ambition, political opportunity and the European governance of patenting: The case of human embryonic stem cell science. *Social Science & Medicine* 98: 286–292. The UN debate on human cloning is examined by George J. Annas (2005) The ABCs of global governance of embryonic stem cell research: Arbitrage, bioethics and cloning. *New England Law Review* 39(3): 489–500; Mahnoush H. Arsanjani (2006) Negotiating the UN Declaration on Human Cloning. *The American Journal of International Law* 100(1): 164–179.

Sources for 'Governance *through* bioethics' are the following. The four functions of global bioethics are from: Ayo Wahlberg et al. (2013) From global bioethics to ethical governance of biomedical research collaborations. *Social Science & Medicine* 98: 293–300. For the examples from countries, see: Carmel Shalev and Yael Hashiloni-Dolev (2011) Bioethics governance in Israel: An expert regime. *Indian Journal of Medical Ethics* 8(3): 157–160; Joy Yueyue Zhang (2012) *The cosmopolitanization of science: Stem cell governance in China.* Palgrave/Macmillan: Houndmills; Maria Hvistendahl (2013) China's publication bazaar. *Science* 342: 1035–1039; Calvin Wai Loon Ho, Leonardo D. de Castro, and Alastair V. Campbell (2014) Governance of biomedical research in Singapore and the challenge of conflicts of interest. *Cambridge Quarterly of Healthcare Ethics* 23: 288–296.

The problem of representation and expertise: Susan E. Kelly (2003) Public bioethics and publics: Consensus, boundaries, and participation in biomedical science policy. *Science, Technology & Human Values* 28(3): 339–364; Aurora Plomer (2008) The European

Group on Ethics: Law, politics and the limits of moral integration in Europe. *European Law Journal* 14(6): 839–859.

For the problem of public participation, see: Lonneke Poort, Tora Holmberg and Malin Ideland (2013) Bringing in the controversy: Re-politicizing the de-politicized strategy of ethics committees. *Life Sciences, Society and Policy* 9: 11; doi: 10.1186/2195-7819-9-11.

The two forms of governance are distinguished by L.E. Paula (2008) *Ethics committees, public debate and regulation: An evaluation of policy instruments in bioethics governance.* Thesis Vrije Universiteit Amsterdam.

Sources for the section 'Governance *of* global bioethics' are: Robert Baker (2005) A draft model aggregate code of ethics for bioethicists. *The American Journal of Bioethics* 5(5): 33–41; Erich Loewy and Roberto Springer Loewy (2005) Use and abuse of bioethics: Integrity and professional standing. *Health Care Analysis* 13(1): 73–86; Gerard Magill (2013) Quality in ethics consultations. *Medicine, Health Care and Philosophy* 16: 761–774; Eric Kodish and Joseph J. Fins (2013) Quality attestation for clinical ethics consultants: A two-step model from the American Society for Bioethics and Humanities. *Hastings Center Report* 43(5): 26–36; Stuart J. Murray and Adrian Guta: Credentialization or critique? Neoliberal ideology and the fate of the ethical voice. *American Journal of Bioethics* 2014: 14(1): 33–35.

About bioethics institutions: Jean-Christophe Galloux, Arne Thing Mortensen, Suzanne de Cheveigné. Agnes Allansdottir, Augli Chatjouli and George Sakellaris (2002) The institutions of bioethics. In: M.W. Bauer and G. Gaskell (eds) (2002) *Biotechnology: The making of a global controversy.* Cambridge University Press: Cambridge (UK): 129–148.

For 'epistemic community': Peter M. Haas (1992) Epistemic communities and international policy coordination. *International Organization* 46(1): 1–35. For bioethics, see: Eric Vogelstein (2014) The nature and value of bioethics expertise. *Bioethics*; doi:10.1111/bioe.12114; Jeremy R. Garrett (2014) Two agendas for bioethics: critique and integration. *Bioethics*: doi:10.1111/bioe.12116.

Useful sources for 'Governance *of* global bioethics': Educational programmes: Global Bioethics Initiative: www.globalbioethics.org; Global Health Impact project: http://global-health-impact.org/aboutindex.php; Erasmus Mundus Master in Bioethics: https://med.kuleuven.be/eng/erasmus-mundus-bioethics; Fogarty International Center: www.fic.nih.gov/Programs/Pages/bioethics.aspx; Collaborative Institutional Training Initiative: www.citiprogram.org/. The UNESCO bioethics core curriculum is downloadable at: http://unesdoc.unesco.org/images/0016/001636/163613e.pdf; WHO: Casebook on ethical issues in international health research. WHO, Geneva, 2009 (http://whqlibdoc.who.int/publications/2009/9789241547727_eng.pdf).

For professional associations, see: IAB: http://bioethics-international.org/index.php?show=index; IALES: www.iales-aides.com/mission.html; SIBI: www.sibi.org/; ISCB: www.bioethics-iscb.org/; IAEE: https://www.ethicsassociation.org/.

For global networks, go to: Bioethics International: www.bioethicsinternational.org/index.php5; Law, Ethics, Health Network in Senegal: http://rds.refer.sn/; Bangladesh Bioethics Society: www.bioethics.org.bd/; Universities Allied for Essential Medicines: https://uaem.org/; For the UAEM University Global Health Impact Report Card see: http://globalhealthgrades.org/about/; Physicians for Human Rights: http://physiciansforhumanrights.org/; Access to Medicine Index: www.accesstomedicineindex.org/; Global Health Impact Index: http://global-health-impact.org/aboutindex.php.

Relevant information concerning global bioethics infrastructures is in the following: NIH Bioethics Resources on the Web: http://bioethics.od.nih.gov/; Ethics CORE (Collaborative Online Resource Environment): https://nationalethicscenter.org/;

Bioethics and Law Observatory, Barcelona: www.bioeticayderecho.ub.edu/en; Global
Ethics Observatory, UNESCO: www.unesco.org/new/en/social-and-human-sciences/
themes/global-ethics-observatory/

See also: Henk ten Have and Tee W. Ang (2007) UNESCO's Global Ethics Observatory.
Journal of Medical Ethics 33(1): 15–16; WHO, National Ethics Committees Database
(ONEC): http://apps.who.int/ethics/nationalcommittees/; Global Summit of National
Bioethics Advisory Bodies: www.who.int/ethics/globalsummit/en/; Global Network
of WHO Collaborating Centres for Bioethics: www.who.int/ethics/partnerships/
global_network/en/.

For WHO activities, see: Marie-Charlotte Bouësseau, Andreas Reis and W. Calvin Ho
(2011) Global Summit of National Ethics Committees: An essential tool for international
dialogue and consensus-building. *Indian Journal of Medical Ethics* 8(3): 154–157.

For UNESCO's capacity-building activities, see: Henk ten Have (2006) The activities of
UNESCO in the area of ethics. *Kennedy Institute of Ethics Journal* 16(4): 333–351; Henk ten
Have (2008) UNESCO's Ethics Education Programme. *Journal of Medical Ethics* 34(1):
57–59; T.W. Ang, H. ten Have, J. H. Solbakk and H. Nys (2008) UNESCO Global Ethics
Observatory: Database on ethics related legislation and guidelines. *Journal of Medical Ethics*
34: 738–741; Henk ten Have, Christophe Dikenou and Dafna Feinholz (2011) Assisting
countries in establishing National Bioethics Committees: UNESCO's Assisting Bioethics
Committee project. *Cambridge Quarterly of Healthcare Ethics* 20(3): 1–9.

The role of international organizations is discussed in: Martha Finnemore (1993) International
Organizations as teachers of norms: The United Nations Educational, Scientific, and
Cultural Organization and science policy. *International Organization* 47(4): 565–597;
Adele Langlois (2013) *Negotiating Bioethics: The governance of UNESCO's Bioethics
Programme.* Routledge: London and New York; German Solinis (ed.) (2015) *Global
bioethics: What for? Twentieth anniversary of UNESCO's Bioethics Programme.* UNESCO,
Paris.

Chapter 11: Global practices and bioethics

The Baby Gammy case is discussed in: Claire Achmad (2014) How the rise of commercial
surrogacy is turning babies into commodities. *The Washington Post*, 31 December 2014
(www.washingtonpost.com/posteverything/wp/2014/12/31/how-the-rise-of-comme
rcial-surrogacy-is-turning-babies-into-commodities/); Amel Ahmed (2014) Offshore
babies: The murky world of transnational surrogacy. Aljazeera America, 11 August 2014
(http://america.aljazeera.com/articles/2014/8/11/offshore-babies-thebusinessoftransna
tionalsurrogacy.html).

For the broader context of commercial motherhood: Sally Howard (2014) Taming the
international commercial surrogacy industry. *British Medical Journal* 349: g6334; Louise
Johnson, Eric Blyth and Karin Hammarberg (2014) Barriers for domestic surrogacy and
challenges of transnational surrogacy in the context of Australians undertaking surrogacy
in India. *Journal of Law and Medicine* 22(1): 136–154; Leslie R. Schover (2014) Cross-
border surrogacy: The case of Baby Gammy highlights the need for global agreement on
protections for all parties. *Fertility and Sterility* 102(5): 1258–1259; John Tobin (2014) To
prohibit or permit: What is the (human) rights response to the practice of international
commercial surrogacy? *International and Comparative Law Quarterly* 63(2): 317–352. See
also France Winddance Twine (2011) *Outsourcing the womb: Race, class, and gestational
surrogacy in a global market.* Routledge: New York and London. The Hague Conference
on Private International Law (started in 2011, convened in 2012, 2014 and 2015) aims

at improving international standards on commercial surrogacy and on human trafficking in general. See: HCCH: The parentage/surrogacy project; an updating note. February 2015 (www.hcch.net/upload/wop/gap2015pd03a_en.pdf) (accessed 15 May 2015).

Literature on changing practices is: Abram Chayes and Antonia Handler Chayes (1993) On compliance. *International Organization* 47(2): 175–205; Wayne Sandholtz and Kendall Stiles (2009) *International norms and cycles of change.* Oxford University Press: Oxford and New York; Thomas Risse, Stephen C. Ropp and Kathryn Sikkink (eds) (2013) *The persistent power of human rights: From commitment to compliance.* Cambridge University Press: Cambridge, UK; Emilie M. Hafner-Burton (2013) *Making human rights a reality.* Princeton University Press: Princeton and New York. For the idea of human rights as modes of practices, see Fuyuki Kurasawa (2007) *The work of global justice. Human rights as practices.* Cambridge University Press: Cambridge (UK).

Sources for the section 'Global bioethics practices' are: Martha Finnemore and Kathryn Sikkink (1998) International norm dynamics and political change. *International Organization* 52(4): 887–917; Harold Koh (1999) How is international human rights law enforced? *Indiana Law Journal* 74(4): 1397–1417; Oona A. Hathaway (2002) Do human rights treaties make a difference? *The Yale Law Journal* 111(8): 1935–2042; Joshua W. Busby (2010) *Moral movements and foreign policy.* Cambridge University Press: Cambridge (UK). For the example of PEPFAR, see: John W. Dietrich (2007) The Politics of PEPFAR: The Presidents' Emergency Plan for AIDS Relief. *Ethics & International Affairs* 21(3): 277–292.

The section 'Driving forces for change' has used: Mary Kaldor (2003) *Global civil society: An answer to war.* Polity Press: Cambridge (UK) and Malden (MA). Donatella della Porta *et al.* define global social movements as 'supranational networks of actors that define their causes as global and organize protest campaigns that involve more than one state', Donatella della Porta, Massimiliano Andretta, Lorenzo Mosca and Herbert Reiter (2006) *Globalization from below: Transnational activists and protest networks.* University of Minnesota Press: Minneapolis and London, p. 18). See also, Margaret E. Keck and Kathryn Sikkink (1998) *Activists beyond borders: Advocacy networks in international politics.* Cornell University Press: Ithaca and London; Jeremy Brecher, Tim Costello and Brendan Smith (2000) *Globalization from below: The power of solidarity.* South End Press: Cambridge (MA). The examples of co-optation of social movements and NGOs are from Peter Dauvergne and Genevieve Lebaron (2014) *Protect Inc. The corporatization of activism.* Polity Press: Cambridge (UK) and Malden (MA). See also Lisa Ann Richey and Stefano Ponte (2011) *Brand aid: Shopping well to save the world.* University of Minnesota Press: Minneapolis and London.

For the sub-section on 'Media' the following publications are useful: Kenneth W. Goodman (1999) Philosophy as news: Bioethics, journalism and public policy. *Journal of Medicine and Philosophy* 24(2): 181–200; Albert Rosenfeld (1999) The journalist's role in bioethics. *Journal of Medicine and Philosophy* 24(2): 108–129; Gary Schwitzer, Ganapati Mudur, David Henry, Amanda Wilson, Merrill Goozner, *et al.* (2005) What are the roles and responsibilities of the media in disseminating health information? *PLoS Medicine* 2(7): 0576–0582; Marjorie Kruvand and Bastiaan Vanacker (2011) Facing the future: Media ethics, bioethics, and the world's first face transplant. *Journal of Mass Media Ethics* 26: 135–157.

The positive interaction between bioethics and media is elaborated in Peter Simonson (2002) Bioethics and the rituals of media. *Hastings Center Report* 32(1): 32–39.

Important publications about Framing are: Erving Goffman (1986) *Frame analysis: An essay on the organization of experience.* Boston: Northeastern University Press (original publication

1974); David A. Snow, E. Burke Rochford, Steven K. Worden and Robert D. Benford (1986) Frame alignment processes, micromobilization, and movement participation. *American Sociological Review* 51(4): 464–481; Robert M. Entman (1993) Framing: Towards clarification of a fractured paradigm. *Journal of Communication* 43(4): 51–58; Robert D. Benford and David A. Snow (2000) Framing processes and social movements. An overview and assessment. *Annual Review of Sociology* 26: 611–639; Ronald Labonté and Michelle L. Gagnon (2010) Framing health and foreign policy: Lessons for global health diplomacy. *Globalization and Health* 6: 15; doi: 10.1186/1744-8603-6-14.

Collective action is advocated in Michael F. Maniates (2001) Individualization: Plant a tree, buy a bike, save the world? *Global Environmental Politics* 1(3): 31–52; Todd Sandler (2004) *Global collective action.* Cambridge University Press: Cambridge, UK.

Chapter 12: Global bioethical discourse

The need for another bioethical discourse is advocated in: Paul O'Connell (2007) On reconciling irreconcilables: Neo-liberal globalisation and human rights. *Human Rights Law Review* 7(3): 483–509; Salmaan Kesgavjee (2014) *Blind spot: How neoliberalism infiltrated global health.* University of California Press: Oakland (California); Solomon R. Benatar, Abdallah S. Daar and Peter A. Singer (2005) Global health challenges: The need for an expanded discourse on bioethics. *PLos Medicine* 2(7): e143. See also: Solomon R. Benatar (2005) Moral imagination: The missing component in global health. *PLos Medicine* 2(12): e400.

The 'imperative of responsibility' was the title of the English translation of Hans Jonas's book *Das Prinzip Verantwortung: Versuch einer Ethik für die technologische Zivilization* (Insel Verlag, Frankfurt am Main, 1979; English translation as *The imperative of responsibility: In search of ethics for the technological age.* University of Chicago Press: Chicago, 1984). See also: World Parliament of Religions (1993) *Toward a Global Ethic,* 1993 (www. parliamentofreligions.org/_includes/fckcontent/file/towardsaglobalethic.pdf);

Commission on Global Governance (1995) *Our global neighbourhood.* Oxford University Press: Oxford (www.gdrc.org/u-gov/global-neighbourhood/); InterAction Council (1997) *Declaration on Human Responsibilities* (http://interactioncouncil.org/universal-declaration-human-responsibilities); United Nations General Assembly A/RES/55/2: *United Nations Millennium Declaration,* 18 September 2000 (www.un.org/millennium/declaration/ares552e.pdf); Andrew Kuper (ed.) (2005) *Global responsibilities: Who must deliver on human rights?* Routledge: New York and London, pp. 37–52.

For respect for human vulnerability, see Henk ten Have (2015) Respect for human vulnerability: The emergence of a new principle in bioethics. *Journal of Bioethical Inquiry,* DOI: 10.1007/s11673-015-9641-9; Henk ten Have (2014) The principle of vulnerability in the UNESCO Declaration on Bioethics and Human Rights. In: Joseph Tham, Alberto Garcia and Gonzalo Miranda (eds), *Religious perspectives on human vulnerability in bioethics.* Dordrecht: Springer Publishers: 15–28.

The literature on solidarity is rapidly growing. For this paragraph the following literature has been used: Rahel Jaeggi: Solidarity and indifference. In: Ruud ter Meulen, Wil Arts and Ruud Muffels (eds) (2001) *Solidarity in health and social care in Europe.* Dordrecht/Boston/London: Kluwer Academic Publishers: 287–308; Darryl Gunson (2009) Solidarity and the Universal Declaration on Bioethics and Human Rights. *Journal of Medicine and Philosophy* 34: 241–260; Barbara Prainsack and Alena Buyx (2011) *Solidarity: Reflections on an emerging concept in bioethics.* London: Nuffield Council on Bioethics, (http://nuffieldbioethics.org/wp-content/uploads/2014/07/Solidarity_report_FINAL.pdf).

For cooperation, see: Samuel Bowles and Herbert Gintis (2011) *A cooperative species: Human reciprocity and its evolution.* Princeton and Oxford: Princeton University Press; Jennifer Prah Ruger (2011) Shared health governance. *The American Journal of Bioethics* 11(7): 32–45.

For the example of joint ethics review, see Eric M. Meslin, Edwin Were and David Ayuku (2013) Taking stock of the ethical foundations of international health research: Pragmatic lessons from the IU-Moi Academic Research Ethics Partnership. *Journal of General Internal Medicine* 28 (Suppl 3): S639–645.

For equality, justice and equity, see Gillian Brock (2009) *Global justice. A cosmopolitian account.* Oxford: Oxford University Press. See also Angela J. Ballantyne (2010) How to do research fairly in an unjust world. *The American Journal of Bioethics* 10(6): 26–35; Gorik Ooms and Rachel Hammonds (2010) Taking up Daniels' challenge: The case for global health justice. *Health and Human Rights Journal* 12(1): 29–46; Kok-Chor Tan (2013) Global distributive justice. In Hugh LaFollette (ed.) *The International Encyclopedia of Ethics.* Oxford (UK): Blackwell Publishing, pp. 2142–2151.

For social responsibility, see Susanne Soederberg (2007) Taming corporations or buttressing market-led development? A critical assessment of the Global Compact. *Globalizations* 4(4): 500–513; UNESCO (2010) *Report of the International Bioethics Committee (IBC) on social responsibility and health.* Paris: UNESCO (http://unesdoc.unesco.org/images/0018/001878/187899E.pdf); Stefano Semplici (ed.) (2011) Social responsibility and health. Thematic issue. *Medicine, Health Care and Philosophy. A European Journal* 14(4): 353–419; John Gerard Ruggie (2013) *Just business: Multinational corporations and human rights.* New York/London: W.W.Norton & Company.

For sharing of benefits, see: Doris Schroeder and Julie Cook Lucas (eds) (2013) *Benefit sharing: From biodiversity to human genetics.* Springer: Dordrecht. For the issue of virus sharing: Siti Fadilah Supari: *It's time for the world to change: In the spirit of dignity, equity, and transparency.* Penerbit Lentera: Jakarta, 2008. See also: WHO Executive Board: *Pandemic influenza preparedness: Sharing of influenza viruses and access to vaccines and other benefits.* Geneva, Director General 2009, EB124/4 ADD1.1; D.P. Fidler (2010) Negotiating equitable access to influenza vaccines. Global health diplomacy and the controversies surrounding avian influenza H5N1 and pandemic influenza H1N1. *PLoS Medicine* 7(5): 11000247.

For protecting future generations, see: Hans Jonas (1984) *The Imperative of responsibility: In search of an ethics for the technical age.* University of Chicago Press: Chicago (quotation on p. 11); Emmanuel Agius: Environmental ethics: Towards an intergenerational perspective. In: Henk A.M.J. ten Have (ed.) (2006) *Environmental ethics and international policy.* Paris: UNESCO Publishing, pp. 89–115.

For protection of the environment, the biosphere and biodiversity, see: James Garvey (2008) *The ethics of climate change: Rights and wrong in a warming world.* Continuum: London and New York. See further: James Dwyer (2009) How to connect bioethics and environmental ethics: health, sustainability, and justice. *Bioethics* 23(9): 497–502.

An example of an ethics of harmony: Miguel D. Escoto and Leonardo Boff: Proposal for a Universal Declaration on the Common Good of the Earth and Humanity: http://servicioskoinonia.org/logos/articulo.php?num=118e

Sources for the section 'Biopolitics' are: Thomas Lemke (2011) *Biopolitics: An advanced introduction.* New York and London: New York University Press; Timothy Campbell and Adam Sitze (eds) (2013) *Biopolitics: A reader.* Durham and London: Duke University Press; Miguel de Beistegui, Giuseppe Bianco and Marjorie Gracieuse (eds) (2015) *The care of life: Transdisciplinary perspectives in bioethics and biopolitics.* London and New York: Rowman & Littlefield.

'Global bioethics as social ethics' have used: Global Health Watch. *An alternative World Health Report;* four editions (2005, 2008, 2011 and 2014). www.ghwatch.org/who-watch/about). See further: Simon Critchley (2012) *Infinitely demanding: Ethics of commitments, politics of resistance.* London and New York: Verso; Alain Badiou (2015) *Philosophy for militants.* London and New York: Verso.

General further reading

Van Rensselaer Potter (1988) *Global bioethics: Building on the Leopold legacy.* East Lansing: Michigan State University Press.

In this monograph Potter argues that bioethics should be extended into a global bioethics. He builds on the ideas of Aldo Leopold who developed an ecological ethics concerned with human survival. Potter shows how ecological bioethics and medical bioethics can merge into a global bioethics. Potter elaborates dilemmas in medical bioethics (from teenage pregnancy to euthanasia) with a separate chapter on fertility control. In the last chapter he discusses the same issues from the perspective of global bioethics. The book is a strong statement that a broader scope in bioethics is necessary beyond the medical one but does not systematically elaborate what global bioethics entails. It also hardly addresses the worldwide scope.

Michael W. Fox (2001) *Bringing life to ethics: Global bioethics for a humane society.* Albany: State University of New York Press.

The author, a veterinarian, elaborates Potter's broad notion of bioethics. He thanks Potter in the Introduction, and presents a Life Ethic that includes the interests of the entire natural world and the biotic community next to human interests. The book covers topics such as: environmental ethics, animal rights, conservation of the biosphere, sustainable agriculture, biotechnology, economy, cultural diversity, and universal bioethics. Bioethics is taken as a very broad holistic framework with peace, justice, fulfilment, and integrity of creation as basic principles. The book is deliberately not academic but offers personal reflections and an eclectic approach.

H. Tristram Engelhardt (ed.) (2006) *Global bioethics. The collapse of consensus.* Salem, MA: M & M Scrivener Press.

This collection is the result of a number of conferences of like-minded colleagues arguing that global bioethics does not and should not exist because there is intractable moral diversity. In ethical matters, pervasive and persistent disagreement reigns, making any hope for consensus elusive. Proclamations of moral consensus are not only deceptive and rhetorical but in fact another manifestation of bioethical imperialism. Global bioethics is a plurality of approaches; it can only be visualized as a marketplace of moral ideas. The book is an eloquent elaboration of moral impotence.

Solomon Benatar and Gillian Brock (eds) (2011) *Global health and global health ethics.* Cambridge, UK: Cambridge University Press.

In 29 contributions, this edited volume presents relevant aspects of present-day global health: its relations with trade, debt, international aid, health systems, climate change, biotechnology, food security, taxation, and research. It provides analyses of global health ethics, especially in connection to justice, human rights, and global responsibilities. Separate chapters discuss the teaching of global health ethics, values in global health governance, and whether there is a need for global health ethics.

Catherine Myser (ed.) (2011) *Bioethics around the globe.* New York: Oxford University Press.

The book provides comparative anthropological and sociological studies of globalizing bioethics. The assumption is that global bioethics is globalizing of Western bioethics. Chapters are included on the development of bioethics in diverse countries such as Chile, India, China, Malawi, France and South Africa. It does not have introductory chapters about global bioethics as a new discipline.

I. Glenn Cohen (ed.) (2013) *The globalization of health care.* Oxford/New York: Oxford University Press.

This collection of essays offers an ethical and legal examination of many relevant global issues. In 23 chapters, an overview is presented of subjects that illustrate the globalization of health care. The first and largest section of the book addresses medical tourism. Subsequent sections focus on medical worker migration, the globalization of research and development, and telemedicine. The last section discusses healthcare globalization, equity, and justice. The book does not explicitly address global ethics issues, though some chapters do.

Andrew D. Pinto and Ross E.G. Upshur (eds) (2013) *An introduction to global health ethics.* London and New York: Routledge.

This collection of essays is primarily intended for global health students. It examines theoretical issues such as definitions of global health, governance, human rights, education, and indigenous health, but also practical issues such as clinical work, research, partnerships, advocacy, the political context and teaching. All chapters include interesting cases and examples. Although the book has a specific contribution on ethics and global health, a coherent ethical framework is not presented. The difference between global health ethics and public health ethics is not clear.

Wanda Teays, John-Stewart Gordon and Alison Dundes Renteln (eds) (2014) *Global bioethics and human rights: Contemporary issues.* Lanham: Rowman & Littlefield.

A range of issues is covered by 34 contributions. The chapters are arranged in four parts: Theoretical perspectives (debating common morality), Human rights (with cases on torture, immigration, lethal injection and reproductive freedom), Culture (sex selection, euthanasia, informed consent and research on aboriginal people), and Public health (global aging, public safety and environmental disasters). Each part ends with discussion topics. The book is not rigorously edited (it refers, for example, to the draft UDBHR). It provides useful suggestions for further reading, an overview of electronic resources on global bioethics, and an extensive list of relevant movies and videos.

Alireza Bagheri, Jonathan Moreno and Stefano Semplici (eds) (2015) *Global bioethics: The impact of the UNESCO International Bioethics Committee.* Dordrecht: Springer Publishers.

This collection of 17 contributions analyses the work of the UNESCO International Bioethics Committee in the area of global bioethics. Thematic issues are addressed such as: human rights, consent, traditional medicine, biobanks, discrimination, nanotechnology and national bioethics committees. Other chapters examine the impact in various regions of the world: Central and Eastern Europe, the Arab region, Latin America, Africa and East Asia. The book is published in a special series *Advancing Global Bioethics* that includes a range of studies in global bioethics.

INDEX